TechTV's Security Alert:

Stories of Real People Protecting Themselves from Identity Theft, Scams, and Viruses

Becky Worley

Contents at a Glance

TechTV's Security Alert:

Stories of Real People Protecting Themselves from Identity Theft, Scams, and Viruses

Trademarks

Warning and Disclaimer

Bulk Purchases/Corporate Sales

The publisher offers discounts on this book when ordered in quantity for bulk purchases and special sales. For sales within the United States, please contact: Corporate and Government Sales at (800) 382-3419 or corpsales@pearson-techgroup.com. Outside of the United States, please contact: International Sales at (317) 428-3341 or international@pearson-techgroup.com.

650 Townsend Street
San Francisco, California 94103

Associate Publisher
Stephanie Wall

TechTV, Vice President, Strategic Development
Glenn Farrell

Production Manager
Gina Kanouse

TechTV Press Project Manager
Sasha Zullo

Acquisitions Editor
Wendy Sharp

Development Editor
Michael Thurston

Copy Editor
Keith Cline

Senior Indexer
Cheryl Lenser

Composition
Wil Cruz

Manufacturing Coordinator
Dan Uhrig

Interior Designer
Alan Clements

Cover Designer
Aren Howell

Marketing
Scott Cowlin
Tammy Detrich
Hannah Onstad Latham

Publicity
Susan Nixon

Table of Contents

About the Author

Becky Worley is a relatively normal human being from Maui, Hawaii, who now lives in the San Francisco Bay Area. She has an undergraduate degree from Middlebury College in American literature, religion, and Japanese.

She is now clawing her way toward the completion of a masters degree at Stanford in an education and computer science program.

She has worked at TechTV since 1998, when the network was known as ZDTV. She was the first producer of *Call for Help* and was involved in the creation of *The Screen Savers*. She is now a reporter/producer on TechTV's daily news show, *Tech Live*, where she tries to bring any possible trace of humor or intrigue to the job of reporting viruses, cybercrime, and scams. She also reviews products and generally makes an ass of herself on TechTV's weekly gadget show *Fresh Gear*.

About the Technical Reviewer

These reviewers contributed their considerable hands-on expertise to the entire development process for *TechTV's Security Alert*. As the book was being written, these dedicated professionals reviewed all the material for technical content, organization, and flow. Their feedback was critical to ensuring that *TechTV's Security Alert* fits our readers' need for the highest-quality technical information.

Robert Blader has worked at the Naval Surface Warfare Center, Dahlgren Division, since 1985. Since 1999 he's worked specifically in computer security and computer forensics. Robert has edited training manuals for SANS and has done technical editing for Sams Publishing (including *Maximum Security* and *Maximum Windows 2000 Security*). He has taught computer forensics at the International Association of Computer Investigative Systems (IACIS) yearly training conference. He graduated from Long Island University with a degree in computer science, and earned a certification in computer forensics (Certified Forensics Computer Examiners) from IACIS.

James F. Kelly is co-owner of Those Computer People, Inc., a Houston-based IT consulting company that specializes in networking and hardware/software integration. He has more than 9 years of experience in the IT arena, and has MCSE, Network+, Security+, and MCT certifications. When not assisting clients, he can usually be found at Java House Coffee, taking advantage of its wireless network and answering email.

Acknowledgments

Mom for being an idealist. Dad for being a realist. I'm hoping this is somewhere near a B paper.

Jane, for not making me untangle all the wires in the office until this project was finished. For all your patience, thank you.

Emalia, Jesse, Sarah, Eddie, Brookie, E-dog, Z3, Kath, Emma, Di, and Laura—for bringing so many good things to my life and helping me remember there is life outside of work.

Carolyn, Scott, Brandon, Monet, Dan, and Johnny—for being so flexible and helping me get this thing done.

Leo, a mere 3 years after we pitched this thing, I started writing. From the very beginning, thanks for all your support.

Brooke, Aunt Peg, Molly—you help me remember what it's like to be completely flummoxed by computers—Keep plugging away; they're worth it.

Lindsey, Erica, David, Marc, Tracey, Barb, Brendan—thanks for your encouragement
and for lending an ear.

Glenn, Sasha, Annie, Michael—for all your hard work to make this book a reality.

Wendy—for saving the day.

Introduction

Technology makes us vulnerable in ways we can't fully comprehend, and that freaks most of out. No need to panic—the sky is not falling—but now, more than ever, it's raining computer viruses, identity theft, and online scams. The good news is that you can shelter yourself from the storm.

That's what this book is for. From it, you learn the real truth about computer crimes and learn simple ways to protect your computer, your privacy, and your identity.

I won't make you a slave to time-consuming routines that overprotect you for the sake of lining the pockets of those in the security community. I won't force you to lock down your computer to the point that you can't enjoy all the freedom and content that the Internet provides. With a few simple tricks and a whole lot of increased awareness, you're good to go.

The Stories We Tell

In any book about computers, you expect lists of what you should do: software vulnerabilities that should be patched, habits you should adopt, and safety checks you should put in place. With security, all these "shoulds" come from the hard lessons of others and the warped minds that instigate digital crimes. As a technology reporter assigned the beat of security, I come across stories of real people facing all kinds of high-tech crimes, and there's no need to embellish how widespread computer crimes have become.

This book gives you the straight truth about people who have been victimized. Long before Aesop, stories have burned indelible images in our mind. Hearing a story of one person's experience stimulates our ability to process that experience. No longer is a warning abstract: It's tangible and applicable. That's the goal here, to offer true stories of other victims as a warning and then show you how to protect yourself.

Some of these stories come directly from the articles I've written and posted to TechTV.com. You'll know the material is from an article when you see the Tech Live icon. I've also provided a URL for each of these stories in case you want to read the full article or find more information about the topic online.

Behind every computer victim and crime is a fascinating story of greed, cunning, and sometimes even lust. Take the Melissa virus, a computer worm that spread so fast and with such explosive results that it cost American corporations $80 million in resources and manpower. Behind this simple little piece of code was one love-struck programmer, David Smith. When arrested, he told authorities his worm was an ode to a Florida stripper whom he frequently ogled. Her name, Melissa.

Now you're thinking, "Look lady, I didn't buy this book as a thriller. Patricia Cornwell and John Grisham can kick your butt in that department. So where's the beef? Where's the hardcore technical programming you're going to show me? I mean, shouldn't I be learning to rewrite the code for Internet Explorer to lock out viruses or start encrypting all the email I send out?"

Here's the big secret of this book: Protecting yourself from these new bad guys is not very technical. By that I mean you will never need to make a Registry modification: typing in an unintelligible string of HKEY_CURRENT_USER.

This book is not for system administrators and high-end geeks (and I mean that as a compliment). If you want to delve into the theoretical possibilities of polymorphic viruses mutating through a network running both Windows 2000 and Linux servers, this book is not for you. For the rest of us, that's good news. It means this book is written in English.

Becoming an Unappealing Target

I promise not to bore you with this book, and not to overdramatize crimes, but I will help you lock down your PC and your life so that you will be an unappealing target. Criminals look for the path of least resistance. After reading this book, you will not be part of the path of least resistance, the low-hanging fruit of the uninformed who bad guys depend on for their trade.

Sometimes the way to avoid a certain crime is merely to broaden your understanding of the methods used by criminals. Think of the stories in this book as real-life fables.

For example, you read the tale of some poor guy who sends all his personal data to a crook, all the while thinking he's updating his AOL account. From his story, you learn that if someone sends you an email asking for your credit card number and it looks like it's from AOL, check the header of the email to see whether it was spoofed. (Don't worry, I'll show you how to do that.) Then call AOL to ask, "What's up?" Even after all that, you should still be a little suspicious, because no legitimate company will ever ask you to update your account via email.

However, this book is not just full of stories and allegorical learning; it's a tool. Some chapters show you how to modify your system settings to protect your computer. We've written out the instructions in the chapter and then again in the Appendix, "Homework," at the end of the book. Very few people will actually read and use this book while they sit at their computer. Instead, when you read a set of instructions for a computer modification, a protocol for locking down your identity online, or how to install a security program, go to the Appendix, cut out the second set of instructions, and tape them to your computer's monitor. The next time you boot up, run through the instructions, and then throw them away, knowing you are better protected.

Who Are These New Bad Guys?

Succinctly: They are a bunch of jerks.

Technically, these new bad guys (and girls) are criminals who use computers and technology to get past our defenses and exploit the emerging vulnerabilities in our infrastructure. They are virus writers or virus distributors who remotely place spying software on our computers to log passwords and account numbers. A similar snoop physically installs key-logging software on public computers, and then comes back later to read a digital log of all our doings online.

They are web masters who put up online stores, take a few orders, and then disappear from the web with no intention of delivering the goods. They are burglars and shoplifters who fence stolen merchandise through web auctions. They are scam artists who steal the identities of highly rated eBay sellers, put up a phony auction, and then walk away with the auction winner's money.

They can be insiders at credit companies who see a flaw in the system and exploit it. They can be crackers who probe the networks of our banks to find a tiny hole through which they can drain funds or steal millions of credit card numbers, placing a charge here and a charge there to make millions.

They are egomaniacal boasters who bring corporate networks to a standstill so that they can brag to their buddies that they "owned" the servers of IBM or EarthLink or TechTV. They are script kiddies stealing code from other hackers so that they can play pranks and bring teenaged meanness to the Internet.

They are real-world bullies who use instant messaging and cell phone text messaging to threaten and intimidate other kids. They are pedophiles and con artists who play upon our most basic human emotions, enticing us into taking foolish chances, such as meeting them in the real world.

Most of the time, these new bad guys nickel and dime us so that they can stay below the radar. Sometimes, however, they go for the big jackpots, like a programmer who exploited code glitches in racetrack software, manipulating the program to win millions of dollars in prize money for his frat brother cohorts.

What they do entails some organization, but much of it is still random. There are big identity-theft rings creating structured approaches to the theft and distribution of our credit. They work hard at their business and make big money. There is hierarchy, promotion, and strategy in these groups. On the other hand, there are lone ID thieves who steal whatever information they can easily obtain. All of them are opportunists looking for easy targets.

They rely on the fact that many victims will be embarrassed and ashamed to admit that they have fallen for scams. Which one of us wants to admit that we fell for a ruse? Thousands of online scam victims have never come forward, never even bothered reporting their losses to the authorities. Many of the victims believe they made foolish mistakes and deserved to lose money.

A friend of mine was distraught for her 73-year-old father. He'd fallen for the Nigerian letter scam and had sent tens of thousands of dollars overseas and drained his retirement account to dangerously low levels. She knew he'd survive financially with the help of his family and friends, but she was worried her father wouldn't survive the loss of his dignity.

They Have Us Scrambling

Corporations are scrambling to protect themselves from the new bad guys. IT managers already overtaxed by the need to set up new employee accounts or help the CFO with his fancy monitor are struggling to stay current on critical software patches. (This book isn't for corporate system administrators; however, an explanation of some of the doings at the network level will help readers understand why a denial-of-service attack aimed at Yahoo! indirectly affects all of us online.)

Law-enforcement authorities are also completely flummoxed by these new bad guys. These criminals exploit areas that don't specifically fall into any one organization's jurisdiction. Some criminals know the intricacies of the law so well that they plan their crimes in ways that intentionally make it hard for victims to get help.

I interviewed a man from Pleasant Hills, California, who only wanted to disclose his first name, Steve. Steve is a savvy, wealthy businessman who lost $44,000 in an escrow fraud scam. He thought he was buying a Porsche from eBay, but actually he wired his money to a crook in Latvia. When he realized he had been scammed, Steve called the local police.

The police took Steve's complaint, but told him they wouldn't be able to do much against an international scam artist. The FBI wouldn't take the case because the total damages were less than a hundred thousand dollars. They referred Steve to their Internet Fraud Complaint Center (which only takes reports online). From the site, Steve dutifully filled out a web form describing how he was victimized. A *web form*! That's like pouring your heart out to a black hole. Obviously, Steve has gotten nowhere against the bad guys. But it's not for lack of trying; he's made it his mission to stop the man who victimized him. Short of a trip to Latvia, however, Steve is screwed.

Taking a Stand

The new bad guys know more than the authorities. Most detectives know how to talk to victims and suspects, interpret their reactions, and anticipate how criminals will act on the street. Most cops are low tech, relying on computer forensic labs and their station IT guys to help them find important data on computers, use the Internet to track communications, and understand how computer criminals are able to avoid detection. Without having those skills first hand, most cops rely on a translator (the resident computer geek) to help them understand the very basics of computer crimes. Many agencies realize this is a problem and are recruiting madly to create a new breed of cybercops, but that's a work in progress.

Relying on the police to help you after the fact is a flawed plan when it comes to cybercrime. Learning in advance about your computer, your identity, and the methods used by computer criminals is the best defense. Even better, if you end up being targeted, you may be savvy enough to bust the bad guys.

Jill Maggio is a California businesswoman who sells mobile phones. When one of her customers tried to take her for a ride, she set up a sting. Julian Torres (our accused bad guy) used a bad check, a document he had dummied up based on the identities he'd stolen in a big, local ID-theft ring based in San Jose, California. Authorities say Torres kept the cell phones he bought from Maggio active even though his checks bounced.

Maggio, a sweet and good-natured woman in her forties, rerouted Torres's cell phone to her own number. I'm not sure how "street smart" Maggio was to begin with, but she told me she pulled out as much lingo as she could muster to act like a girlfriend of the alleged ID thief. Maggio wanted to find Torres so she milked information from all of Torres's associates who called his cell phone number. Eventually she had a call from a sales rep at Sony who was trying to confirm the shipping information for a laptop Torres had purchased. With the address Sony had on file, Maggio called the San Jose Police Department, who then had Torres arrested.

He and his partners in crime stand accused of stealing identities from more than 75 people and amassing more than a quarter of a million dollars in illicit funds. Jill Maggio beat these criminals at their own game. It's a little on the Clint Eastwood side, and maybe she's a cybervigilante, but Jill Maggio is one of the new good guys. After reading this book, you'll be one too.

Hacking 101

Ever since *WarGames* first hit movie screens in 1983, we've imagined hackers as teenage boys hopped up on caffeine in the wee hours of the night madly pounding away at the keyboard. With one phrase, "I'm in," this social exile unlocks the secrets of any computer and takes control of our information. These images represent the personification of our fears about technology, our computer inferiority complexes. *WarGames*, *Hackers*, *Sneakers*, and *The Net* are all manifestations of the same underlying theme: Some kids out there know a lot more about computers than you ever could, and they hate us. That kid can instigate nuclear war, ruin your credit, or steal all your savings just for fun.

When real-life accounts of such hackers began to trickle out, the media jumped onboard. The stories made headlines and sometimes lacked context, but they fed into the perception that a subculture existed just out of sight, a subculture of anarchists and criminals typing us toward the next apocalypse. It's a great image, but one that doesn't always fit with reality.

In the real world, *hackers* are curious guys and some girls from age 15 and up who see computer networks as targets for exploration. They find security holes in software, create computer code, or *hacks*, to exploit these holes, and then try to gain access to remote computers running the vulnerable software. Old-school hackers see themselves as explorers with a code of ethics and morals—as noble anarchists, who empower the People. Their code may differ dramatically from that of mainstream society, but it is not about stealing passwords and credit card numbers from your individual computer at home.

On the other hand, if an online business were to store credit cards on an unsecured computer network, that would be a target for a different kind of hacker, one with different motives. (Many refer to these hackers as *crackers*.) In fact, as these lines are being written, the Internet is abuzz with thousands of credit card numbers being harvested from a credit card processing center. Millions of dollars are at stake.

> **Note**
>
> **Hackers Versus Crackers** A semantics issue among the hacking community can be a little cumbersome: It's the hacker versus cracker terminology. Some see hackers as an umbrella term that describes anyone who manipulates computers in ways not originally intended, both for good and for bad. Others say hacking is the good stuff, and criminal computer intrusions and modifications should be called cracking. Even more complicated, some say that white-hat hacking is exploring weaknesses in remote computers for the benefit of society, whereas black-hat hacking (cracking) is for the benefit of the criminal and to the detriment of society. Clear as mud, right? Let's just keep it simple here and side with the folks who say that the term hackers encompasses the people who manipulate remote computers for good or for bad.

You Are Not a Target

Let me put to rest some of your fears: A hacker with the skill to break into any computer, a real wizard, couldn't care less about you. You are a lame target. As an individual, you are a boring target. Don't take that personally, but think about it: What new and inventive security measures do you have on your home PC? What about your security setup represents the Everest, the K-2 of hacking challenges? Nothing.

You might be running a firewall, but they've seen all those before and have workarounds. They could email you a Trojan horse program, an executable you think is a joke or a photo. You double-click and unwittingly give someone a conduit into your computer. If you use any software that hasn't been patched, a hacker could attack you through the vulnerabilities provided by those programs. But don't freak; I'm telling you this to reassure you. You may be low-hanging fruit, but you are probably a boring target.

More importantly, you are too much work for the payoff. If a hacker has to spend 2 hours, or even 20 minutes, breaking into your system, what could the hacker find? Your kid's first typed letter to Santa, your last four purchases at Amazon.com, the annoying jokes forwarded to you by that friend who sends you everything he finds on the web that he thinks is funny. (We all have "that friend" these days.) Don't get me wrong; there is sensitive data on your computer that a hacker could use. When preparing your taxes, for instance, maybe you scanned in images of your W-2 forms, your IRA retirement account statement, or other sensitive financial data. It's highly unlikely, however, for a sophisticated hacker to go to the trouble of pinpointing you as the individual target of a computer-to-computer hack. Think about it: When was the last time a friend or a coworker complained on a Wednesday morning, "Damn, I got hacked again last night."

If you have a fear of planes, people always tell you, "You have more chance to die in a car accident on the way to the airport than you do to get killed in a plane accident." My phobia is sharks. I love the ocean and before I get in the water I always remind myself, "I'm 30 times more likely to get killed by a bolt of lightning on the golf course than eaten by a shark." But no one freaks out when getting into a golf cart.

The same is true of the hacking fear. You probably have a bunch of viruses on your computer right now and are susceptible to even more because you're not taking the right precautions, but the thing that sticks in your mind is hacking. Why? Because it's a tangible human concept that a technically sophisticated bad guy is trying to get into your computer, and the media has fed into your anxieties.

Airport, Jaws, WarGames! All these movies have played upon our fears.

So relax about the hacking concern. At the end of this chapter, you'll find three practical steps to make your computer pretty safe. You're not in a lot of danger from a one-on-one hack right now; but with three steps, (three free steps I might add), you will become even more of an unappealing target for a hacker.

That being said, we need to make it clear that hackers are out there and they do have targets. Who's being targeted? Big corporations, the government, and other hackers.

The History of Hacking

In the mid-1960s the word hacker was coined at MIT, and it wasn't a bad word. The early hackers were the brightest and best young programmers, and they had a very revolutionary mission: power to the people, or more precisely computational power to the people. A hack was a clever use of a system's features in ways beyond its intended usage. It was a mark of cleverness, not a species of maliciousness.

One of the earliest hacks happened on ARPA network, the Defense Advanced Research Projects Agency. ARPA had funded a project to link computers together so that research teams could share files and programs. The idea was that research could go on in different labs and institutions. About the time the number of computers in a lab reached 25, Ray Tomlinson came up with a great hack: In addition to sending files from one computer to another, the hackers could send "private" mail. Thus email, one of many hacks that revolutionized the planet, was born. It was something no one had initially foreseen. Tomlinson's hack included a way of separating the user from the machine in the address. He chose the at symbol (@). It seems to have caught on.

ARPAnet changed the world as it eventually grew into the Internet. Businesses, education, research, and banking are based on linked computers. If you are like many people, you bank on the Internet, you check your email daily, you don't even drive to a new location without using MapQuest. You live in a world where the great source of power is interconnectivity. Now days, there are a few more than 25 original users. In September 2002, NUA Internet estimated the total at more than 605 million machines.

The Internet was developed to let computers share files, but it was grown in a culture that favored anarchy; that was built around pranks and showing off. It was a boys' toy. Police officers have commented on the desire the old-style hacker has to brag. Pick him up, and he'll be spilling the beans before the squad car reaches the police station. He wants to tell people how clever he is, how he did it. Hackers have always shared files and boasts. Even today, numerous illegal sites provide hacking tools for entering various government or corporate entities.

Operation Sundevil

In 1990, things changed. The government began to notice that hacking could be serious; it was no longer a kid's thing. Sure, a group called 414 had hacked into the Los Alamos military computers as far back as 1982, but that still smelled like a prank. In 1990, however, hackers stole code from AT&T, and posted it publicly. The Secret Service was worried, and in an episode known as Operation Sundevil, they started hauling in people and their computers. Bruce Sterling writes about the Secret Service's bungling attempts at law enforcement in a territory that no one understood in his book *The Hacker Crackdown*. But suddenly hackers weren't clever programmers or kids having fun, they were enemies of society.

Three things came out of Operation Sundevil:

- A civil liberties group for computer users, called the *Electronic Frontier Foundation*, was established.
- Popular (mis)understanding of the hacker threat grew.
- The government and big industry started paying attention. This meant that there were high-paying jobs for hackers in private industry and so-so paying jobs in the government. After all, if you're going to protect a system, it helps to know how to break it.

Today's Hacker

Here is what a hacker looks like today. He's probably still a young man (the average age of a hacker is 16 to 25); he does well to average in school; he is mildly antisocial; and he's got more money to burn than he should have. Let's look at his crime:

Ralph's Hacking

Ralph sits at his computer screen for 12 hours straight. Last year he played at hacking, using a dialing program to scan hundreds of phone lines with an eye to finding an open computer that might be interesting; tonight he has a specific target in mind.

From his computer, he goes via the Internet to a phone with an 800 number that is calling one of the servers at his target company. Servers are the hubs that all computer communications go through. They allow client computers to share data, which is what makes modern companies work. Ralph knows something about the configuration of this server; he finds an open port, and he's in. On the other side of the server is a router: Ralph infests the router with a small bit of code called a Trojan (short for Trojan horse) that will help him get back in. Then he uses his access to finger external hosts, commanding the machine to tell him where the servers are and where the connections to the outside world are. Finally, he has his remote phone hang up.

The next night he goes for his target: credit card information. It's stored in a database, and all he needs is access to the database. By the end of the night, Ralph has 15,000 credit card numbers with names. Ralph can cut another notch on his PC tower.

If you think attacks like Ralph's are rare, consider that a recent survey of 503 American corporations said that the vast majority of them had electronic security breaches in 2001. Only 37 percent reported these breaches. Companies thrive by having good reputations; they can't afford to let the general public know that they are under attack.

Today, the hacker's use of computer worms to place malicious programs on victim's computers has changed the way data is stolen. These programs are called *Trojan horses* or just *Trojans*. They are malicious programs that weasel their way onto a victim's computer through harmless-looking email attachments disguised as one thing (naked pictures of Jennifer Lopez, a love letter from a secret admirer, a file needing your thoughts) when they are actually computer programs that send information out of, and allow a remote attacker to gain control of, your PC. For example, family.jpg.scr might really be a malicious attachment that executes a program that relays data to its creator. (Chapter 4, "The Virus Threat," covers these types of viruses and worms in more detail.)

This is not hacking in the traditional sense. Virus writers and data thieves who use Trojans are usually on fishing expeditions: trolling for big targets. These aren't the targeted hacks we think of from movies about hacking and media portrayals of the lone computer nerd out to get you.

One of the more recent hacker sports is the distributed denial of service (DDOS) attack. The hacker sends massive amounts of data to a company's server. To do this he needs allies: He creates a DDOS attack. He gets these allies by infecting home computers, with a Trojan that enables him to run your machine. In many ways it is like giving a posthypnotic command, "Little machine, little machine, you are very sleepy, you will forget the sound of my voice, but at 13 hundred hours on the twentieth, you will rise up and attack Three Initial Company.com."

The infected machines, known as *zombies*, are a willing army to the hacker. There have been some dramatic DDOS attacks in the past few years targeting Microsoft, the White House website, various Bells, and other media websites. In fact about the only interest hackers will have in your home system is recruiting it as a zombie, and you learn ways to prevent that later in this chapter.

It takes a great deal of work to hack into a system, so targets are chosen with great care. It isn't cost efficient to spend weeks of research and hours of hacking just to compromise one individual computer. But if that one hack has big payoff or big prestige, that's a different story. Let's look at common targets.

Companies That Are Research Intensive

The juiciest targets spend a lot of money and time on research. A pharmaceutical firm may spend a year developing a new drug. There are hundreds of pages of files about dosage, side effects, crystallization issues, formula, manufacturing tests, and so on. Other companies are willing to pay handsomely for that data.

Banks and Financial Institutions

As Willie Horton said, "That's where the money is." Everything from transferring funds to stealing data about clients has been tried and worked. The best reason for cracking a bank is that it won't tell. Fearful of their customers' reactions, banks hide their attack history.

Uncle Sam

Hackers attack the government for three good reasons:

- Most of its branches have historically had a very low security budget, so it has been much easier to hack the government than a corporate target. Many hackers get their training by pulling up secure files from the government. Terrorist threats against government networks are changing their approach and budgets for computer security. As a result, hacking Uncle Sam is starting to get more difficult.

- It appeals to the hacker mindset. The government is the great symbol of everything hackers want to thumb their noses at. Yes, the FBI website was hacked. There is no possibility of financial profit in hacking a website, as real goods are never connected to the web server, but the coolness factor should not be overlooked.

- Hacking the government can give a hacker practice for the real payoff jobs: hacking defense contractors. Serious espionage money is to be had there.

Internet Service Providers

Here's a real plum: Hackers frequently go after *Internet service providers* (ISPs). They get revenge on ISPs they don't like, they can show off their power and expertise, but above all they can read email. They can read credit card numbers, bank access codes—they can read the material that you should have encrypted on your own system, but felt it was okay to send just once. Never send sensitive data through email, and use a proven ISP that takes its security seriously. While some mom and pop ISP's might do a decent job of securing their servers, you are better protected using a big ISP that has resources to devote to security.

Big Corporations

Shutting off an entire company can be a thrill for a hacker. Some people will pay hackers to shut down a company for a while, but most of these attacks are still adolescent demonstrations of power.

techlive

A Hacker Attacks

On March 10, 2000, the Nasdaq reached an all-time high, breaking the 5000 mark for the very first time. Internet Trading Technologies (ITTI) wasn't participating in the market upswing, however. The company was too busy working to fend off an online attack.

According to Craig Goldberg, president and founder of ITTI, an attacker overwhelmed the company's servers by submitting a constant stream of fake trade requests. As a result, ITTI's customers were unable to make automated trades several times during the course of the day and in the last half-hour before the market's close.

"Somebody was attacking the system who had a very intimate knowledge of the way our system worked," Goldberg told TechTV. "Because of his unique knowledge of the system, [the hacker] was able to access the demo part of our site and, by putting through some packets of information that somebody else would not be able to do, was able to crash the system."

That was when Goldberg decided to call Eric Friedberg, senior litigation counsel at the U.S. attorney's office in Brooklyn, New York.

"You can't have a trading firm that processes trades on the Nasdaq down three or four hours a day," Friedberg said. "So we chose in this case to pursue a much more reactive approach, so that we could try to get to the heart of the matter and stop the denial-of-service attacks immediately."

The first step in this process involved locating the attacks' origins. This task fell to ITTI network engineer Alexander Parker.

"We observed that every time a person would log in from a certain IP address that the server would crash," Parker recalled.

It turned out that the IP address belonged to a computer at the science building at Queens College in New York City. Another IP address used in the attacks originated from a publicly available computer at a Kinko's copy shop located in New York's Citicorp building.

"Usually if you're going to go into an attack of that nature, you'll do something to mask the source of the attack," Parker said. "And the intruder did nothing of the sort this time, so I guess we got lucky."

ITTI and law enforcement agents would have to get lucky again in order to track down the attacker. Although police knew the locations of the attacks, they still had no way of knowing who had staged them. "When you launch an attack from a Kinko's, it's very difficult to put a particular person at that keyboard at a particular time," Friedberg explained.

If the attacks' locations couldn't reveal the identity of the attacker, however, the nature of the attacks could. Friedberg was sure that the hacker was somehow connected to ITTI.

"The person [who] did this denial-of-service attack was an insider, and not only was he an insider, he was a programmer," Friedberg said. "He was equipped with information to be able to easily exploit any weaknesses in the system, so he was essentially able to bring the system to [its] knees with very little effort."

An Inside Job

Goldberg agreed that the attacker was an insider and, in fact, already suspected someone within his own company: Abdelkader Smires.

Smires, who was a programmer at ITTI and a part-time computer teacher at Queens College, had recently had a falling-out with company management.

"At that time, Abdel and his brother requested an increase in salary and a greater equity participation in the company," Goldberg recalled. "Once we thought we had reached an agreement...Abdel and his brother basically said, 'We want more,' at which point we said, 'This is no longer a good faith salary negotiation.' We felt that we were being held hostage."

In fact, the company was being held hostage by Smires. When Nassau County police, along with US Secret Service agent Bob Sciarrone, went to Queens College to examine the scene and interview potential witnesses, they found someone who had seen Smires at the computer used in the attack.

"I believe it was the teacher [who] was in there at the time that [Smires] was in there, knew him, and pointed out where he was sitting," Sciarrone said.

Police seized the computer used to stage the attacks, and Secret Service agents recovered files indicating that Smires had originated the attacks on ITTI's website.

continues

"It turns out that the person was a little sloppy in launching [his] attack, because at the same time as launching the denial-of-service attack against ITTI, the defendant was reading his emails," Friedberg said. "I think that although he may have had the technical skills to do a better job, to hide his tracks, I think that his anger got the better of him."

Smires was arrested, charged under the Computer Fraud and Abuse Act, and eventually indicted by a grand jury. He was sentenced to eight months in prison.

In his confession, Smires confirmed that he tried "to slow down the ITTI systems by making the computer think it was getting a lot of orders for trades." He also apologized and said that he never intended to hurt anyone.

He had hurt ITTI, however. "In terms of reputation, in terms of consulting charges…it cost us quite a bit of money," Goldberg said. "There were no market losses per se, but easily this incident cost us a few hundred thousand dollars in terms of lost opportunity and just costs to replicate the software code of these two individuals." ITTI also claims it sustained more than $54,000 in damage as a result of Smires's attacks.

The company lost more than just money as a result of the attacks. It also lost the ability to blindly trust its own security and its own people.

"This [was] an insider, using confidential information, using his personal knowledge of the system, not only to get into the system but to cause damage," Friedberg said. "That's a serious attack, and we haven't seen a lot of them, but I think we're going to see more."

Online Games

Another popular focus of hacking energy revolves around online gaming. Popular multiplayer games, such as Unreal or Counterstrike, provide ample opportunity for a hacker to jack up his score and seem like a "total Jedi" when really it's his hacking skills earning the points.

Hacking Other Hackers

A lot has been written on the culture of hacking. To delve into the "who did what and why" is a whole other book. What's important for you to know is that many hack attacks are targeted at other hackers. This is a game in which adolescent pranks and turf wars determine who is King of the Mountain. Website defacements are a very popular endeavor for the hacking community. Defacing the websites of big targets, such as the Department of Defense or Microsoft, puts a notch in the belt of an up-and-coming hacker. However, many of the biggest and baddest hacks come not from attacking corporations or the government, but from attacking those who should know better, other hackers.

A website called Zone-H.org (www.zone-h.org) monitors all the web defacements that occur online. Look at any of the archived defaced sites and you'll see evidence of bragging and hacker-on-hacker showmanship "Blood BR ownz your box" is posted on a personal site located in Russia.

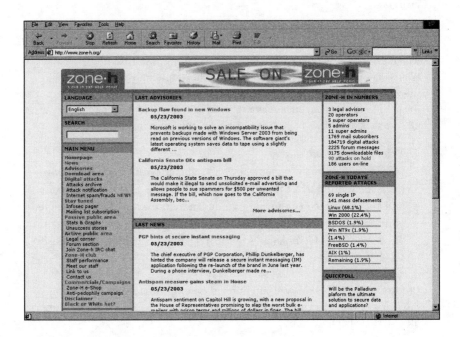

Figure 1.1

Zone-H.org monitors all the websites that are hacked.

An Example Skirmish

One noted hacker and virus writer, Gigabyte, gives us a great example of hacker-on-hacker attacks, but this one had the accidental effect of negatively affecting home computer users.

Born in 1984, this female Belgium hacker and virus writer wrote her first virus at age 14. At age 16, her Sharpei worm got international attention, and she says this type of work is art. "I want to do something original, that not everyone does," she says. "If you write something that's new or funny or special in a way, then I think it is a form of art, yes."

But then in early 2003, somebody pissed Gigabyte off. In an email that is supposedly authored by the Belgian teen, she says her website was hacked by the author of another virus, the Yaha worm. So Gigabyte wrote a worm of her own with good intended—to disinfect the thousands of people infected by the Yaha virus.

The virus she wrote was intended to fend off the Yaha worm and was technically called W32.Sahay.A@mm. It came as an attachment, mathmagic.scr, which executes and then checks for the Yaha family of worms. If W32.Sahay.A@mm found any evidence of Yaha, it attempted to remove the worm. If you want to learn a little more about Sahay, go to `http://securityresponse.symantec.com/avcenter/venc/data/` `w32.yaha.k@mm.html`. Sahay then displayed the following message:

> Title: Exchange viruses?
> Message: Hi there...it seems you were infected with Yaha.k. That worm however, written by an idiot who sPeLlS lIkE tHiS, abused my website and got me to receive the complaints. Therefore, I have just disinfected you. Don't worry tho...as I didn't wanna steal from you, I gave you this virus (Win32.HLLP.YahaSux) in return :) Greetz, Gigabyte [Metaphase VX Team]

Unfortunately, Gigabyte's well-intentioned cleanup virus meant to thwart the writer of the Yaha virus backfired. It crashed systems and corrupted data files on some computers.

Bottom line: This very unique public skirmish between hackers/virus writers shows the one-upmanship at play in the hacking community. As in the case of the Sahay virus and web defacements of sites we may be trying to use, it shows how the general public is occasionally caught in the crossfire of such hacker-on-hacker attacks.

Hacktivism

Another type of hacker claims motives that are more altruistic than ego-maniacal. *Hactivists* take political and social issues into the battleground of cyberspace. They hack the websites and networks of countries known for human rights violations, or countries that perpetrate aggressive acts against the hacker's home country. More commonly, hacktivists say they aren't hacking for money or fame, but for social change.

Deceptive Duo: Patriots or Vandals?

In one unique case of hacktivism, a pair of hackers attacked U.S. government sites and networks they claim support critical infrastructure in the United States.

They called themselves the Deceptive Duo and say their motives were to expose holes so that terrorists wouldn't find and exploit them. Just as Gigabyte's adventures give us insight into the dynamics of hacker-on-hacker contests, the Deceptive Duo represent a glimpse into the motivation and methodology of a hactivist.

Superheroes or crackers, the Deceptive Duo penetrated computer networks in some of the nation's most secure organizations: NASA, the Federal Aviation Administration, and the Space and Naval Warfare Systems Command. But analysts were quick to point out that the Duo accessed only the "low-hanging fruit" of medium-security databases and third-tier government agencies such as the U.S. Geological Survey.

continues

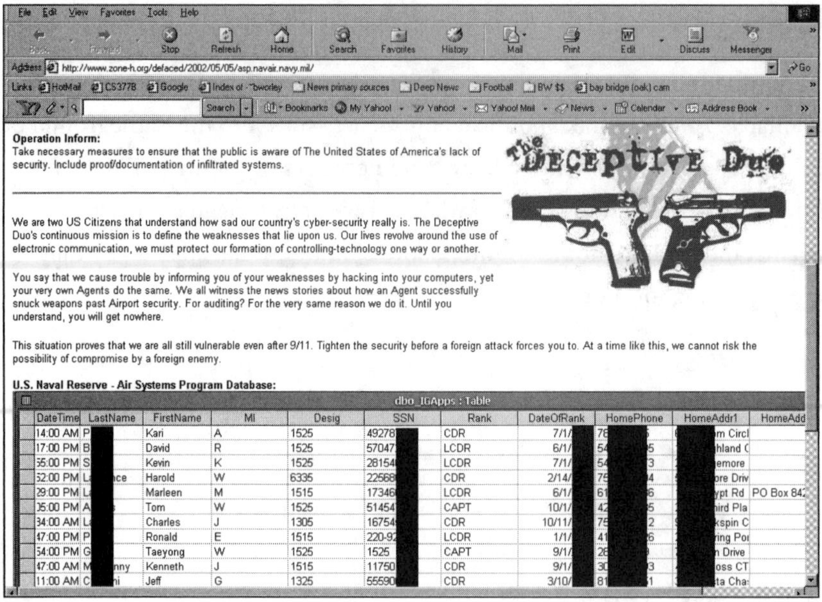

Figure 1.2

The Deceptive Duo hacks some of the country's most secured sites to expose holes that terrorists could exploit.

In the altruism versus publicity debate, critics of the pair claim they are in it for the ink, but they refute that statement.

In an email interview, the Duo told me, "If we were in it for the publicity, prison time is quite the price to pay for attracting media attention to a name that keeps our real identities anonymous."

In our interview, the Duo stressed its "mission": exposing threats to system administrators, publicly embarrassing them in an effort to shore up the national cyber-infrastructure.

In their own words they explained, "It doesn't take extraordinary skill to do what we have been doing in the past few weeks. Al Qaeda can easily gain intelligence just as we have. It's just a matter of time before they use our own vulnerabilities and energy against us."

Companies trying to test their security often pay corporate hackers big money to perform penetration tests: They hire "white-hat" experts to test their systems. Kevin Poulsen, noted ex-hacker turned security journalist for *SecurityFocus Online*, said the Duo is "definitely performing a service for the companies. The price (those companies) pay is an embarrassment."

Poulsen added that the media has paid extra attention to the Duo despite the fact that 30 to 40 web defacements of a similar technical nature take place every day. The patriotism angle post-9/11, Poulsen said, "may have us asking if there's more tolerance for hacktivism, hacking for a cause."

Although Poulsen said he sees many conflicting messages in the mission and work of the Deceptive Duo, he does say the hackers' actions shine a light on the vulnerability of our personal data stored on corporate and government networks. But Poulsen adds, "Nobody thinks Osama bin Laden is after their Social Security number," referring to the type of data the Duo were able to access.

In May of 2002 after a few months of defacements, the Duo got pinched. The FBI issued sealed search warrants against Robert Lyttle, an 18 year old from Pleasant Hill, California, and a second suspect, Ben Stark in Florida. Officials say both suspects have a history of hacking. The two have taken a very low profile since their arrests. Their intentions may have been good, the side benefits of publicity not such a bad thing for them, but the media exposure reinforced the general feelings of anxiety in your average computer user. If these kids can hack the government and banks, there must be lots of hackers out there trying to get me.

If you want the full story go to:
`http://www.techtv.com/news/security/story/0,24195,3384181,00.html`.

Note

The Full List of Hacks the Duo Performed According to Zone-H
See `http://www.zone-.org/en/search/what=deceptive+duo/`.

Defense Logistics Agency, Sandia National Laboratories (Warhead Monitoring Technology Program), Federal Aviation Administration, Office of the Secretary of Defense, Midwest Express Airlines, Rio Grande Airlines, Cameroon Airlines, Saudi Arabian Airlines, NASA Ames Research Center, Department of Transportation, California Department of Transportation, NASA Jet Propulsion Laboratories, Space and Naval Warfare Systems Command, Uniformed Services University of the Health Sciences, Durango, Colorado Airport, South Bend Regional Airport, Southeast Iowa Regional Airport, National Institute of Standards and Technology, U.S. Geological Survey, Peoples State Bank, Arkansas Community Banking Association, Bank of West Baton Rouge, Community Bankers Association of Kansas, Bank of Dumas, Merchants & Planters Bank, Merchants & Marine Bank, Copiah Bank, Madison Bank and Trust, The Evangeline Bank & Trust Company, Iowa Independent Bankers, IBanc Virtual Bank, Greers Ferry Lake State Bank, Gartner Inc., U.S. Naval Reserve — Air Systems Program, U.S. Government Export Portal, Federal Housing Finance Board, Health Resources and Services Administration.

Protecting Yourself from Hackers

Although the chances of being targeted for a one-on-one hack are very slim for your average home user, it's still prudent to make yourself an unappealing target. Three things can protect you from most hacks:

- Install a firewall.
- Turn off file sharing.
- Encrypt sensitive material on your hard drive.

Further, these three things will make you much less susceptible to viruses, Trojans, and data theft from people who have physical access to your computer.

Step 1: Install a Firewall

A *firewall* is hardware, software, or a combination of the two that keeps unauthorized people or programs from remotely accessing a computer or computer network. The best analogy I've heard is that it's like customs and immigration for the Internet. The firewall is the administrator that checks each item entering or leaving the network through port conduits through which data can flow in and out of the computer. Each item needs to conform to the right criteria to pass through. So a hacker attempting to enter the network through the wrong port or with improper goods would be prevented from entering.

Equally important, a firewall controls what data leaves the host computer. If you are infected with a worm that installs a Trojan horse program, the firewall alerts you to the fact that a new program is trying to transmit data from your computer. That could be a list of passwords, a keylog of all your correspondence, or a file containing all the Excel spreadsheets on your computer. The firewall knows that only certain data is allowed in and only certain data is allowed out.

For the home user, a software firewall is perfectly sufficient. You really don't need a hardware firewall to boot unless you are engaging in tremendously dangerous online behavior, such as starting flame wars with known hackers on security message boards (an activity I strongly recommend against).

The Nuts and Bolts of Firewalls

If you like understanding the technical stuff behind software, you'll love this explanation. If you are intimidated by all the techno jargon, have a crack at this because just reading and immersing yourself in the jargon can help you learn a little, even if by osmosis. Finally, if you think it's all techno-babble and you just want your computer to work, skip to installing your firewall.

Firewalls work because you train them. You tell the firewall which programs can transmit data and through which ports. The process of training the firewall is pretty easy. When you first install it, it's like an annoying game of "Mother may I." "Mother may I allow Internet Explorer to transmit data via port 80?" You say yes, and then Internet Explorer always has the capability to use port 80. For the first few weeks, you may have to research which programs use what ports, and understanding ports is an important part of the learning process.

What Are Ports?

There are two types of ports. The first type is at the back of your computer (where you stick hardware cables into): USB, parallel, SCSI, and so on. Those aren't the types of ports we're discussing here, however. We're talking about the ports that facilitate communication between two computers engaged in a client/server relationship on a network.

A client/server relationship is when one computer, the server, hands files and data to the other computer, the client, which has one of its applications ask for the files and data. A common example of this is your computer's web browser application asking a TechTV serving computer for the data that comprises an article.

Let's not forget that the client and server computers are talking using a transmission protocol called TCP/IP. The TCP part is a point-to-point protocol that governs the transmission of data streams between the two connected computers. The next layer, IP, doesn't deal with streams of data but rather with packets (discrete bundles of data also called *datagrams*).

How Do Ports Work?

To illustrate this concept, think of the server part of the network as a Chinese restaurant and the client side as my apartment, where I hungrily await some mu shu pork and pot stickers. For me to get the Chinese food, I need to tell the delivery driver what my street address is. Because I live in a big building, however, I also need to specify my apartment number; otherwise my irritating neighbor McNubbins might hijack my mu shu.

The street address for my whole building is like the IP address of my computer. This unique number distinguishes my computer from all others on the huge network we call the Internet. My apartment number is like a port number. The port number describes which application in my computer needs the data, just like my apartment number tells the delivery driver which door to knock on with my mu shu and pot stickers.

Port numbers range from 0 to 65,535. (My apartment building isn't that big, though.) Ports numbered between 0 and 1023 are restricted. (If you're programming, don't have your applications bind to them.) Well-known ports and their corresponding numbers are as follows:

- ftp (File Transfer Protocol): 21/tcp
- telnet (Telnet): 23/tcp
- smtp (Simple Mail Transfer Protocol): 25/tcp

- domain (Domain Name Server): 53/tcp
- gopher (Gopher): 70/tcp
- finger (Finger): 79/tcp
- http (World Wide Web HTTP): 80/tcp
- pop3 (Post Office Protocol version 3): 110/tcp
- nntp (Network News Transfer Protocol): 119/tcp
- irc (Internet Relay Chat Protocol): 194/tcp
- ipx (IPX): 213/tcp
- https (HTTP protocol over TLS/SSL): 443/tcp

These are standards, but you can change port-number assignments if you're worried about hackers sniffing at your ports. Changing port numbers confuses the hackers. It's like watching TV. If you want to watch **TechTV**, you need to know its station number. Likewise, if someone wants files off your computer, he needs to know the right port number to gain entry. But changing port numbers is pretty advanced; it's better just to install a firewall to keep ports closed to unauthorized entries.

An important thing to know: When you change your port number, you must change the server's port number as well; otherwise the machine won't talk with its server.

> **Note**
>
> **The Router Option** Many people say that you don't need a firewall if you are using a router—a piece of hardware that attaches to your computer, networks them together, and/or allows them to share a broadband connection. The router effectively hides your IP address, your computer's unique (sometimes changing) numeric identifier online (remember the Chinese food delivery guy). Many think this IP obfuscation is enough, but I disagree. Firewalls do a lot more than keep your IP address hidden. They also help you keep track of traffic coming into your computer, and, more importantly, they log the data trying to leave your computer. In a world where one-on-one personal hacks are uncommon and Trojan horse programs stealthily sending out your personal data are incredibly common, firewalls have a place, router or no router.

Installing ZoneAlarm

At the time of this printing, I recommend three firewalls: ZoneAlarm, BlackICE Defender, and Norton Personal Firewall. Many others are on the market, but these specific products are most tailored to the home user and keep the technical aspects to a minimum. Of the three, I use ZoneAlarm for one key reason: It's free for personal use, and it's the best firewall I've come across. It's easy to install, has a great graphical interface, it's easy to train, and it's tailored to home users. You can download ZoneAlarm, and the other firewalls mentioned, from Download.com.

Here's how you install ZoneAlarm.

1. Go to Download.com (CNET.com's clearinghouse for downloadable programs).
2. Search for ZoneAlarm.
3. Choose the free version or the plus version if you want tech support.
4. Click the Download button.
5. Save the file to a location you will remember (a folder you create called Downloads or on your desktop, for instance).
6. Double-click the downloaded ZoneAlarm setup file.
7. Accept all the installation defaults. Your computer will automatically reboot.
8. Follow the ZoneAlarm instructions for training the firewall to allow or prevent certain programs from accessing the outside world. Then start the training or configuration process.

Training ZoneAlarm

- Do you want ZoneAlarm to notify you when it blocks Internet traffic or do you want it to protect in silence? If you're easily annoyed by pop-up windows, choose to be protected in silence. You will still be asked to verify programs.

- Do you want ZoneAlarm to configure your browser's security settings right away or the first time you launch your browser? It's safe for most users to do this right away. Advanced users will want to customize access and server permissions. Most novice users should stay away from the Advanced options.

Now that you're finished with setup, you can customize even more settings. Here's what you can do in each part of the interface:

- **Overview**

  You can quickly view how much traffic ZoneAlarm has blocked, which programs have attempted to go online, and how many email attachments are quarantined.

  - Go to the Product Info tab to get version, licensing, and registration information, as well as product updates and help.

  - The Preferences tab contains ZoneAlarm's display properties, enables you to decide how to communicate with Zone Labs, and enables you to specify how you want to check for updates.

- **Firewall**

  Firewall settings are divided into two categories: Internet Zone Security and Trusted Zone Security.

  - The Internet Zone Security option includes all computers on the web. Putting this setting on Low turns off your firewall protection. Medium is recommended for limited Internet use. (On Medium, other users can see your computer, but can't share its resources.) High is recommended for always-on Internet users.

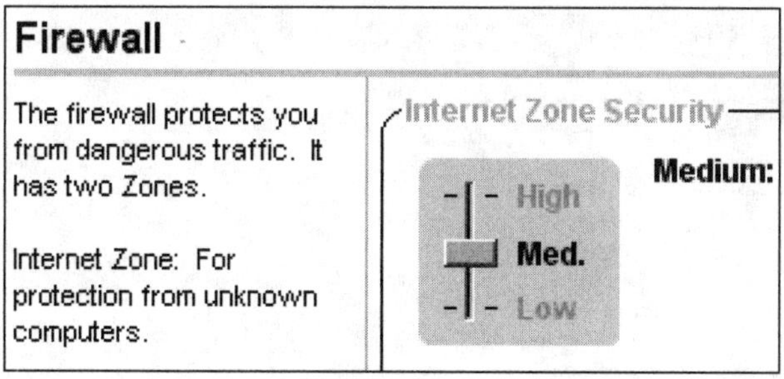

Firewall

	Internet Zone Security
The firewall protects you from dangerous traffic. It has two Zones.	**Medium:**
	– High
Internet Zone: For protection from unknown computers.	**Med.**
	– Low

Figure 1.3

A medium setting is recommended for Zone Alarm's Internet Zone Security option.

  - Trusted Zone Security enables you to share files with other "trusted" users. Low turns off the firewall. Medium lets you share files. High hides your machine and keeps it operating under hackers' radar.

- Use the Advanced button to tweak your security settings by blocking specific types of incoming and outgoing traffic.
- Go to the Zones tab to add computers to your trusted zone.

- **Program Control**

  It's recommended that you keep Program Control on the Medium setting so that each program requests permission to access the Internet. Here's how to use the other options in this field. (You also can access the Program Wizard if you want to change any of the original options you chose during setup.)

  - Automatic Lock shuts off Internet access after a period of inactivity. Click the Custom button to specify what amount of time determines "inactivity" or choose to have it activate when the screen saver comes on. You can also determine whether you want to block all Internet traffic or grant permission to pass-lock programs.
  - Go to the Programs tab and left-click one of the symbols next to a program's name to change its access: Allow, Block, or Ask.

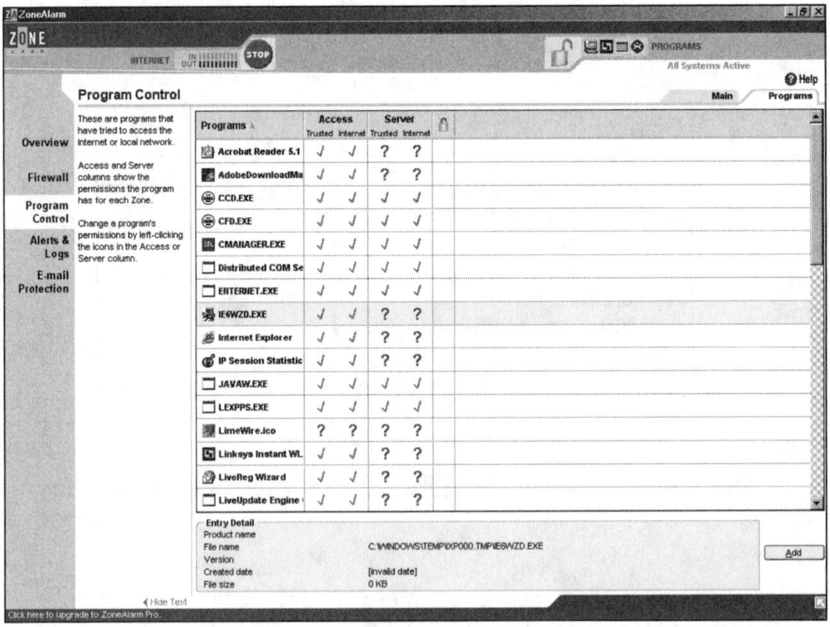

Figure 1.4

Use Zone Alarm's Program Control to change your programs' permission status for accessing the Internet.

- **Alerts and Logs**

  Indicate whether you want to get alert pop-up messages for things that are not programs. The Log Viewer enables you to look over all the alerts you have received.

- **Email Protection**

  Turn MailSafe on and off. This feature spots questionable email attachments that may contain viruses and puts them in quarantine. In general, keep it on.

It's easy to minimize ZoneAlarm's screen. If you want to turn off the program for any reason, right-click the icon in your system tray and choose Shutdown ZoneAlarm. Firewalls are "noisy" at first—that is, the firewall is quite active while it customizes itself to your computer—but then they quiet down.

Testing Your Firewall

If you really want to be thorough, here are some ways to test your new firewall:

- **ShieldsUp!** (www.grc.com) is a free 20K application developed by Internet privacy/security advocate Steve Gibson of Gibson Research Corporation and designed just for Windows users. When installed, it contacts the ShieldsUp! web server and tests your firewall's integrity from the outside.

- **Atelier Web Security Port Scanner** (AWSPS) v4.0 is an incredible utility used to report and test TCP and UDP ports. You want to verify that no ports are reported open unless you've opened them yourself. To test your firewall, just install this program on an outside computer and ping every port on your IP address.

To test from inside, consider the following:

- **Leak Test** (www.grc.com) is another great free download from GRC. Leak Test is designed to test from the inside out, so you'll want to install it on the computer where your firewall is located. With the push of a button, it tests your firewall and generates a report identifying possible security issues. The best part about Leak Test is the information and step-by-step instructions it provides on how to improve your computer's security if security issues are found.

Step 2: Turn Off File Sharing

File sharing is the act of letting users on multiple computers access documents through a network. This is great for businesses and families that want to share printers. Or for coworkers who want to access, modify, read, or print the same document at the same time. However, file sharing is also an easy way for hackers to access your system.

Computers on a network using Microsoft file sharing open up the directories on their hard drive to others on the network. With file sharing enabled, Susan in accounting can access an expense report on your computer even though you are at a different desk. Similarly, a remote attacker can access the files on your hard drive at home through the file-sharing feature.

Microsoft ships its Windows operating system with file sharing turned off, but you never know what your helpful cousin was up to when he was "optimizing" your system. For most of us, we aren't networking our computers and don't need this feature, so follow these steps to make sure file sharing is turned off.

1. Click Start.
2. Choose Settings.
3. Open the Control Panel.
4. Click Network.
5. Toward the bottom of the window that pops up, click the File and Print Sharing button.

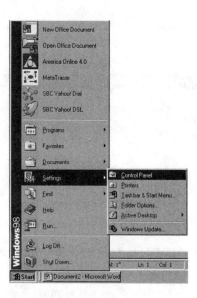

Figure 1.5

Open the Control Panel from the Windows Start menu.

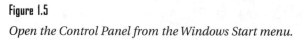

Figure 1.6

Click the File and Print Sharing button in the Network dialog box.

6. Uncheck the two options for files and printer(s) so that the boxes are empty.

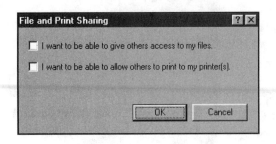

Figure 1.7

Uncheck the options in the File and Print Sharing dialog box.

7. Click OK twice to close the Network windows.
8. Restart your computer if prompted to do so.
9. Close the Control Panel.

Step 3: Encrypt Sensitive Material

Whether from a hacker on the outside or from someone you know on the inside, your sensitive data needs protection. Financial documents, medical records, love letters—whatever you want to protect, the Windows boot-up password for your computer doesn't do a thing. You need to encrypt the data to keep it safe from prying eyes.

If you are emailing anything sensitive, it should be encrypted. Anywhere along the chain of computers relaying your message, a hacker could snoop through the emailed message.

Cryptography is the process of storing information in a form that appears scrambled or hidden from all but authorized viewers. The original message, known as *plain text*, is scrambled using a software application called an *encryption engine*. The engine takes this plain text and applies other data (usually mathematical) known as a *key* to create the scrambled message, which is called *cipher text*. To unscramble the cipher text, the recipient needs to have access to the key and decryption software.

The encryption process can be as simple as substituting numbers for letters: A = 1, B = 2, C = 3, and so on. You then provide the key to the people whom you want to read the encrypted text.

Most forms of encryption used for military purposes in the first half of the past century involved a more complicated kind of substitution, but it was essentially the same process. The U.S. military began using Native Americans as voice encryptors for military communications during World War I. The Marines perfected the use of these human encryptors during World War II as they used Navajo speakers, known as *codetalkers*, exclusively. The Navajo speakers' codes were not broken during the war.

In World War II, the Axis Powers relied on a device called the *Enigma machine*, a rotor-based machine that created cipher text with a typewriter-like system (originally meant for commercial use) that transposed letters of the alphabet. It was broken during the war, thanks to the work of Polish and British mathematicians, allowing the Allies access to German plans.

With modern encryption, plain text tends to be scrambled by computers using complex mathematical algorithms that are only theoretically breakable by a concerted effort involving supercomputers over a long period of time. So far, no encryption has proven absolutely secure, just practically secure.

Public Key Encryption

There's a problem with this kind of cryptography: How do you get the key to the people to whom you want to send encrypted messages? Ideally, you would physically hand the key to the person with whom you want to communicate. That isn't practical in most cases, however, especially for commercial transactions such as Internet shopping or international communications between people who have never met. The problem is compounded by the fact that to prevent previous message recipients from being able to read messages you don't want them to see, you need a new key for each transaction. That's where a relatively new form of encryption enters the picture: public key encryption, invented in the early 1970s by Whitfield

Diffie and Martin Hellman. Previously, cryptography was a closely guarded science practiced by governments and a handful of shady characters with quasi-governmental roles. Its applications were largely military, with only a few business uses. With public key encryption, cryptography exploded right alongside the personal computer revolution.

In most encryption, the key for encrypting a message is the same as the key for decrypting it. What public key encryption does is split the key into two parts: a public key (widely distributed and available in public directories), and a private key (held as private, like your ATM PIN code).

Someone using your public key to encrypt a message to you is assured that only you can read that message, decrypting it using your private key. You never have to meet that other person or worry that the she can read other messages encrypted with your public key. The other person can only "lock" the message she sends, not "unlock" it.

This public key can be used for another purpose, too. Messages encrypted using your private key can be decrypted by this public key, creating what's called a *digital signature*, which can be used to verify the authenticity of digital exchanges.

Although other forms of encryption are available, public key encryption is the darling technology of privacy advocates and a group of self-proclaimed "crypto-anarchists" who call themselves *cypherpunks*. Public key cryptography made its first really big splash on the Internet via a program called PGP, which stands for *Pretty Good Privacy*.

PGP was first based on algorithms created at MIT. After a roller-coaster ride during the dot.com hay days, PGP is back and available for free personal use. You can download it from the PGP site (www.pgp.com) or from Download.com; just search for "PGP freeware." PGP is the de facto standard for encryption, but new computer users may find it cumbersome. Other free encryption products are on the market, but they either contain spyware, only work on certain platforms (Windows NT/2000), or have extremely complicated interfaces. The one I find easiest and that's devoid of all the previously mentioned bad stuff is called File2File, by

Cryptomathic (available at Download.com). Because of its basic functionality—File2File just encrypts and decrypts files—File2File has an easier installation and setup than PGP.

The file-encryption functions in both File2File and PGP basically work the same way: Just right-click the file you want to encrypt. You select Encrypt, enter your password, and the file is scrambled. Note that the file extension changes. (For instance, the Word document sensitive_information.doc becomes sensitive_information.doc.f2f.) Only by double-clicking or right-clicking the file and entering your password can you access the encrypted data. Forget that password and you can kiss that data good-bye!

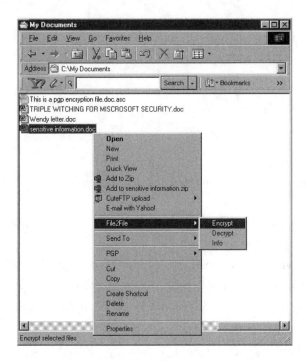

Figure 1.8

Right-click and select File2File, Encrypt to encrypt a file with File2File.

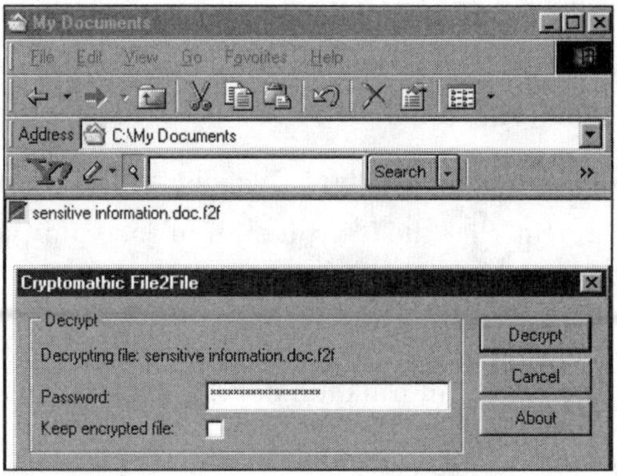

Figure 1.9

The only way to open a file encrypted with File2File is to enter the password that was set when the file was encrypted.

How to Encrypt a File

Office 2002 has a built-in file encryption. Here's how to use it:

1. Open the document you want to encrypt.
2. Go to Tools, Options, and then the Security tab.
3. Enter a password for your document.
4. Write down or memorize this password. You will not be able to read your document if you lose it.

Your document is now an encrypted file. You can open it in other applications, such as Notepad or DOS Edit, but you won't be able to read its contents. You also can use the same menu to require a password from anybody who wants to modify the document.

Windows XP Professional also has a built-in encryption program. You can encrypt files only on volumes that are formatted with the NTFS file system. Here's how you encrypt a file with this program:

1. Select Start, All Programs, Accessories, and then Windows Explorer.
2. Select the file you want to encrypt, and then click Properties.

3. On the General tab, click Advanced.

4. Under Compress or Encrypt attributes, select the Encrypt Contents to Secure Data check box, and then click OK.

5. If the folder the file is located in is not encrypted, you receive an Encryption Warning dialog box. From here you have two options:

   • If you want to encrypt only the file, click Encrypt the File Only, and then click OK.

   • If you want to encrypt the file and the folder, click Encrypt the File and the Parent Folder, and then click OK.

When someone tries to access the encrypted file, he receives a message similar to the following:

Word cannot open the document: *username* does not have access privileges. (*drive*:*filename*.doc)

If he attempts to copy or move the encrypted document to another location on the hard disk, he receives this message:

Error Copying File or Folder
Cannot copy *filename*: Access is denied.

The Importance of Encryption

Encryption is at the heart of most digital commerce done over the Internet. However, encryption tools haven't been particularly intuitive. To make encryption easy to use, it needs to be transparent to users. So the standards organizations that control Internet protocols are trying hard to push encryption technology right into the network itself. In the meantime, only a few commercial products exist for consumer use.

Part of the reason for the slow spread of encryption is that, under pressure from law-enforcement agencies that view strong encryption as a threat to their ability to investigate crimes and terrorism, the government has classified this technology under the same export restrictions reserved for weapons and munitions. Privacy advocates and business interests point out that the technology is already available internationally, and that imposing restrictions on them is just closing the barn door after the horses have gone.

In any case, more and more of our private information is making its way into public places, thanks to the spread of the Internet and other digital networks. When used to secure information from credit cards to love letters, encryption allows a modicum of privacy in an increasingly public world. Cryptography is no longer a spy-versus-spy tool, but the cornerstone of an emerging digital marketplace.

Wireless Security

If you have more than one computer in your home, you might decide to network them. Networked computers can share printers, data, and most importantly a broadband connection. But creating a network between computers in different rooms can be a real hassle. The main problem is the thick cat-5 Ethernet cables snaking through your house connecting the computers. Because a relatively new technology fights the cable mess and gives laptop web surfers portability, wireless or Wi-Fi networks are gaining real popularity.

You plug your broadband connection into a wireless hub, install wireless cards in your computers, and you've got Internet access all through the house. The wireless hub connects to the computers through radio signals at high speeds—basic models work at about 11MB per second, almost 20 times faster than a 56k dialup modem and 3 or 4 times faster than most DSL and cable modem downstream speeds.

Because Wi-Fi radio signals broadcast up to 300 feet, anyone cruising for signals in proximity to your base station could gain access to your network. This act of drive-by hacking is called *wardriving*. Unsecured wireless access points make your network vulnerable to wardriving and put the data on your computers at risk. It also enables a hacker to launch an attack through your bandwidth.

More commonly, unsecured wireless signals allow neighbors to act as parasites on your broadband access. Living in tight quarters or in an apartment building, Wi-Fi hijackers install a wireless card and scan for open connections. As soon as they find one, they use it to access the Internet for free. It's not a huge infraction, but the rightful subscriber is paying $40 a month for a fast connection while the hijacker is slowing that connection to a crawl downloading porn and uploading music.

You can lockdown your wireless connection by following a few simple steps:

- Change all the default account names on your router. Most wireless routers and access points come with a default service set identifier (SSID). This is the unique name your base station uses to name the wireless local area network (WLAN) to which it broadcasts. Use a name you can remember, but not one so obvious that a wardriver or neighbor can guess. Don't use your address: A security journalist for the magazine *ExtremeTech* drove through a group of office parks and used the street number of each office as a possible SSID sign in name. He was shocked that his simple guesswork gave him access to more than a few corporate networks.

- Change the default passwords. Again, use something that's simple to remember, but hard for an outsider to guess.

- Activate the Wireless Equivalent Privacy (WEP) controls that come with your wireless router. WEP is not an unbreakable standard of encryption, but it certainly makes your network a more difficult target for drive-by hackers. Most routers come with some sort of configuration utility.

  The Linksys wireless router (a popular home wireless product) has a web-based configuration tool that enables you to turn on WEP. If you are using the Linksys router, in the WEP settings area, choose Mandatory or Enable, and then set a passphrase. You will then have to reconfigure the wireless cards in each computer, enabling WEP and inputting the correct passphrase so that all encrypted signals from the base station/router can be decrypted by your wireless card/computer.

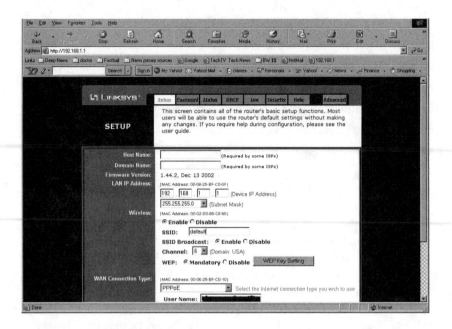

Figure 1.10

The Linksys wireless router has a web-based configuration tool that lets you turn on WEP and encrypt your wireless connection.

There are people who want to access your data and computers, but as you'll learn in later chapters, there are easier ways than hacking to gain that access. Hackers get all the ink, and with the advent of every new technology (like wireless networks) curious, mischevious, and sometimes, nefarious hackers will try to circumvent that new technology's security. The key for home users is to make yourself an unappealing target. Taking these simple measures will take you off the 'easy victim list' and give you peace of mind knowing you're protecting yourself.

Identity Theft:
Who Owns Me Now?

The Federal Trade Commission says identity theft is the fastest growing white-collar crime in America. In 2002, 380,000 Americans reported that their identity had been hijacked, and American companies lost $25 billion to identity-theft crimes. That's billion with a *B*. Individuals lose time and money trying to regain their good name, and the corporate losses that credit card companies pick up is a drain on our national economy. When someone runs up $50,000 bill, everyone involved pays and pays. The Federal Trade Commission says that nearly half (43 percent) of all the complaints they received in 2002 were about ID theft.

In the age of data, we are numbers: Social Security, driver's license, home address, phone number, PIN, credit cards. Each of these numbers has a value. For example, your ZIP code tells a bad guy something about your worth. Your driver's license number lets you cash checks, rent cars, and is often used for certain simple security deposits (for renting DVDs or roto-tillers, for instance). Your Social Security number lets you open bank accounts, work for a wage, and is how most universities track you when you are a student. Many of these numbers that describe you are already being bought and sold (more or less legitimately) every day. Companies want your name for mailing lists, your phone number for telephone solicitation. They want to know what magazines you read, so they know what products you're most interested in buying. However, some people want your numbers so that they can be you.

The people who want to be you come from all economic classes and have a wide range of motives. They may need a job, but lack citizenship papers—or they may want to use the community hospital. They may want to open a little bank account for moving questionable money around. They may want what your credit cards can buy, or they may be happy renting as many DVDs as they can one weekend without planning to return them. The consequences can be serious. Take, for example, Jonathan, a California resident who lost his identity and his privacy in 2000. Jonathan did not want to further jeopardize his identity, so he asked us to use just his first name, but he wants his story told so that others can learn from it. Jonathan was first alerted to an identity problem when he got an unexpected phone call from Verizon.

A Victim's Story

Verizon, a telecommunications company, wanted to verify Jonathan's information, but he hadn't applied for an account. "[The company representative] said that somebody had used my identity to apply for a cell phone account, and they were calling to verify my information," Jonathan said. The representative who called said there was a discrepancy in the address, adding this was typical with cases of fraud. Although he put a stop to that attempt, 6 months later Jonathan found out someone had successfully used his identity again. This time, however, he was told he would have to pay a high price.

Jonathan received a bill for $1,200 from a collection agency for 6 months of unpaid service with a different cellular carrier. Jonathan had put fraud alerts on his credit reports with the three major credit reporting agencies, but the telephone company said no alerts had appeared when the person applied for an account. It took a year, but he finally resolved the bill. "I had to go through all my bank accounts, brokerage accounts," he said. "I had to contact my payroll services…all of those things are linked to your Social Security number and your address and all those bits of information."

Although Jonathan still isn't sure if the information was found on the Internet, he isn't taking any chances. At his request, the few websites that listed his address or phone number removed the information. Jonathan no longer offers any personal details online. If a site requires an address or phone number, he enters false information. He still monitors his credit reports and shreds all documents before throwing them out.

Liar Liar

Sue Peters says she has become a shameless liar to protect her identity. That's because her ordeal both frustrated and frightened her.

Peters, a San Francisco-based artist and editor, didn't know she was the victim of identity fraud until it was too late. She had applied for a new credit card, and for the first time in her life was denied. A woman with a different name had appropriated Peters's Social Security number and had run up so many bills that Peters's credit had been damaged.

"I don't know [how it happened], and that's the most frightening part of this story for me," she said. "It's scary to think how often people ask us for our Social Security numbers, and ask us that in public. It was very creepy, actually, was my first reaction. And then I started to get really angry. I thought, 'How dare this woman do this, and how did the bank let this happen?'"

How the woman got a hold of Peters's Social Security number remains a mystery. But private investigator David Cook, regional managing partner with security firm Noesis, says this kind of fraud happens all the time—via both the mailbox and the email inbox. "It's a very common practice, and it's fairly easy," he said. "Basically, if someone's determined to do it, they can do it." Cook says identity theft is a lot easier to perpetrate than one would think. "A lot of people feel that if they gave up their name or their Social Security number making an online purchase, that's how it's done," he said. "Oftentimes it's simple things, like items you discard in the trash, credit card applications, or pre-approved credit cards in the mail. People just toss them out, don't rip them up."

Shred Everything

Cook says the only way to prevent theft is to shred everything. Additionally, if you're not careful, the information you put out about yourself could come back to haunt you online. "If you're using your real name and real address, real phone numbers, Social Security number, those things are possibly available to other people to misuse," Cook said.

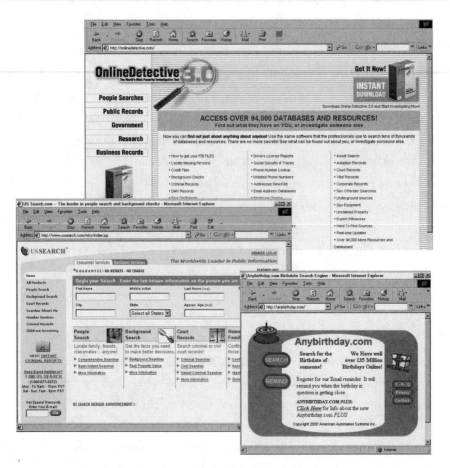

Figure 2.1

Some websites provide personal information that could be used by identity thieves.

Thanks to a growing number of websites that put a price tag on your personal information, the identity-theft problem seems to be growing. For instance, AnyBirthday.com serves up people's birth dates, OnlineDetective.com reveals individuals' criminal histories, and US Search.com returns names, numbers, and addresses—personal data that could aid a would-be identity thief. However, Rick Heitzmann, senior vice president of corporate development with US Search.com, says the information his company and companies like it gives out is relatively harmless. "We're not giving out things…that you couldn't find through public availability like a phone book or public records of any kind," he said.

After her ordeal, Sue Peters reclaimed her true identity by eradicating it online. "I'll use pseudonyms, I'll use lots of different passwords, I don't give the accurate information for the most part," she said. "I'll often lie about my gender, lie about my birth date, all of that. So I'm a total schizophrenic online. And I think that's the safest thing to do because most of this information is nobody's business."

Identity Theft Through Email Scams

How do identity thieves get your identity? The most obvious source of your information is you. Believe it or not, you may provide the identity thief with everything he or she needs to know—and you may do it willingly. One of the most common types of identify theft occurs through email scams.

Every week, TechTV gets email about scams like this. You get an email that looks like it's from AOL, eBay, PayPal or EarthLink. The From address is "support@aol.com" or "billing@paypalcom." It appears to be a legitimate request for updated account information, but it's actually an identity-theft ploy that provides easy pickings for con artists.

Here's how the scheme works: Con artists send out thousands of emails to every name they can find at AOL.com or EarthLink.com, or to random email addresses for services such as eBay and PayPal. The bad guys use a technique called *spoofing* to make the email look like it's official, as if it's actually from support@aol.com. They forge the "from" address so that it doesn't say conartist@randomisp.com, it says billing@paypal.com.

The first generation of these scams asked you to email back your credit card number, account name, and password. However, people wised up: A legitimate company would never ask you to send your personal information via email.

Now the bad guys have taken it a step further. ID thieves register a domain name (a website or URL) with an address that looks a lot like a legitimate site: www.billing-aol.com, www.earthlinksupport.com, www.cgi-paypal.com. In the spoofed email asking for an account update, there is a link to the fake website the thief set up. Clicking the link takes the victim to a website that is a carbon copy of a real site's billing page. All the data-input fields work and most people don't notice that the website address is slightly off. Victims input their personal data, click Submit, and don't think anything of it until months later when they are turned down for a home loan or denied on a credit card application. Only then do they realize they're victims of identity theft.

> **Note**
>
> **Secure Socket Layer** Secure Socket Layer (SSL) is a secure encryption feature that responsible websites use to protect customer data during transfer over the Internet. If a website is using SSL, it will have a gold padlock symbol at the bottom of the browser window. Be aware, however, that bad guys can use SSL technology on dummy websites used to steal your personal data. SSL ensures that the transmission of your data is encrypted, but it's not a seal of approval.
>
>
>
> **Figure 2.2**
>
> *A padlock symbol at the bottom corner of your browser tells you the website uses SSL to protect data transferred on the site.*

A Viewer Falls for an eBay Scam

A TechTV viewer submitted this story. "Richard" (not his real name) said he received an email that looked like it was from eBay. It asked him to click an embedded link to update his eBay account, but the link led to a website that looked exactly like eBay.com, but wasn't actually affiliated with the auction site. Richard submitted all of his credit card and personal data to the dummy site. "I filled out half of the info myself and became frustrated with the level of private information required for the 'update,'" he wrote. "Unfortunately, I still hit Send and sent vital information."

Richard later thought the site was asking for too much personal data, became suspicious, and called eBay. "At first I asked them if they knew about this fraud involving the duplication of their site, and they replied that they did." Richard then asked why they didn't send a warning letter: "The reply from customer service was that they would have to send too many emails!"

Richard had no choice but to go through the arduous task of changing his bank accounts, PIN numbers, and credit cards. He's thankful he figured it out, however, before his credit was ruined or charges were put on his account.

eBay spokesperson Kevin Pursglove says these types of scams do happen. As he told us, "Depending on the sophistication of the scammer, they could send out just a few dozen spoofed emails, but others send out hundreds of emails that look like they are from us."

Pursglove says many people are automatically suspicious of the information requests. "Most people know that these emails are scams," he said. "But to spread the word, we post announcements on our message boards every 3 to 4 weeks warning about attempts to trick eBay users."

Pursglove further explains that eBay doesn't ask people to update their information. "You put your information in when you register, but that's it."

eBay wants to protect its trademark, but says it's tough to find criminals such as the email scam artist. "It's very hard to track these types of fraud," Pursglove said. "Most of the people who receive the emails do not respond to them or alert eBay. Another issue is that the criminals who post dummy sites are quick opportunists. The sites are up and gone within hours."

Tony Recognized EarthLink Message as Scam

Tony in Seattle wrote TechTV to thank us for the information we broadcast about these types of scams. He said knowledge of the con helped him figure out that he was the target of a scam before it was too late. "I received an email, ostensibly from EarthLink, stating that I needed to update my account info. It directed me to the website EarthLink-Billings.com, where I found a form asking for my personal and credit card info."

Tony was immediately suspicious because the URL for the site ended in .com, rather than the traditional .net used by EarthLink in all of its official corporate URLs. However, noticing these small details is no easy task for persons just trying to keep up with all the requests and "action items" that come through their inbox. Tony says he is suspicious of any email, piece of snail mail, or cold call over the telephone that asks for his personal information, and it was this skepticism that saved him from the scam.

Once he made the ".com" rather than ".net" observation, Tony started looking for other clues that this wasn't a real EarthLink site. He saw that the site wasn't transmitting information using SSL, another tip-off to Tony that the site wasn't EarthLink.

His suspicions in full force, Tony called EarthLink's customer service department to find out whether the site was legit. EarthLink confirmed that the site wasn't affiliated with the company in any way. The site was fully operational for only 10 days. Now if you type in EarthLink-Billings.com, you get a "Cannot find server" error page.

"EarthLink cautions Internet users about any email or website that asks them to input personal information," EarthLink's chief privacy officer Les Seagraves said in a statement given to TechTV. "It could very easily be the work of an identity thief. Internet service providers do not typically ask for information in this way. It is always safer to call if in doubt."

Seagraves offered a list of red flags for Internet users wary of fraud:

- An email asking for personal information.
- An email asking for any information that you have already given.
- A website or email with a different domain name than what you typically use (EarthLink.net).
- An input form that isn't secure. ("https:" should be in the URL, and a closed lock [SSL symbol] should appear in your browser.)
- Claims about the security of an input form.
- Claims of lost or "flushed" information.
- No requirement asking users to log in.

How Not to Lose Your Identity in an Email Scam

The only way to protect yourself is to act like Tony: Be skeptical! Know that none of the web-based services will ask you to update your information via email. Check the URL of any site where you're inputting sensitive data. If it doesn't exactly match the site you think it is, go to the front page of the actual site (AOL.com, eBay.com, PayPal.com) and drill down to the Billing section. Overall, when in doubt call the customer service number on your bill and ask them to advise you.

If you want to get really geeky, and this is something I recommend, you can perform a Whois lookup through the Verisign WHOIS service. This enables you to search the database of all registered web addresses. The Whois lookup gives you some of the information provided by registrars when they listed their websites. Most importantly, it can tell you the official address used in the registration process, where the site is hosted (where the computers that actually serve up the site's pages are located), and when the site was registered. For the site Tony reported, EarthLink-Billings.com, no address was given, the site was created 7 days before he received the "account update" email, and it appears to refer to a web server in Germany. These are all red flags: Any legitimate corporate site lists company headquarters in their domain name registration information and the site will have been registered a long time ago (a "long time" is relative here—remember we're talking Internet years). As for the actual location of the servers, the website creater may outsource web hosting to a contracted company at a remote location, but AOL, EarthLink, eBay, and so on are not likely to host their sites in Eastern Europe.

Whois

Whois, pronounced "who is," is a service that enables you to look up the account information of a registered domain name. Each website's URL or domain name is tied to an account in the Network Solutions/Verisign Registrar database. This is the company that organizes websites into the working entity that is the World Wide Web. Whois can also be thought of as a reverse lookup. You have the web address, now you want to know who is really behind it: Where was it registered, by whom, what physical address did they provide, and when was the domain name originally registered? All this information can help you fact check an online business.

How to Use Whois

Go to http://www.verisign-grs.com/whois/. On the page, you will see an open box that reads "Whois Lookup www._____." After the "www," enter the remainder of the web address you are researching.

A pop-up window should give you a physical address and contact information, but there is no guarantee that information is correct. In one recent case involving Premier-escrow.com, the name used to register the site belonged to a man who'd had his identity and credit card numbers stolen.

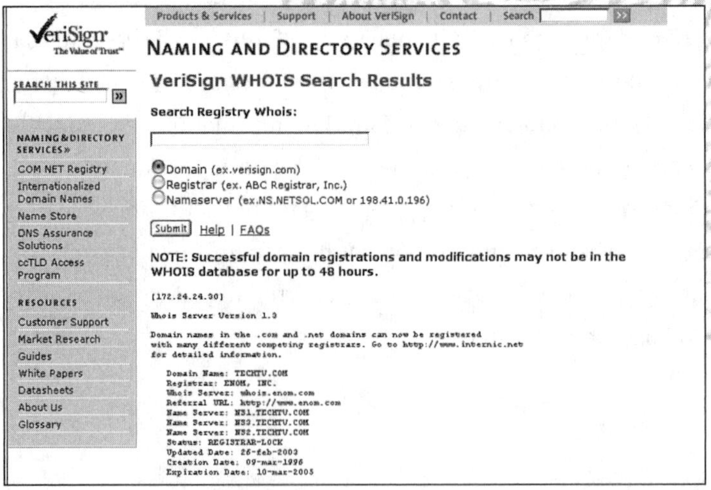

Figure 2.3

Whois enables you to look up account information for a registered domain name.

Giving Your Information Away

Assessing when you can feel safe giving out your personal information is a tough task, especially as identity thieves get more and more sophisticated. Take the case of "Jim," an Internet-savvy marketing rep who fell victim to an incredibly plausible identity scam. (Many of the "victims" whose stories we are telling will not divulge their last names to the press. Victims of identity theft are a cautious bunch and live by the motto "Once bitten, twice shy." Jim's story comes from a report by Bob Sullivan at MSNBC).

Jim replied to a job listing on Monster.com, a big job-search website. According to the posting, a known insurance company offered the job, and to Jim it looked completely legitimate. After he had submitted his resumé, Jim received an email back, supposedly from the company's Human Resources hiring manager. The email stated that the company was interested in Jim, liked his experience, and thought he would be just the employee to work with company's valuable clients. However, the HR manager insisted that Jim submit to a background check because the job involved working with sensitive corporate data and a large budget.

Eager to get the job, Jim sent off all the key information in his life, including his age, Social Security number, bank account numbers, height, weight, and even his mother's maiden name. This was all a ruse for an identity-theft scam. The fake HR manager even asked Jim for a four-digit PIN number so that Jim could check his job application status at the company's website. The thief knew that most people use the same set of numbers for all passwords, including ATM PIN numbers. A few days later, Jim called the phone numbers provided by the fake HR manager and found the lines all disconnected. Jim knew then he'd been taken and started the long process of canceling credit card numbers and putting fraud alerts on his credit records. Telling a prospective employer that you are not willing to provide a Social Security number may sound like a quick way to get passed over for a job. However, doing some investigating and fact checking before you release data may be the best thing you can do to protect yourself and show a company you know how to perform your due diligence.

Here are some tips to help you think critically about any request for your personal data:

- Never give out your Social Security number online unless you are 100 percent sure to whom you are giving it. Make calls to organizations, ask them how they will use and store your data, assume a data request is malicious and investigate the request. Work backward to prove someone is legit, instead of kicking yourself later for not being skeptical.

- Never give out your bank or credit card number. Unless you are setting up an online banking or bill-paying service or working with a known company to have them bill your credit card for services, assume any request for your data is malicious and work backward to prove it's legitimate.

- If you are posting your resumé online, include only the most relevant personal details and keep details of your work history to a minimum.

- Lots of people love to post their genealogy; if you are serious about protecting your identity, however, keep information to a minimum.

- Look for red flags on any website or data request such as misspellings or bad grammar. Be skeptical. Check domain names using a Whois service and see who registered the site.

- Opt out of websites that offer public information on you. Many have privacy information pages where you can check a box to get your information out of their databases.

- Remove your email and snail-mail addresses from direct-marketing lists at the Direct Marketing Association's website (http://the-dma.org/).

- Limit the amount of information you share, and approach every data request with skepticism.

You Can't Control Everything

In the spring of 2001, I received a phone call from my gym warning me that they had a problem. A burglar had broken into the administrative office of the workout center and stolen hundreds of member files. Those files contained our membership applications, complete with name, address, Social Security number, height, weight, and fitness goals. But that wasn't the worst of it. Not only did the thieves know that I wanted to drop

10 pounds and increase my aerobic endurance, they had my credit card number and its expiration date. The gym was billing my credit card every month instead of sending me a bill in the mail, and that number was in my file. Now, that personal financial info was in the hands of the bad guys. Luckily, I was never hit with a charge on my account, and I never had an ID problem, but it scared me enough to take control of my credit and identity.

Despite the damage it might have done to their image, the gym called every person affected and warned us to either cancel our credit cards or check our statements rigorously. Not every victimized business or organization will be so forthright about a breach. I know of a business that had data stolen from its databases. Many employees had money drained out of their bank accounts, and only after a few coworkers commiserated about the theft did they realize that the breach might have come from the Human Resources/Payroll department.

These are examples of victims who had no control over the data that was stolen from them. The organizations tasked with safeguarding their information let them down. Aside from living in a small hut on a remote tropical island, you will have to release some of your data and hope that the institutions that control your personal data info do a good job of safeguarding it.

However, one of the best ways to make yourself less susceptible to identity theft is to minimize the information you give out. Treat all requests for information as hostile, especially when the request is for your Social Security number. The *Federal Trade Commission*'s (FTC) website advises consumers to hold that nine-digit unique identifier close to the chest.

The exact advice from the FTC is this: "Your employer and financial institution will likely need your SSN for wage and tax reporting purposes. Other businesses may ask you for your SSN to do a credit check, like when you apply for a loan, rent an apartment, or sign up for utilities. Sometimes, however, they simply want your SSN for general record keeping. You don't have to give a business your SSN just because they ask for it. If someone asks for your SSN, ask the following questions:

- Why do you need my SSN?
- How will my SSN be used?
- What law requires me to give you my SSN?
- What will happen if I don't give you my SSN?"

Sometimes a business may not provide you with the service or benefit you're seeking if you don't provide your Social Security number. Getting answers to these questions will help you decide whether you want to share your SSN with the business. Remember, the decision is yours.

Stolen Property and More

Okay, so you're not going to fall for an email scam and you're going to be very careful about what information you share online and with companies. Does that mean you're safe? Unfortunately, old-fashioned criminals—the ones who steal property—are discovering the profits in identity theft.

The Federal Trade Commission uses this example to explain how identity theft works. It's taken from an actual complaint filed in February 2001:

```
http://www.ftc.gov/bcp/conline/pubs/credit/idtheft.htm#occurs
```

"My wallet was stolen in December 1998. There's been no end to the problems I've faced since then. The thieves used my identity to write checks, use a debit card, open a bank account with a line of credit, open credit accounts with several stores, obtain cell phones and run up huge bills, print fraudulent checks on a personal computer bearing my name, and more. I've spent the last two years trying to repair my credit report (a very frustrating process) and have suffered the ill effects of having a marred credit history. I've recently been denied a student loan because of inaccurate information on my credit report."

All from a stolen wallet.

When thinking about computer crimes and digital bad guys, we see remote attackers lurking in cyberspace. With identity theft, however, the bad guys could be right under our noses, people in our homes:

Roommates, hired help, or workmen could access personal data from obvious locations, such as a file cabinet or desk drawer. Many identity thieves cruise through neighborhoods, opening old-fashioned mailboxes and stealing mail in plain daylight. Without ever leaving their cars, they could have a pre-approved credit card, your Social Security statement, your bank statements, and mortgage information. Burglars are also becoming more sophisticated. Where's the last place they might stop on the way out of your house? The office, to get data they could sell to an identity thief.

For Serena, in Berkeley, California, the office wasn't the last place the thieves stopped: It was the first. The person who robbed Serena's home went straight to her files: She took passports, Social Security cards, an expired driver's license, a credit card...all the available identity papers, and nothing else. Why do I call the thief a she? Well, Serena knows something of what's happened since. The woman, using the expired driver's license with a faked picture, goes to a bank and attempts to withdraw $5,000 as a cash advance on the credit card. The card is declined, of course: It's long since been reported stolen. The woman protests—something is wrong, her credit card is fine, and she needs this money for a car purchase. She asks to call her credit card company. The bank agrees, so fake Serena gets on the phone and makes a call. Her "credit card company" obligingly agrees that the card is fine, and that fake Serena is in fact real Serena, and the bank hands over $5,000. Think this couldn't work? Think the bank would surely have a way of determining that the call isn't real? So far, the thief has gotten away with at least $60,000. The FBI is involved.

But all is not lost: You can protect yourself, even if your wallet gets stolen or your house gets robbed. How?

- **Put your Social Security card somewhere safe.** Take it out of your wallet! Finding a Social Security card or number in a stolen purse or wallet is a jackpot for ID thieves. So many instances of identity theft spawn from muggings or pickpockets that it's imperative you remove your Social Security card and store it safely.

- **Secure your personal data in your own home.** Use a locked firebox and keep it someplace a little more obscure, or just choose a more out-of-the-way spot for your really key personal data. The really important stuff to protect includes your passport, Social Security cards, birth certificates, mortgage documents, bank statements, and credit card statements. Most importantly, don't write your passwords on a post-it note and stick it on your computer monitor. (You know you've done this before.)

- **Opt out of pre-approved credit card offers.** You probably receive a hundred of these direct mail offers a year. The promise of low interest rates doesn't entice you to get a new credit card, so you toss the envelopes, unopened, into the garbage or recycling bin. An enterprising ID thief needs only to make an early morning jaunt through a neighborhood to pick up the recycling before the garbage man. The thief changes your address to a Post Office box, and they have a credit card in your name within days. They max the card out, dump the Post Office box, and you spend months trying to prove to the credit card company that it wasn't you. Bad guys in these schemes don't just steal the offers from your trash; they will raid your mailbox before you get home. Therefore, the best protection is to opt out of the offers entirely. Call 1-888-5-OPTOUT (1-888-567-8688) and request to no longer receive these offers. Press 2 for the opt-out option, and choose the permanent removal option. You will be asked for your home phone number. Enter it. Then you are asked to say and spell your name. After that, you are asked to enter your ZIP code. They will ask you to say and spell your address. Finally, you will be asked to enter your Social Security number: In this case, you must submit it. It takes 5 days to process your request, and you will stop receiving mail only from companies that use the credit services to acquire names and addresses.

- **Secure your mailbox.** I suggest purchasing a locked mailbox. (The postman just slides the mail in through the slot, and you use a key to unlock it). You can also get a Post Office box and check it a couple of times a week.

- **Consider shredding.** Enron employees and those really paranoid about identity and information theft swear by the devices, but do you really need to shred at home? Realistically, I can't in good conscience advise that you run out to Office Depot to purchase a $50 shredder and commence "Operation Home Info Blackout." As with all things in this book, the goal is to make you a less desirable target for the new bad guys, without making computer security the central focus of your day-to-day routine. So here's the short answer on shredding. Rip up paperwork that contains sensitive data: pre-approved credit card applications, old bills, check stubs, family historical data, any old ID cards, driver's licenses, applications for anything, pay stubs, ATM receipts, credit reports, investment statements, any documents relating to your passwords, medical histories, any items with your signature, resumés, tax forms, and used airline tickets or itineraries. Some identity-theft warnings advocate tearing anything with your name or address on it, but if an identity thief just wants your name and address, he could get it from the tax office or any number of other sources. If you have room for a new gadget in your office or have a whole bunch of this paper mess that you need to destroy, get the shredder, because you'll get tired of ripping stuff up.

If you are a super-organized person, you don't need me to help you come up with a plan to keep track of all your important financial documents. For the rest of you (read, disorganized, frenzied, and barely controlling-the-chaos types), however, the best bet is to have a file folder into which you dump all your opened, paid, and "to file" bills. Keep all of these documents, and use them to do your taxes at the end of the year. Keep this file in a locked box or obscure drawer out of your office to keep it out of the wrong hands. There are varying theories about how long you should keep your financial documents. That's a personal decision. When you do throw them away, however, cut them up or shred.

What Else Can You Do?

There are lots of ways to protect yourself: some more drastic than others. You might not be ready to buy a shredder, and even the locked box might seem inconvenient. But there are basic steps that everyone should take.

Know Where You Stand with Your Credit

Start by ordering a copy of your credit report. This document is a vital collection of information that tells lenders how well you repay debt. Credit card companies, loan agencies, prospective employers, and others use your credit report to help determine credit limits, loan interest rates, and more.

A credit report contains information such as the names of your creditors, your account numbers, when the accounts were opened, your balance, and whether you've made timely payments. It contains information on where you work and live, if you've been sued, arrested, or even filed for bankruptcy.

The three major credit bureaus in the United States are Equifax, Experian, and TransUnion. These companies do not share information with one another, so you should order a report from all three.

- **Equifax Credit Information Services, Inc.**
  800-525-6285 / TDD 800-255-0056 and ask the operator to call the Auto Disclosure line at 800-685-1111 to obtain a copy of your report.

  P.O. Box 740241
  Atlanta, GA 30374-0241

  www.equifax.com

- **Experian Information Solutions, Inc.**
  888-397-3742 / TDD 800-972-0322

  P.O. Box 9532
  Allen, TX 75013

  www.experian.com

- **TransUnion**
  800-680-7289 / TDD 877-553-7803 Fraud Victim Assistance Division

  P.O. Box 6790
  Fullerton, CA 92834-6790

  www.transunion.com

It costs less than $10 each to order the reports separately from each company. You can also view all three reports online instantly at QSpace for $29.95. Another company, EZcredit Report Retrieval lets you order credit reports from all three credit bureaus right from your desktop. You can download a free demo, but registration for the full version is pricey ($179.95).

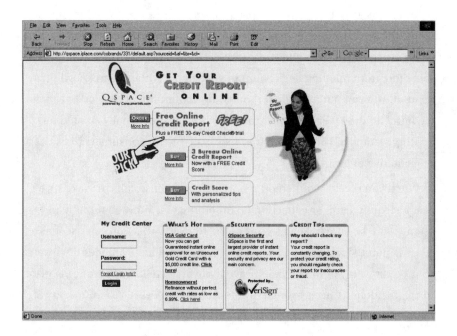

Figure 2.4

QSpace.com is one of several sites from which you can purchase all three of your credit reports instantly.

In some cases, you can get your credit report for free. You may qualify under one of the following conditions:

- Your state allows one free credit report a year.
- You're unemployed.
- You've been turned down for housing or credit in the past 60 days.
- You have a fraud alert placed on your account.

Download the PDF file, Your Credit Report, from the Consumer Credit Counseling Service of San Francisco's Consumer Library to find out more about your credit report and to see whether you qualify for a copy at no cost.

When you order your credit reports, ask each bureau to put a fraud alert on your account. This is a flag tied to your name and Social Security number that tells any credit card company or lender to contact you for approval if any new accounts are opened in your name. This will hold you up a little if you are trying to get a quick low-interest Visa card, but it will also prevent some jerk from opening an account in your name without you knowing about it. You can put a fraud alert on your account for 90 days or 7 years. I recommend the 7-year option. This fraud alert was originally created for existing victims of ID theft, but it is also available for consumers to use as a preventative measure.

When you receive your credit reports, go over the details to make sure every account, card, or collection is something you know about. If it all seems right, be sure to keep a copy of the report so that you can use it as a starting point if you ever do have a problem. It will help you identify when your credit went south and help prove that you were in good standing prior to any incidents. Check your credit reports at least every year and every 6 months if you are the paranoid type.

If you do find something that doesn't fit, contact the creditor and get details about the discrepancy. Sometimes the opening of a credit line or a collection happened so long ago that you might have forgotten about it. Another common occurrence is that a company might use a slightly different or unfamiliar name as their corporate identity. Therefore, double check with the creditor first to get more details about the red-flagged item on your credit report.

If that doesn't clear things up, call the Federal Trade Commission's toll-free Identity Theft Hotline at 1-877-ID-THEFT (438-4338, TDD 202-326-2502) or go to their website, http://www.consumer.gov/idtheft/, to start the process of clearing your credit and your name. The resources on the FTC site are outstanding, and they streamline the process as much as it can be.

Credit-Monitoring Services

If you really want to stay on top of your credit and don't have the discipline to manually check your report on a regular basis, sign up for a credit-monitoring service. I recommend TrueCredit.com. This monitoring service from Lehman Brothers and TransUnion charge between $35 and $80 a year to watch and alert you to changes in your credit. Weekly emails point out status changes, including new lines of credit in your name, inquiries made by others on your credit, and address changes filed.

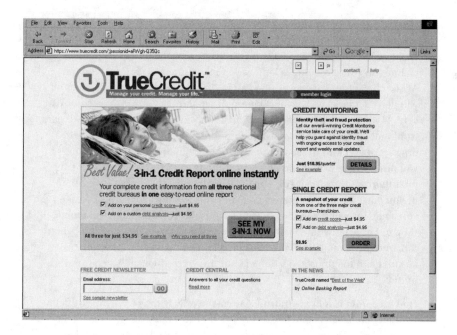

Figure 2.5

Using a credit-monitoring service, such as TrueCredit.com, helps you to stay on top of your credit reports.

Bank Online and Check Your Accounts Regularly

One trick identity thieves use is to change the address for your bills so that you won't be able to check statements to see that they are making purchases on your credit cards or withdrawing money from your accounts. An immediate awareness of a fraudulent transaction puts you on notice, and enables you to act promptly to protect your identity—instead of trying to do something later, long after the damage has been done and the theft has progressed to epic proportions. However, you can't spot fraudulent activity when you don't have a copy of the bill. To stay on top of your accounts, you have to track when bills should arrive, in case they are rerouted.

Your Liability

With credit cards, you are liable for no more than $50 of any fraudulent charges on your account, as long as you report them as fraudulent. With ATM or bank fraud, however, you can lose all the money in your account if you don't act quickly. The most common scenario is that you lose your ATM card. If you report the loss within 2 business days after you realize your card is missing, you are not responsible for more than $50 of fraudulent withdrawals. If you wait to report the loss for more than 2 business days after you discover the card is missing, you could lose up to $500 because of an unauthorized transfer. If you don't realize the card is gone for a long time, or you don't report a withdrawal on your statement that you didn't make, you could lose all the money in your account. If you fail to report an unauthorized transfer within 60 days after your bank statement containing unauthorized use is mailed to you, you could lose all the money in your bank account and the unused portion of your line of credit established for overdrafts.

One exception is if funds transfers are made only with your debit card number, but you haven't actually lost your debit card. In that case, you are liable only for transfers that you fail to report. You have 60 days after the fraudulent withdrawals are noted in your statement to alert the bank or lender.

The easy way to track when your bills should arrive is to enter a recurring item in your online or computer/PDA calendar. If your credit card bill always arrives by the last day of the month, put a recurring item on the first day of every month in your digital calendar that reads "has the credit card bill arrived?" If an ID thief has diverted your bill or statement, this reminder will help you quickly recognize that something is wrong.

Another option is to direct all your bills to an online bill paying service such as PayTrust. All your bills are sent to PayTrust's remote location, scanned into digital format and placed on a secure website where you log in and pay your bills. They also email you a notification that the bill has arrived; more importantly, they'll notify you when one doesn't show up on time.

When a credit card processing company was hacked in early 2003, 8 million card numbers were stolen. The extent of charges made on those stolen accounts is still publicly unknown. For those worried that their accounts could be in the hands of the bad guys, the best advice we could offer at the time was to check your statements mid-billing cycle. Credit card thieves have a very short window of opportunity to make charges to your account. As soon as a transaction is identified as fraudulent, the credit card number is flagged as compromised and further charges are declined. Checking your transactions in between paper bills arriving in the mail is one of the best ways to shorten that window of opportunity for the bad guys.

Almost every credit card company has a phone- or web-based method for checking recent purchases. On the back of your card, there is a customer service number. Call it and ask how you can check transactions online. If they don't have a web-based tracking system, they will most likely have a way for you to check the record of recent purchases by phone. If you have any reason to suspect that your account may be compromised, use these methods to check your transactions.

Most banks now offer online banking for free, and I recommend signing up and checking your statement every week for security purposes. As noted in the scary legal explanation earlier about your liabilities in case of debit card theft, noticing and reporting fraudulent activity on your bank account is a lot more crucial because you can lose all the money you have in the bank. Online banking is not only a good practice to adopt for safety, it's an incredible way to stay on top of your money and have access to your financial records.

Online banking and credit card access are all done through encrypted Internet transmissions. The data that you send and receive from trusted financial organizations is scrambled as it travels from their servers to your computer so that bad guys can't intercept the data. When you look at all the crimes committed against banks, interception of web-based data transmission is not one that happens much. It's too much work, with very little chance of success. Breaking the encryption algorithms of the data being transmitted is not a task many thieves want to undertake.

Note

Beware of Who's "Watching"   Warning: An easy way to get control of people's online banking or financial information is to steal that data from a victim's personal computer. Never let anyone see you put in a password or account at work or at your personal computer. Never use a public computer, such as in an Internet cafe or airport kiosk, to access your sensitive financial data. Savvy thieves can access these computers acting as a paying customer, and then install a key logger that records every key typed and website accessed. The bad guy turns the logging feature on, and then walks away. An unsuspecting online banking customer types in his account number and password, looks at his account, and leaves. The bad guy comes back later, accesses the hidden key log, and has all the information needed to transfer funds out of the victim's account.

Create Effective Passwords

When you attempt to obtain or change any information with your credit card company or bank—for instance, to submit a new address, get a balance over the phone, or increase your credit line—you will usually be asked you for your mother's maiden name. How secure is that? Not very. An enterprising identity thief can use any number of genealogical sites to find out the last name of your maternal grandparents. Therefore, when setting up accounts, tell the bank or credit card representative that you want to use a password instead. For your main credit card and bank accounts, call them now and change to a more secure password. For other accounts, change your password details as you replace or update other information with the institution(s).

A Note About Passwords   Your child's name, your birth date, or any information that lives in your permanent record is not a good password. A combination of numbers and letters is the most effective password. I know managing all your account passwords can be difficult, so one strategy is to create a strong password, such as tyu876ghj, and use it for all your accounts. Another strategy is to use many different, easy-to-remember passwords, so that if an ID thief cracks one, he won't have the rest. I firmly believe that one strong password for sensitive accounts and one password for web sign-ups and less crucial accounts are better than a lot of different weak passwords. However, guard those two passwords dearly!

Be Alert

In the end, your awareness of the danger of identity theft is your best defense. Pay attention when you're asked for information. Be suspicious of any information request, guard the nine digits of your Social Security number like gold, and ask questions about how your personal data will be used before you release it.

Buying Online: What's Safe, What's Not?

When you're walking down the street, it's easy to determine which storefronts represent a trusted merchant. Macy's, Wal-Mart, and Safeway all have brand names you know, not to mention large storefronts, extensive staff, and an overall feeling of established credibility. After all, creating a real store and a trusted brand takes time and money.

If you see a small storefront with handwritten paper signs and one or two shifty salespeople selling no-name merchandise, you get a different feeling. You know that if you make a purchase, you are taking a chance that the service will be bad or that the merchandise may be shoddy. To a greater extreme, if you come across a guy selling computer software out of the trunk of his car, it's almost a sure thing that the merchandise is pirated or stolen and that you'll never see this guy again if you have a problem with what you bought.

Making distinctions about the credibility or quality of merchandise of an online business or other vendor is a lot harder. The only storefront you see is their web page or their customer review rating. However, there are some sure ways for you to determine whether a merchant is good, marginal, iffy, or straight-up bad news.

By the end of this chapter, you should have a good idea of where it's safe to buy online and where it's not. More importantly, you'll be able to spot an online scam. Many of the auction scams discussed in this chapter sound perfectly legit, but the key to doing business online is skepticism. You have to approach every deal with an air of suspicion and research all the details until you are comfortable. If you don't get comfortable, don't do the deal.

Shopping Online

Not all the cases covered in this book happened to some distant, unknown victim. These things can happen to anyone regardless of what he or she knows. Let's look at what happened to my dad.

My father was having a hard time getting in touch with an online retailer, AllYouCanInk.com, where he had made a purchase. He found the website through a promotional offer (spam) he received in his email, and the prices they listed beat Office Depot and Office Max by more than 30 percent.

He was happy with their prices and ordered about $200 worth of ink cartridges for his printers. Three weeks after placing the order, he had received nothing and became worried. He decided to contact AllYouCanInk.com, but the 800 number they listed on their site only worked in certain areas of the country, and he couldn't find any other phone numbers listed on the site.

Because I was in one of the states where the toll-free number worked, I called the company for him. What I got didn't sound like your typical business. A woman answered the phone, and I could hear a television program in the background along with what sounded like a crying baby. I told the woman my dad's problem, and the woman tried to look up the order in the company's computer. The woman reported back that they'd had a problem with the approval process; she said that my dad had transposed a number on his credit card and the order couldn't be processed. Instead of calling the phone number my father had entered on the AllYouCanInk.com form or emailing him that there was a problem, the company did nothing. No one from the company followed up on the stalled order. Even worse, no one had responded to the seven emails my dad had sent asking about his ink cartridges.

After I figured out what happened, I went ballistic on the poor woman. (Can you tell I feel a little guilty?) The company's business practices were shoddy and a huge waste of time. At least I took solace in the fact that the company had the wrong credit card number for my dad, and he was safe from their misuse of his information. I cancelled the order, which was probably a moot point at that stage—it's not like the site would have ever followed through on his unresolved credit card number.

I found inkjet cartridges for a few bucks more at OfficeDepot.com and ordered them for my dad. Hoping I wasn't being a nagging, lecturing daughter, I then called my dad with the following advice, which any online consumer would benefit from knowing:

- **Never buy anything from spammers.** Sending out unsolicited emails not only disrespects all of us with flooded email inboxes, but it says something about the company sending out the spam: They are desperate and don't have the resources of an established company to market themselves in any other fashion.

- **Look critically at the website of any company you are doing business with.** Is it professionally designed? Does it have typos or misspellings? Is there a real street address for the business (not a PO box)? Do they have multiple telephone numbers, not just the 800 number or main phone-mail jail? Do a "Whois" lookup to see how long the website has been registered. Does the address that the company is registered to online match the address listed on the company's website? Go to www.nic.com, follow the steps, and see who owns the domain. Then search that name on Google for complaints.

- **Think about the price of what you're about to buy.** Are the listed prices just below the big boys (in this case, any established office-supply company) or are the prices obscenely low? If items are priced that far off retail, wise up! The item being sold is stolen, pirated, unsupported, unreturnable, or it's just a plain old piece of junk. Caveat emptor!

The fact that no one returned my dad's emails, and AllYouCanInk.com never called him to fix his order, only confirmed the fact that this online business was no bargain-hunter's dream, rather it was a shopper's nightmare.

Skepticism you apply to a business online needs to be even more acute than the critical thinking you apply to retailers in the real world. It's much cheaper and easier for a bad guy to set up a fake shop online than it is to set up a shop in the real world. For less than $100, a scam artist can set up a website that looks like a legitimate online business. With a few thousand emails sent out as spam to advertise the site, a bad guy could get hundreds of people to place orders and enter their credit card numbers. In a few days, the shysters could set up shop, rip you off, and then disappear off the web.

Some online scam businesses are very well disguised, and many offer real-world services. As of this writing, there are several online moving companies ripping people off. On their websites, they offer a smaller fee than other moving companies, hooking you like the AllYouCanInk.com site hooked my dad. After you hire them, they pick up your goods. Only after loading the moving truck, and sometimes even at the delivery spot, do they tell you the fee is going to be much larger (often twice the original price), and they refuse to unload your goods until they get their money. These scam artists change their company's name every few months to avoid being ousted by Better Business Bureaus, and to clear their lists of complaints. And with each new start, the websites look just as good.

I'm not trying to scare you away from shopping online. In fact, I make a lot of online purchases. It's easy, cost effective, and keeps me from shopping impulsively in a big department store. However, my advice is to make smart choices about the websites where you shop. If you are a newbie to web shopping, start with brand name stores that you know from the real world. For online retailers that don't have a brick and mortar presence, choose widely known sites, such as Amazon.com or Buy.com.

Internet Auctions: Going, Going, Gone

Auctions are a big industry, with an estimated $7 billion in sales a year. eBay is the largest electronic auction house in the world, commanding 90 percent of the online auction market. It's a multibillion-dollar business; and most eBay auctions are legitimate, and customers are usually happy with the transaction—otherwise, it wouldn't be so popular. There's also a lot of money to be had there. Anywhere money flows, bad guys hang out.

Fraud or Innocent Error?

Karen, 32, from Oakland, California still hasn't decided whether the seller who scammed her was a con artist or an innocent victim herself. But the lesson Karen learned was to stay away from cosmetics, perfume, and handbags on eBay.

In 2001, Karen won an auction for an unopened jar of Crème de la Mer, a very expensive brand of face cream. As Karen described it, "A jar of the stuff goes for about $90 per ounce. It's the caviar of cosmetics. Wealthy socialite women swear by its healing properties. I'd tried it on in a department store once—it's thick and rich, almost like spackle."

Unfortunately, when Karen opened the jar—which had been shipped in its original packaging—what was inside was not the fabled Crème de la Mer at all, but common hand lotion.

Irked beyond belief, Karen sent a follow-up email to the seller, accusing her of fraud. The seller responded right away, seemingly mortified, letting Karen know that she'd bought the jar on Canal Street in New York, an infamous street known for its knockoff handbags, perfume, and jewelry. Although the seller's concern and embarrassment seemed genuine, when Karen asked her to at least split the cost of the product, the seller never responded. Karen was out $40 for hand lotion she could buy for $3.49 at Target.

The $2,500 Telephone Book

Dennis Barringer thought he'd purchased a laptop computer. But when the FedEx package arrived, it contained a Montreal telephone book.

According to a story on MSNBC.com, "Clever scammers now regularly ship reams of paper, or even rocks, to buyers. That buys the scam artist a few more days before arousing suspicion, and often a FedEx tracking number is enough to convince a buyer to send the money."

For Barringer, the fraud was enough to turn him into an eBay vigilante, one of a group of individuals attempting to battle online fraud and scam artists. Since his loss, Barringer has searched for fraud and scams, and has successfully spoiled "hundreds of fraudulent auctions." This hasn't resulted in his getting his $2,500 back, but he has received death threats from the con artists. The FBI is investigating.

Not Too Humble About Hummel

Stewart Richardson seemed to have gone legit after a youthful indiscretion of car theft. He had set up a little business on eBay and had his own commercial website. Even his wife thought Stewart had turned over a new leaf. That is until he scammed customers out of a large sum of money, drained his bank accounts, and left town.

From his collectable figurine shop in Oakland county, Michigan, Stewart bilked eBay customers out of more than $300,000 before his disappearance. He was the perfect scam artist. His business started off as legitimate. For 4 years, he sold Hummel figurines on consignment. He had a long string of good auctions: 6,270 between 1998 and early 2002. He had 6,170 positive ratings that emphasized his quick delivery and good merchandise, and only 47 complaints. Then he posted more than 100 auctions claiming that he had recently bought a large number of figurines and was ready to sell.

It was a figurine collector's dream; almost every piece was rare and sought after, and prices were high. A lot of people bid; those who lost an auction, Stewart emailed privately. He offered to sell a similar piece at the same price, but in reality he was selling the same piece over and over again. When the bad posts began showing up for Stewart, he emptied his bank account and left town. His wife was looking for him about the same time as the Oakland County Computer Crime Unit became involved.

Methods of Payment

Because most credit companies only hold you liable for a small amount if a seller defrauds you, using a credit card is the safest way to pay online. For most online retail stores, you use a credit card for your purchases. For items bought through auctions or other person-to-person channels, however, credit cards are not an option. Individuals don't usually accept credit cards. If you want to use auction sites, you have to find other ways to transfer money, methods that ensure you won't get taken for a ride.

You learn about the main methods people use for money transfers a little later in the chapter. First, it's important to show you how auction fraud makes the issue of buying from sites, such as eBay or Yahoo! Auctions, a little more complicated than just sending a personal check or cashier's check for a purchase. In fact, the old reliable cashier's check is no longer reliable. They are easy to forge and easily used in scams.

A recent ruse involving cashier's checks starts with the victim selling an item in an online auction: a victim such as Shaun Mosch. Shaun decided to sell her husband's 1961 Buick through an online car site. Shaun accepted the bid of a buyer who said he was out of the country but would pay for the shipping himself. Just one problem, the buyer logically explained, he needed to send them a cashier's check that included the cost of the car and the shipping fees. Then after the check cleared, could they send the shipping money on to the freighter? Shaun says she had that funny feeling in the pit of her stomach, but went ahead anyway. "We thought this sounded fishy, but we told him to send the check, and that after it cleared the bank we would contact him to set up the transportation of the car. We thought that we would never really see a check, or that when we brought it to the bank it would not clear; in which case, we just would not set up the transportation and that would be the end of it."

When the check arrived, Shaun took it to her local bank to make sure this was all on the up-and-up.

"While at the bank depositing the check, I asked when the check would clear so that I would know that the funds were *good*. The teller said 24 hours. I said to the teller, 'Really, I thought that it took like 10 days for a check to clear?' He said, 'Not with a cashier's check.' Since I wanted to be sure that I was being clear to him, I said, 'I need to know not just when the funds will show up in our account, but I need to know when we can be sure that it is a good check, that it has cleared, and that it is real money that we can touch and use. I don't want to get a charge or have this come back and bite us in the butt.' The teller laughed, and said, 'Tomorrow afternoon, ma'am, no problems.' I thanked him and left."

When Shaun got word the check cleared, she wired the $7,200 in shipping fees to the freighter, and figured the only thing left to do was clean out the car and transfer the pink slip. However, 6 days later she received a call that made her heart sink. "Our bank called us and told us that the check was counterfeit and that they were deducting $8,800 from our savings account, even though they told us that the check would be cleared in 24 hours. We now have a negative account balance of over $5,000 that the bank says we are responsible for."

In this case, the scammers are taking advantage of a little known loophole in the U.S. banking system. Depending on the type of checks deposited, federal law mandates that banks must offer consumers access to the money within 1 to 5 days. As evidenced in the Mosh's case, some bank employees don't even realize that just because a check has cleared it doesn't mean the money is actually there.

The Moschs didn't lose their merchandise, but lost $7,200 to the scam. They have since filed reports with the FBI and even set up a victims support group online (www.scamvictimsunited.com).

The scams will change, but the premise is the same: bad guys using their knowledge of the system and their verbal skills to fast-talk you into trouble. Currently, there are similar scams involving Western Union, escrow services, and wire transfers. Use a reputable escrow service, such as Escrow.com, don't make any special arrangements to "help out" the buyer or seller, and research like mad before you do anything involving money transfers online.

The FBI's Internet Fraud Complaint Center (IFCC), a joint project of the FBI and the White Collar Crime Prevention Center, gets thousands of emails each week from consumers victimized online. Nearly half (46 percent) involve auction fraud. You needn't take our word for these statistics; check out the IFCC's 2002 Internet Fraud Report at
`http://www1.ifccfbi.gov/`
`strategy/2002_IFCCReport.pdf`.

Let's look at a few cases of auction fraud.

Customer Complaints and Auction Sites

Although most complaints go to the online auction site or the IFCC, some people report to the U.S. Postal Service, the National Consumers League, or the local police. This lowers the number of complaints that auction sites receive and post. And the auction sites don't count cases such as Karen's as fraudulent: Karen did receive her face cream.

eBay provides a feedback service that enables customers to rate sellers and sellers to rate customers. This service provides some protection as it warns customers of bad sellers, but there are still ways for bad guys to maneuver around it. Stewart Richardson, from the previous example, figured out that it took a long time for customers to post negative feedback. The complainant has to approach eBay, show their check was cashed, and show the exchanges between them and the vendor. eBay then evaluates the complaint and finally posts it. Stewart had plenty of time to empty his bank account and leave town before too many complaints showed up on eBay.

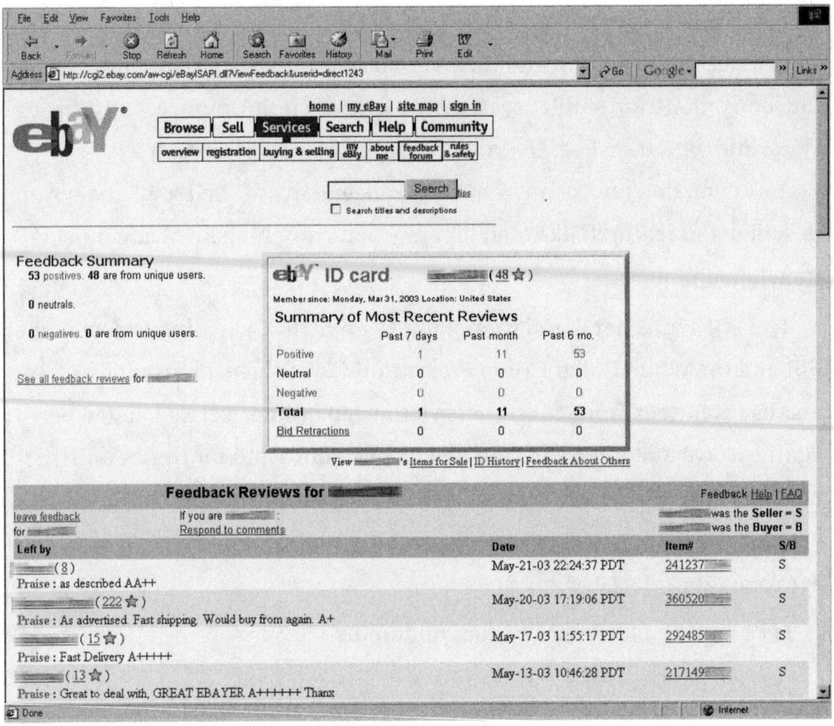

Figure 3.1

eBay's feedback service provides some protection for buyers allowing them to see reviews from people who have purchased items from the same seller.

The feedback system itself has been used in various scams. The simplest scam is shill-bidding rings. Sellers get their friends (the shills) to pretend to buy the first few items they put up on the auction block. The shill "buys" the item, and then posts glowing reports about the seller, giving him a higher and higher rating. The shills also hang around and put in false bids to drive up the prices of other items. When a customer wins a bid, the seller cheats them—by sending the wrong merchandise or no merchandise at all. In these cases, when customers get ripped off, they don't necesarily post bad reviews. After all, who are they to post negative feedback about a seller who has such a high rating? If the consumer does post negative feedback, the dealer responds with retaliatory negative feedback. You've got the picture: a well-liked dealer versus a hot-headed customer.

Buying from Auctions Safely

Internet auctions are fun. They help you find things you've been trying to buy for years. They let you run a garage sale without sticking up a single sign in your yard, and they keep you from being awakened by an early caller about the ad you placed in the newspaper. They are also a great form of entertainment. As you've already learned from the examples in this chapter, however, anywhere there's a lot of money changing hands, there's danger of being ripped off. You have to use common sense and be careful if you are to stay clear of auction scams. Follow these bits of advice to protect yourself:

- **Ask the seller for a telephone number.** We repeat this advice throughout this chapter and this book. Businesses that won't let you talk to them are best avoided. An eBay seller won't post his or her phone number during an auction, but you should expect to talk to the seller if you win the auction, and before you send any money. However, a telephone presence alone does not make a legitimate trading partner. Disposable cell phones are all too common. Talking with a buyer or seller is just a way to get more information, scrutinize it, and use it to inform the ultimate arbiter of a good or bad deal: your gut instinct. Trust your little voice and call off all bets when that little voice starts doubting the deal.

- **Watch out for radical changes in inventory.** If you've looked at a business or seller for a month and they've gone from selling $10 products to $100,000 goodies, it's likely that they're about to pull a fast one and run off with the customer's money without delivering the item.

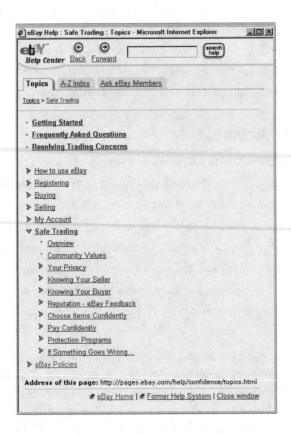

Figure 3.2

eBay's Help menu has a Safe Trading section that provides tips for purchasing items online.

- **Follow the site's advice.** eBay and other auction sites give out good advice to buyers and sellers. eBay has an entire "Safe Trading Tips" section. Review these warnings before diving into online auctions.

- **Ask how they get their merchandise.** One trick you can pull to get a better feel for where a vendor gets its merchandise is to tell them you may have some products to sell them, and ask whether they take items on consignment. If you pretend to offer a product that is rare or collectible, they will want to talk with you. If they have no interest, you should think about why a rare coin/stamp/antique seller isn't interested; they might not be legitimate.

- **Repeat the magic mantra.** "If it looks too good to be true, it probably is." This goes back to the advice I gave earlier. If the items are priced obscenely low, the items are likely stolen or of poor quality.

- **Never deal with anyone outside of the auction floor.** If a dealer contacts you *after* an auction, do not respond. In fact, you should report that dealer to eBay. There's a good chance you are being scammed.

- **If you feel you are being ripped off, complain.** Complain to eBay or whatever auction site you are using. They are open to complaints, even if they are slow to post them. eBay also provides links to the U.S. Postal Inspection Service, the IFCC, and other regulatory agencies with which you can lodge complaints. Remember that you should not feel bad about being the victim of a scam.

- **Use PayPal or another go-between service.** Never give a dealer your credit card number, driver's license number, or anything I warned you about in Chapter 2, "Identity Theft: Who Owns Me Now?." Also do not expect any extra protection from Western Union. Many people have been talked into believing that Western Union can be used as an escrow service, which is not true. Instead, use a reliable go-between service, such as PayPal or Escrow.com, to relay any funds needed for the sale.

Using PayPal

I've convinced you not to send that personal check, but instead to use PayPal, eBay's official transaction service. Right? (If you don't use PayPal, use another reliable go-between service.) PayPal is a low-cost transfer service. If you're not familiar with it, let's step through the process of how you use it to make a purchase.

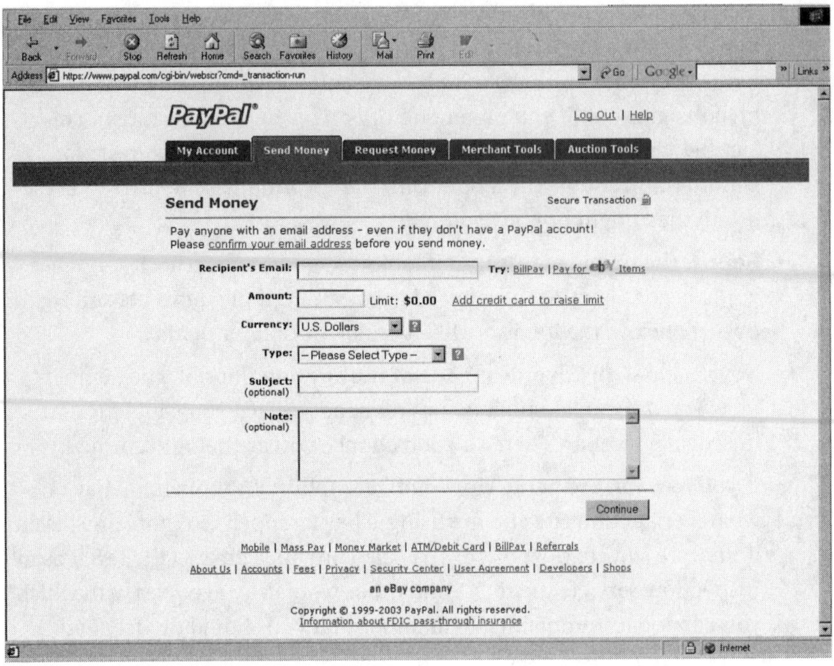

Figure 3.3

eBay's go-between service PayPal is one of the safest methods for buying and selling items online.

Suppose you buy a slightly used fly-fishing rod from an online auction. The seller lives in Montana, and you live in New Jersey. The usual methods of payment put one or both of you at risk. If the seller ships the item before she receives payment, there is no guarantee you will pay. If you pay before the item is received, there's no guarantee the seller will actually send the item or that the sender even truly has the item. How do you exchange the item without putting either yourself or seller at risk of getting ripped off?

Most eBay transactions are done through the PayPal service. When a sale has been made and the price has been agreed upon, both the buyer and the seller set up an account with PayPal. Each person's account is tied to his or her bank account, credit card, or both. The buyer and seller exchange PayPal account numbers, and the money for the items purchased moves from the customer's account to the dealer's. PayPal has a redress system if the buyer never receives the goods, but fundamentally PayPal is just a currency exchange service that guarantees the money is really there. In addition eBay has an included insurance policy on every transaction. If a buyer is cheated out of his or her purchases, they are eligible to receive up to $200 back from eBay as insurance, less a $25 dollar processing fee. For example, if the item you are eligible to receive $175; If the item price is $500, you are eligible to receive $175.

Using Escrow Services

When big-ticket items are involved, such as cars, jewelry, or boats, buyers often insist on using more traditional escrow services, and I strongly recommend their use. These are third-party companies that hold the buyer's money in trust until the goods are certified and delivered. Escrow services are not free, but can give both parties an increased sense of security (and they are easy to use). Be aware, however, that even these services have been co-opted by bad guys. If you are going to use an online escrow service, I recommend you use Escrow.com. There are other legitimate services, but Escrow.com is well known and its website address is the easiest to remember.

Escrow.com is a known legitimate site. Hundreds of others are just knockoffs run by scam artists who are ready to steal your money. Do not use sites whose names look similar to Escrow.com, but have slight variances (such as EzEscrow.com, Escrow.net, and EscrowServices.com). I've interviewed a few different people who fell victim to these dummy escrow sites. Their stories are similar in the details and the sentiment, each with immense frustration for losing thousands of dollars in an escrow fraud.

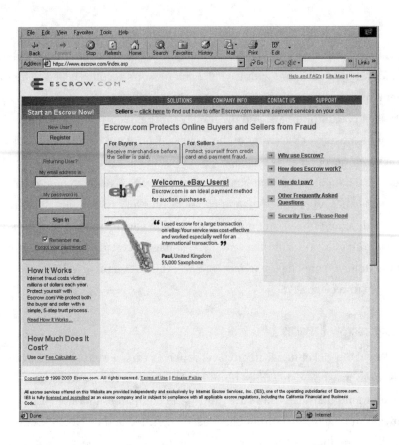

Figure 3.4

The safest method for buying and selling big-ticket items online is to use an escrow service, such as Escrow.com.

Don't Get Burned on Big-Ticket Web Auctions

"Steve," an eBay user in the market for a new Porsche, was taken for a ride in the spring of 2002, but in a way that he never imagined. He didn't want his real name used in this story because his case is still under investigation and because he's embarrassed that he lost thousands of dollars to an online scam artist.

Steve's nightmare started after he purchased a new Porsche Boxster online. The seller of the Porsche seemed legitimate, claiming to be a doctor. The seller initially asked Steve to wire the money directly to him, but Steve knew better, and he asked whether they could use an escrow service to handle the payment and delivery of the automobile. The seller agreed, but insisted on using USescrow.com. That's when things went terribly wrong. Usescrow.com was a fake site. The supposed seller of the car had set up the dummy site and waited for Steve to wire in the $44,000 for the Porsche. After the money was wired, Steve expected the seller to send the car.

Steve started to get suspicious when the car had not arrived after several weeks. He began digging around to figure out why his Porsche wasn't in the driveway. He contacted the seller, who stalled Steve with bogus excuses for why the Porsche delivery was delayed. Steve tried to contact the escrow service but found the site no longer existed. Steve received a rude awakening: The car wasn't for real; the man who had sold it to him didn't exist; and Steve's money was now with a scam artist, a scam artist Steve later learned was well beyond his reach; the whole con was perpetrated online from Latvia!

Steve visited eBay's corporate lobby to file a report with company security. They directed him to the FBI, with whom he filed another report. The FBI said they couldn't do anything for him because he had only lost $44,000. For Internet crimes in which the victim loses less than $100,000, the FBI has only one policy: They have you fill out a form, a web form no less. Victims complete the five-page form via the FBI's IFCC website (www.ifccfbi.gov). The FBI says all the data is put into a database connecting Internet crimes regardless of the geographic location of the victims. Steve put his data into the website, but has never heard another word as a result of that claim.

Dan Larkin, a representative of the IFCC, says the $100,000 monetary limit makes victims fume. He says, "There is often a frustration because the individual filing the complaint is told the threshold—the loss isn't high enough, so they think their case isn't getting any attention."

However, Larkin explained that cases like Steve's are combined with additional, low-value cases. "Actually," he said, "that's part of the reason we set up the Internet Fraud Center. We wanted to build those complaints into a bigger case that will be worked by somebody, where there's one victim of an Internet scam there are usually lots more. This is a way of aggregating them."

For Steve, however, the experience left him cold. He's out a lot of money and the only hope he has of getting it back is the case number the IFCC's automated web form spat out to him when he completed the form. That's all he got. No visit from a field agent, no call from his local FBI office...nothing. If the FBI makes any headway on his case, he might get an email or phone call, but it's unlikely they will. As of now, Steve hasn't heard anything from the IFCC, and doesn't know whether he'll ever see his $44,000 again.

Limited Resources

The FBI's Larkin says it's the best the FBI can do. "We have budget issues, only so many people...and we distribute the packaged, combined complaints that fit the same profile—sending them to the appropriate FBI offices or other law-enforcement agencies."

Larkin says the FBI's database of IFCC complaints is helping to find criminals who use the Internet to spread out their crimes. So what happens to complaints such as the one Steve filed about the $44,000 he lost to escrow fraud?

"It goes into the cycle at the IFCC and is matched up with like complaints that we already have: the URL, the names, phone numbers, anything else you could derive from the transaction matched up against other data that we have in the database," says Larkin.

Is that process working? Larkin says, "I can tell you that victims ought to have a growing comfort level that action will be taken."

Quantifying that action is tough, however. Because the IFCC parses bundled complaints out to other parts of its organization and different branches of law enforcement, Larkin can't say how many cases have been solved or how many bad guys have been prosecuted.

Heed eBay's Warning

"Well, I didn't think anything was fishy," Steve says about the escrow service with which he was doing business. "It looked so real. You know, when you go to the website it looks real."

Unfortunately for Steve, it wasn't real, and he's now out $44,000. Steve points the finger at eBay. "They won't do anything about it. They say that there's very little fraud, but they're just not...making this public," he says.

"We see it mentioned on our message boards from time to time, but it's far from an epidemic," eBay spokesman Kevin Pursglove says. "Since eBay is not directly involved in this part of the auction process, we don't get direct reports on all the fraud that's happening out there. But if the escrow problem became more widespread, our customer support and fraud investigation teams [would] keep us in the loop so we could make a decision to warn our customers more formally."

Pursglove points to the $40 million exchanged on eBay auctions each day, and says it's a big target for fraud. But much of the information needed to protect yourself, he says, is freely available. "Our community shares information readily. Use the message boards, research the web, and check a seller's rating to stay safe, bottom line," Pursglove says. "It's the buyer's dollar. Research wisely."

Although eBay hasn't indicated that escrow fraud is a big problem, the escrow company recommended by eBay, Escrow.com, calls attention to the problem on its site and warns users to avoid other sites:

> Escrow.com *only* provides services using the URL displayed as follows: `https://www.escrow.com` or `https://escrow.com`. If you are not using escrow services at this URL, please be careful. We are not affiliated with *any* other escrow sites no matter what they may tell you.

eBay's biggest competitor, Yahoo! Auctions, lists escrow sites in its directory, but no links appear to be endorsed by Yahoo! Auctions itself.

For his part, Steve says his days shopping online may be through. "I don't know if I would buy anything online again," he says. "You have to really check out the escrow company and all that, but then it goes back to everything...you get really paranoid, and you're afraid of everything."

Look for Legitimate Services

To ensure your escrow company is legitimate, use the escrow service suggested by eBay, Escrow.com, which is backed by the real-world Fidelity National Financial, a well-known, Fortune 500 company.

With any business, it's a good idea to use the Whois registry (as discussed in Chapter 2) to see whether the online registry information fits with the corporate information on the site. If it doesn't, find out why. Or choose another business to use.

Finally, check with your bank to see whether it offers an online escrow service or can recommend one. If you have *any* doubts, trust your instincts and find a new escrow company.

Crying in the Wilderness

Despite FBI agent Larkin's words of support, one of the biggest frustrations for victims of escrow fraud is the lack of attention the FBI seems to give them. Out tens of thousands of dollars, it's understandable for victims to feel as if they're being victimized once by the escrow scammer and again by law enforcement authorities who appear to do nothing.

For victims of escrow fraud, the embarrassment of being fooled, the loss of their hard-earned money, and their frustration with law enforcement's handling of Internet crimes simply adds up to one miserable experience.

Developing Online Shopping Skills

The online shopper is trapped by the illusion of safety. She is looking at a website that has been designed to separate her from her hard-earned cash. While shopping online, there will be plenty of opportunities for her to make a mistake and become a victim of someone's scam.

However, people can rapidly develop good online shopping skills. First they have to realize that they need to use the skill set they acquired in the real world, and second, they have to become accustomed to looking for quality in the cyberworld. Time, practice, and reading this book will help with the latter.

You already know how to find good businesses online, because you're a good shopper. After all, you were smart enough to buy this book, which shows that you have a will for better consuming. You just have to take the real-world skills you have and translate them into the cyberworld. Just as the bad guys have taken old cons, scams, and simple incompetence into the cyberworld, you can take your skills. Use these skills and remember how you have found good, real-world businesses in the past.

A few brief guidelines follow. Share them with your friends and you'll seem very computer savvy; more importantly, the more people you lead into the practice of looking for quality merchants, the fewer scams will succeed.

- **Ask your friends and family to recommend stores.** This is the best method possible; you've used it for years. In the age of the search engine, we forget that the personal databases we call our friends are better than any algorithm. Remember to share your good and bad experiences with your friends.

- **Find out when the store came into being.** An older business with an established clientele is less likely to have shoddy merchandise or inferior services. Otherwise, it wouldn't have stayed around for so long.

- **Ask, ask, ask.** Ask when you can expect delivery, ask how you can resolve problems or make exchanges, ask the vendor about his or her business (future plans, can you visit the store the next time you are in their city, and so on). These questions establish a sense that the store has a reality, roots, and a plan to be around for a while.

- **Look for a phone number.** Be wary of a business with no phone number. A merchant that plans to stay around is looking to increase rapport with customers. Sadly, more and more sites aren't listing phone numbers, so be sure and thank the ones you call, and tell them that was a deciding factor in doing business with them. This helps us all out.

- **Repeat the magic mantra.** "If it looks too good to be true, it probably is."

- **Review the guidelines in this chapter.** Use the positive points to try to find your way to a store first. If you can't find a store via positive guidelines, at least use the negative ones to filter out the ones you know are bad.

- **Seek satisfaction.** Don't assume the Internet is full of uncaring, incompetent people. If you have a problem with a good or service you've bought, call the vendor and ask for help. Many merchants, if approached with respect and a calm voice, are more than glad to help people get a good deal. It makes for repeat customers. Many people accept bad merchandise from a web-based business because they can't imagine that the person on the other end of the fiber-optic cable could actually be a warm human being.

- **Feel free to seek out consumer advice.** You can always contact the Better Business Bureau of the town the vendor lives in, or you can call the Federal Trade Commission toll free 1-877-FTC-HELP (1-877-382-4357), TTY 1-866-653-4261, or visit their web page (www.ftc.gov).

- **If all else fails, complain.** The IFCC's website has a simple complaint form you can fill out at www.ifccfbi.gov. Don't run screaming "fraud," however, unless you think you really are being ripped off. Although your complaint may not be the one that changes things—after all, the government looks for large amounts of money, many people ripped off, and so forth—that list can never come into being unless every person shares their problem. Complaining is part of being a good guy!

Internet shopping is here to stay. With prudence it can lead you to a much wider variety of goods and services than you can find locally. It can even lead to better prices, if you carefully compare local prices against the total price of the Internet goods (including shipping and handling). However, with the freedom of buying online comes the danger of getting conned by the new bad guys. Take your common sense with you and you'll have a great time.

The Virus Threat

Today's bad guys love computer viruses. Viruses are a cost-effective way to steal data and mess people up. For all of us trying to stave off these insidious attacks, however, viruses are a royal pain and provide an even more painful lesson. If you don't protect yourself, you **will** lose time and data. Virus protection is not a lot of fun, but if you get hit even once, you will kick yourself as you hear that nagging voice inside your head, "An ounce of prevention is worth a pound of cure."

So how do you beat computer viruses? It's not as simple as installing an *antivirus* (AV) program—you have to understand how they work and implement a comprehensive strategy to fend off viruses. The first step is to see where viruses come from and how they are written to affect their victims. Understanding the people behind the code, the virus writers, is the first step to getting a comprehensive understanding of viruses.

Viruses are a way for anti-establishment programmers to send a message to corporate America. They are a medium for turf wars between crackers/virus writers. Viruses are a way for bad guys to lash out against society: A virus writer who creates a program to delete files and crash computers is very similar to the angry youth who smashes store windows and spray paints statues. It's a way to make noise and tell the world you are a force to be reckoned with. For some, they are a way for the little guy to have

power. For those of us on the other side, however, those who are victimized, this is no petty prank. Viruses cause serious damage. A reformatted
hard drive is the damage most people fear as the result of a computer virus,
but the truth is that viruses eat time and productivity. Very few destroy
large chunks of data, but all sap the resources of IT departments or individuals trying to figure out the age-old question "why is the computer acting
so weird?"

In this chapter, you learn how and why virus writers are trying to trick
you into infection. Getting a sense of their methods and goals will give you
a leg up on protecting your computer and your data. So that you can go
beyond just installing antivirus software, this chapter gives you the information and technical know-how to stave off viruses.

What Is a Virus?

Viruses are pieces of computer code that modify other programs on a
computer when they are executed. They can travel as email attachments,
wait in peer-to-peer sites for you to download them, or sit on websites
posing as a useful file.

A virus must be executed before it does damage. For example, someone
could send you a virus, you unknowingly download it as an attachment
with your email, and it then resides on your hard drive; until the program is
executed, however, you are not infected.

The most common way a virus is executed is when someone double-
clicks and opens a file that contains a hidden virus. The infected file can
seem like anything from a picture to a music file, or even a setup file for a
new program that was downloaded from the Internet.

At one time, opening an infected attachment was the only way to execute a hidden viral program, but virus writers have evolved the process so
that some viruses execute automatically. Virus writers have found ways to
use features and mistakes embedded in email programs to launch viruses
when we open the email, whether we double-click the infected attachment
or not.

One perception of viruses is that once infected, your computer screen starts blinking, the hard drive makes scratching noises, and smoke puffs out of the keyboard as the CD-ROM tray opens and closes incessantly. The truth is that the infection process is swift and usually very stealthy. Some viruses might pop up an error box on your screen, with a message from the writer saying something to the effect of "You've been had." The more dangerous forms of malicious code quietly infect you or wait for a trigger that executes another set of computer instructions.

When writing a virus, the vxer has to determine three main functions of their virus:

- **Trigger.** Just because a virus is installed on a machine doesn't mean it has released its destruction. It may be waiting for a date to trigger its payload. Perhaps a command from the virus writer or an action from the user of the infected computer launches another series of damaging events. Just because your computer doesn't seem like it's affected by a virus doesn't mean it's not infected.

- **Payload.** The payload is what the virus does after it's installed on a computer. Does it try to reformat the hard drive? Does it selectively destroy data? Does it turn the computer into a zombie machine, waiting for the command to attack another machine? (This is called a distributed denial-of-service attack.) Does it try to disable the operating system? Or is it trying to steal data off of the infected machine and send it back to the virus writer?

- **Replication.** Many viruses have a mechanism by which they replicate and spread to other computers. In many instances, the executed virus mines your computer for new email contacts and new networks it can infect. It might list itself under a phony filename in the victim's music and file-sharing programs, enticing others to download it. It might look for open network shares—other computers connected to the infected computers. This starts the whole process of infection over again on new prey.

Virus Jargon

Before you get too far into this chapter, familiarize yourself with some of the terms typically used when talking about viruses.

- *Malicious code.* Any piece of computer code, normally a program, that can do damage or negatively impact a computer.

- *Virus.* A program that infects a computer and modifies other programs (including the operating system).

- *Worm.* A type of virus that can spread without infecting a specific program or file. Most worms spread via email or through computers linked together through networks.

- *AV scanner.* Antivirus scanner or program that evaluates data on the hard drive or incoming data to assess whether it carries a computer virus.

- *Virus definitions.* The database of known viruses kept by each antivirus company. The database of definitions is updated as new viruses emerge and evolve. The technical characteristics of each virus are used as criteria against which the AV scanner compares files being evaluated for infection.

- *Vulnerability.* Any mistake or feature set that gives a hacker or virus unauthorized access to the machine. When software makers become aware of vulnerabilities, they issue patches that users should download and install to fix the vulnerability.

- *Backdoor Trojans.* Programs that hide on your computer, trying to evade detection while they perform unauthorized actions. Many backdoor Trojans consist of password stealers or keyloggers that log data you type into your computer and then send those logs to the virus writer.

- *Keyloggers.* Programs that record mouse clicks, keystrokes, and sometimes screen shots of your activity on the computer. They create a log that can be emailed out or that a bad guy can read if he has physical access to your computer.

- *SMTP engine.* An email program that can send files without using the email programs installed on your computer. No record of the files emailed out through an SMTP engine will ever show up in the Sent folder of your Eudora, Outlook, Hotmail, or Lotus Notes email programs.

No one expects you to understand all the technicalities of viruses, but understanding the basics is the first step in fighting them.

Who Are Virus Writers?

The easy answer is that they are a bunch of whackos who lash out against the world in a digital form. But that's just my bitter side talking, and is probably how anyone feels who has been infected by a virus. The truth is, virus writers are a very diverse group. Many virus writers never intend to use their work against other computer users. These writers are careful to make the distinction between writing a virus and actually releasing one into the wild with the intent of infecting other people.

Virus writers have their own online community, periodicals, and forums. In fact, I was recently interviewed by one such virus writers' magazine, *Coderz.Net Zine*. The virus writer who interviewed me wanted to know whether the public at large sees virus writers (sometimes know as *VXers*) as bad people.

There is one sure thing among virus writers: Pride in their nefarious work.

Virus writers can become famous in their own communities and gain infamy from media exposure, if not by their names then by the names of their viruses. To achieve success in their pursuits, they have to program eloquently and efficiently. He or she with the most perfectly constructed virus and who infects the most people gets the most respect among his or her peers.

Sarah Gordon, a psychologist who has worked for Symantec and IBM trying to profile virus writers and hackers, says the community is very fluid. "New kids come in all the time; they start as script kiddies and either evolve into creators of original viruses or else they move out of the scene."

Gordon, who communicates freely with many known virus writers, makes the generalization that virus writers are typically in their late teens, usually boys, are of above-average intelligence, and are looking for a community in which they can feel accepted. Their programming skills are put to use creating virus tools, and pretty soon they have credibility within the community. She has made the assertion that very few individuals stay in the virus-writing community for long; most are just experiencing a passing fascination with the craft.

Although most virus writers are boys, you read in Chapter 1, "Hacking 101," about Gigabyte, the teenaged Belgian woman who authored quite a few pieces of malicious code, including the Sharpei worm and the Sahay virus. Gigabyte has exposed herself to a fair amount of publicity trying to show that women can and do exist in the virus-writing community.

Many other writers have other agendas than just pride and acceptance. Some want to make a statement, to send a message; others are after information and use their viruses to steal personal data.

Virus as a Political Statement

Some virus writers have loftier goals than just screwing up people's data. Like the "hacktivists" discussed in Chapter 1, some virus writers have a political message to send to corporations, governments, or the public at large.

The Prestige worm is a classic example. It was something of an anomaly in the virus-writing community, designed to make a political statement. In 2002, the virus spread by promising pictures of the Prestige oil tanker and its environmentally disastrous oil spill. Many speculated the virus writer was trying to make an environmental point.

Melissa Virus: Ode to a Topless Dancer

David Smith gained notoriety for authoring the Melissa worm. In March of 1999, his worm did an estimated $80 million in damages. (That number is based on the man hours used to make fixes, loss of network and employee productivity, and computer resources allocated to fighting Melissa's damage.) Smith, a 31-year-old former computer programmer, was eventually caught and arrested in his hometown of Aberdeen, New Jersey, on April 1, 1999. Smith was charged with creating and distributing the Melissa virus: a Word macro that swept through the email systems of thousands of computers in late March and brought down mail servers around the world.

Although the Melissa worm did not corrupt files, it resulted in significant server slowdowns, and forced the shutdown, in some companies, of entire email systems.

Smith reportedly admitted to investigators at the time of his arrest that he created the Melissa virus. Amazingly, Smith said the worm was named after a topless dancer he ogled at a gentleman's club in Florida. Was the worm an ode to Melissa's skills, a love letter, a way to get her attention? Who knows, but for David Smith his code in honor of the stripper was a move that landed him in jail. Following his conviction in a 1999 trial, Smith read the following statement: "I did not expect or anticipate the amount of damage that took place."

Smith said he created the virus on computers in his Aberdeen apartment and used a stolen screen name, "Skyroket," and password to get into America Online. In the online service's alt.sex newsgroup, he posted a file called list.zip, a listing of adult websites and passwords, which contained the virus.

Virus as a Tool for Data Thieves

For every lofty-minded virus writer, there are criminals after that most precious commodity in the information age: personal data.

A criminal can infect you with a virus that installs a Trojan horse program on your computer, which then sends the virus writer data from your computer. If your computer contains data about your accounts, the criminal can drain money from your bank accounts and open credit cards in your name. These are professional criminals who probably don't talk about their exploits among the VX crowd.

We talked about one protective measure to help thwart data-picking viruses in Chapter 1: encryption. If you have files containing sensitive data on your hard drive that you don't want anyone to access, encrypt them. Even if a virus makes it past your antivirus software, if you have a good encryption program, all the virus can steal is a file the criminal can't read—a useless mess of numbers and letters. Cybercriminals, just like real-world criminals, look for easy marks. Encrypting sensitive data files makes you a tougher nut to crack.

Virus Writers and Social Engineering

Viruses, like every other piece of computer code, are written by pro-grammers—people who put their time and energy into the creation of these programs. They want their programs to succeed, to spread to as many computers as possible. To accomplish this, virus writers use various tricks to get you to open and execute their code on your computer. Some use technical exploits that automate the infection process, bypassing the necessity for you to double-click an attachment; most, however, have to rely on something called *social engineering*. Social engineering is the act of tricking people into performing an act believing they are doing something else (in this case, open an infected file).

The virus writer has to figure out what social-engineering hook will compel a potential victim, what could the virus writer use as bait to entice the greatest number of people into double-clicking or downloading a file that is actually a virus. Social engineering is one of the most fascinating elements of the virus game. If you understand how a virus writer thinks, what elements of human nature he's preying on, it's much easier to spot their tricks in your email or online and identify them as viruses right away.

One of the first viruses to master social engineering was the I Love You, or Love Letter, virus. In May 2000, it hit inboxes with a subject line reading "ILOVEYOU." The attachment, LOVE-LETTER-FOR-YOU.TXT.vbs, conveyed the idea that someone had a secret crush on the recipient and only by open-ing the attachment could the recipient find out the identity of the secret admirer. This ploy played upon our curiosity, and maybe our narcissism, and thousands of people double-clicked and executed a potent worm.

The I Love You virus had the payload of a spurned lover: It deleted data by overwriting files on a victim's hard drive, and it drove system administrators crazy with the massive amounts of data it transmitted over corporate networks.

I won't name names, but the CEO of a significant tech company opened the attachment and sent his IT department into a frenzy trying to control the worm's spread through the network. His embarrassment was matched only by the lost productivity from his employees shut out of the whirling network as the system administrators stomped out the I Love You virus.

Data-Swapping Sircam Virus

A lovely piece of social engineering gave the subject "I need your advice." Who doesn't like to help out their friends? And, so, in July 2001, Sircam was born. But Sircam's social engineering involved more than just the advice line. Sircam stole one random document off of a victim's hard drive and then sent it out to all the addresses it could harvest from that computer. The subject line of the infectious email used the name of the stolen file. Further, that file was wrapped in the program that spread the Sircam virus. Private data left infected computers and traveled to every contact in a victim's hard drive.

Even worse, cached email addresses from web pages were also added to the recipient list. I put my public email address on all of my web articles, so for months my becky@techtv.com account received hundreds of Sircam virus files along with an incredible array of private documents. My favorite came from either the buyer or seller of some sort of aircraft. The subject line of the email read "Thank you for buying a McDonald Douglas Airplane." The body of the message read "I send you this in order to get your advice." Even though I knew it was a virus, I have never in my life been so tempted to open an attachment.

During the height of Sircam, I received attachments that ranged from family photos to spreadsheets detailing the personal finances of the virus's victims. The voyeurism hook of Sircam made its social engineering brilliant. It also did a good job of varying its subject lines. By taking the email subject from the name of the stolen data file, it was difficult for AV scanners and alert recipients of the worm to distinguish whether it was truly Sircam. The only distinguishing feature was that it always asked for "your advice."

Shakira's Hips Shake Up Social Engineering

If you are a member of the MTV generation, in 2002 you were mesmerized with videos from a Brazilian chanteuse named Shakira. Her shaking hips and scantily clad figure gained her name recognition practically overnight, oh and she is a pretty good singer, too. Just weeks after her U.S. debut, a virus writer saw a social-engineering opportunity, and soon his Shakira worm wriggled its way onto thousands of computers. The technical name of the worm is VBS/VBSWG.aq@MM, and it came as an email attachment, ShakiraPics.jpg.vbs. When executed, the virus commanded the infected user's email system to send a copy of the virus to everyone in the user's Microsoft Outlook address book. It also looked for new victims via *Internet Relay Chat* (IRC).

The Shakira worm's payload was minimal. It searched all local and network drives for files with .vbe or .vbs extensions and then overwrote those files with a copy of itself, deleting the contents of the original files in the process. Adding insult to injury, the worm then popped up the message "You have been infected by the ShakiraPics worm."

The replication mechanism for the worm was flawed, but the social-engineering hook was brilliant. Latch onto a burgeoning star's name, promise something unexpected (naked pictures), and know that the curious and gullible will double-click with abandon.

Using Big Events to Hook Victims

Narcissism and curiosity are year-round components of the human psyche, but some viruses play on seasonal events or holidays that garner lots of media attention. The Super Bowl, Christmas, and Halloween have all had the dubious honor of viruses using their theme.

As we approached the 1-year anniversary of the September 11th tragedy, the nation took time to remember the event. As if on cue, a virus writer capitalized on our collective sentiments and wrote a virus promising photographs that provided "new evidence of September 11" and stated that "America and England have begun bombardment of Iraq." Dubbed the Chet worm, it arrived in inboxes as an infected email with a subject line reading "All people!!" and an attachment titled 11September.exe. The worm was buggy and had a weak payload, but the social engineering it displayed probably enticed a few people to open its infectious attachment.

Soccer's World Cup was a huge global event in the summer of 2002. Ronaldo and David Beckham got more ink than J.Lo or Posh Spice. Millions of people turned to the web for real-time reporting of scores and webcasts of the matches. The World Cup event was a prime social-engineering opportunity for its own virus.

Shortly after the first game's kickoff, the Chick.f virus scored one for the bad guys. It promised results from a key match between Japan and Korea, but told users they had to enable ActiveX to see them. In truth, turning on ActiveX scripting allowed the worm to perform more dirty tricks on a user's PC if the user double-clicked the infected Chick.f attachment. After ActiveX was enabled, the worm installed itself, and then searched all the computer's drives for the presence of IRC files. (Internet Relay Chat is a communications method similar to Instant Messaging.) The worm tried to send a copy of itself to any users who were on the same IRC channel. Chick.f also sent itself out to all entries in the Outlook address book. Distribution wasn't very high, but some unsuspecting soccer fans no doubt fell for the worm.

Social Engineering of File-Sharing Programs

Most of the viruses discussed so far replicate via email, which is the most common way viruses spread. You open an infected attachment, the code executes, bad stuff happens to your computer, and at the same time your Outlook contacts list is raided for the addresses of your friends and business associates so that the worm can wriggle on to the next guy. *Peer-to-peer* (P2P) file-sharing services offer virus writers another chance to use social engineering to spread viruses across the Internet.

The rise of Napster and its progenies KaZaA, Morpheus, eDonkey, and BearShare give virus writers a whole other medium for propagation. These services work by allowing a networked group of people using the same software to share any type of file: data, programs, movies, but mostly music.

I open KaZaA on my machine, type in "Johnny Cash," and I can see all the Cash songs that exist on the machines of other people who are using KaZaA.

A lot of questionable material is shared on P2P file-sharing services: pornography, cracking tools, and serial numbers to illegally register software; and users typically trust that what they are downloading is safe. Virus writers have seized on these networks to spread their code, and viruses are continuing to grow as use of the services expands. If you do download through P2P programs, scan all incoming files with your anit-virus program.

> **Note**
>
> One technique virus writers use on P2P services is to use Wrapster/Unwrapper to hide their viruses. Wrapster enables you to take any file and disguise it as an MP3 file. Unwrapper restores the file to original format. These enable you to hide one type of file (virus code) in an MP3.

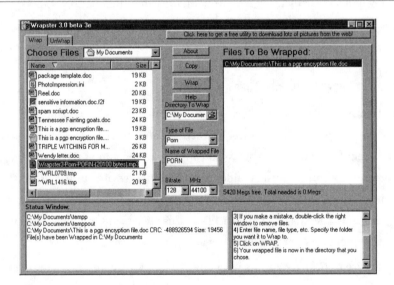

Figure 4.1

Virus writers often use programs, such as Wrapster, to disguise their viruses as MP3 files on P2P sites.

P2P Duload Virus

The Duload virus was one of the first worms to hit P2P networks. Duload disguises itself as free video games and pornography files. When a KaZaA user downloads and executes the falsely labeled file, Duload installs itself to the Windows system folder as systemconfig.exe, and then makes significant modifications to a victim's Registry, the organization chart of the operating system, which can severely affect system behavior.

The worm underscored two new trends in virus writing: disguising malicious code as songs meant to infect song swappers, and the practice of targeting script kiddies or young wannabe hackers with the promise of downloadable cracking tools. Graham Cluely, senior technology consultant at security firm Sophos, said Duload does not reflect kindly on the true nature of virus writers.

"Duload provides a snapshot of many virus writers' minds. Often obsessed with sex and computer games, virus writers are much more likely to be teenage males than crack cyberterrorists bent on the annihilation of the Internet," said Cluley. "Let's all hope that when the new school term begins, these 'script kiddies' will find their time is taken up with homework, giving them less opportunity to write computer viruses."

I should note that Mr. Cluely of Sophos is hated by the virus-writing community for this commentary. Virus writers say they are a much more sophisticated group than Cluely portrays.

In this case, however, some of the filenames Duload uses give a clear example of Cluely's point:

```
Pamela Anderson And Tommy Lee Home Video.exe
Alicia Silverstone Playboy Nude.exe
KaZaA Clone.exe
Napster Clone.exe
Winmx.exe
Website Hacker.exe
Hotmail Hacker.exe
Windows Hacker.exe
Free Porn.exe
Shakira Dancing.exe
J.Lo Bikini Screensaver.exe
Universal Game Crack.exe
Soldier Of Fortune 2 Mutiplayer Serial Hack.exe
Play Games Online For FREE.exe
The Sims Game Crack.exe
```

Klez, The Ingenious Infection

The Klez worm debuted in November 2001. For 13 straight months, it topped the list of top viruses infecting unsuspecting users. Klez achieved such widespread distribution for two reasons: its infection method, and spoofing. With regard to its infection method, Klez exploited a flaw in Microsoft's web browser and email program. A programming mistake in Internet Explorer code caused an email attachment containing a certain type of malicious code to run that code, even if the victim didn't double-click the attachment. Just when the warnings of viral attachments had finally caught on, a virus writer found a way to circumvent the user entirely. When recipients just read their email, Klez began its infection process.

The real genius of Klez came from its use of a technique called *spoofing*. If I send you an email from my becky@techtv.com account but make it look like it's from leo@leoville.com or memberservices@ebay.com, I have spoofed the From address in the email. It's relatively easy to make an email look like it came from one person, disguising the identity of the true sender. Usually worms that email themselves out from a victim's account put the victim's address in the From field to make a recipient think the malicious code attached is really a benign file from a trusted friend. Often this technique worked, but with the spread of AV programs, recipients of infected email were alerted to the incoming virus, and in turn warned the sender that they were infected. The infected and mortified sender disinfected his or her computer, and sent out an apology email. The whole process may not stop a virus from spreading, but it does slow its progression if a significant number of potential victims are warned that the virus has been sent to them.

The writer of Klez realized that masking the identity and email address of the person accidentally relaying the virus would make it a more effective worm. The warning process already in practice wouldn't work.

So Klez grabbed a random email address from either a victim's contact list or a cached web page and used that as the dummy From address. Despite the fact that I am fanatical about keeping a virus-free computer (it would be really embarrassing if a security journalist were Cyber-Typhoid Mary), I received more than a thousand notices from people and corporate networks that I was sending out the Klez worm. In truth, Klez grabbed my email address off the stored web pages on the computers it had recently infected.

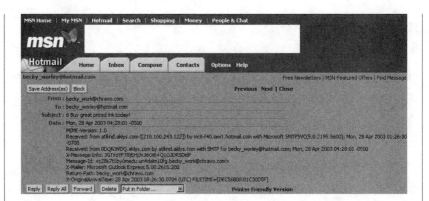

Figure 4.2

Virus writers can spoof the From field on an email to make it appear that the message is from someone else.

Millions of people received warning emails from friends: "Bob, you sent me a virus, I think it's the Klez worm. You should run your AV program and get rid of it, Klez really packs a wallop." Bob, in a panic, scanned his computer for the worm and found nothing. Bob knew he kept his virus definitions updated and didn't open random attachments. He couldn't figure out how he'd been infected and why his AV software wasn't detecting Klez.

Meanwhile, the real infected relayer of Klez had no idea his computer was sending out infectious emails to every address in his contact list and every email address from the web pages stored on his computer. The technical sophistication of the virus caused extreme confusion and made Klez a huge headache for home-computer users. The only good news on Klez was its payload; the virus did little damage. In a very small percentage of the computers it infected, it rewrote some files and destroyed their data. It could have been much, much worse!

Klez was also set apart by being the most prolific virus. Sites that claim to track such statistics for the past year, such as http://www.messagelabs.com/viruseye/default.asp?by=month and http://www.star.net.uk/products/security_antivirus_statistics.as, show Klez to be the fastest breeding virus ever.

Forensics and the Net

It's hard to catch and prosecute virus writers who wreak havoc with the malicious code they distribute. The Internet is about spreading information quickly, not tracking it.

A new breed of cop has sprung up to interpret virus code: *forensic computer analysts*. Like the author of a book, all programmers write in their own unique way, and an analyst studies a virus to determine its author.

To track a virus writer, computer forensic analysts first look at the virus's origination point. Was it initially emailed out or was it posted to a message board, or downloaded as a shared file through a P2P program? If the origination point can't be found or doesn't yield pertinent information, the next step is analyzing the code of the virus itself.

Then the computer forensic analysts evaluate the style in which the virus was written. Each piece of code is written in a *computer language*, which is how a program tells the computer what to do (without the programmer having to write in *machine language*, a very tedious manner of instructing the computer's circuits at the most basic level). Coding in machine language would make a programmer's life miserable and the task of coding much more time consuming. Different computer languages truncate the machine commands into more digestible human terms and concepts. Each language has a different way of doing this. Virus writers use all kinds of computer languages to write viruses: C, C++, Visual Basic. Generally, virus writers have one computer language that they prefer for writing their code.

Computer forensic analysts scrutinize the source code of a virus to see whether it contains any obvious clues. Within the code, there are quirks and habits specific to an individual virus writer. Like the phrasing or patterns that a novel writer repeats, programmers have unique ways of writing their code. These traits also provide clues to the origin of the virus.

Catching VicodinES

Catching a virus writer is no easy task. Identifying "who wrote what?" is a big challenge. Take the case of our friend David Smith, who admitted writing the Melissa virus. Trying to tie Smith to other viruses written under the pseudonym VicodinES is a serious challenge.

The TechTV "CyberCrime" team took on the task, and this (perhaps geeky) explanation of their process shows how a forensic computer scientist would try to unravel a virus's clues to identify the author.

In trying to determine if David Smith is the shadowy virus creator and tutor who calls himself VicodinES, TechTV reporters decided that if Smith and VicodinES aren't the same person, they're close enough to be brothers.

Smith and VicodinES are both linked to New Jersey Internet service provider Monmouth Internet. Melissa was launched onto the Internet using an IP address from Monmouth Internet, and Smith was caught when that IP address was tracked directly to his account on the same day. The IP address was a clue, but certain meta-data embedded in the virus signed his name for all to see.

But the email VicodinES used to cancel his website on SourceOfKaos.Com also came from an IP address assigned to Monmouth Internet. But there's more than just IP addresses linking Smith and VicodinES. According to a 1997 interview with the *VDAT* virus zine, Smith and VicodinES share the same age, location, and pill predilections.

In the 1997 interview, VicodinES says he loves "chocolate ice cream pops from Shop Rite." Shop Rite is a large supermarket chain with stores in the Mid-Atlantic states, but the majority are located in New Jersey. In fact, there's a Shop Rite in Smith's hometown of Aberdeen. In that same interview, VicodinES reveals that he got his start in computers when he "was 14 or 15 and my dad purchased a TI-99 4/A...the timeframe here

continues

was like 1982? Maybe a bit later." That would make VicodinES about 30 or so, the same age as David Smith.

Also, no surprise, VicodinES loves painkillers of all sorts. He took his handle because "I was very high on [VicodinES] when I decided to start writing virii so I thought it was appropriate." Later in the interview he states, "Don't think you can invite me over to your house without me searching your bathroom medicine cabinet for painkillers. I will steal them, you can count on that."

According to the *San Francisco Chronicle*, David Smith has used the alias Zanax.Smith on the Internet. Zanax, aka Xanax, is an addictive anti-anxiety tranquilizer and painkiller. VicodinES and Smith also share the same profession. In 1997, VicodinES was running "the MIS dept. for a large engineering firm." Smith is a contract programmer for AT&T. That's not surprising, given that virus writers are likely to be very good at computers.

In 1998, VicodinES left the Narkotic Network and joined CodeBreakers. The FBI has seized the websites of both SourceOfKaos, which hosted VicodinES's group the Narkotic Network and CodeBreakers. The divergent programming styles between Melissa and VicodinES virii still give some credence to the New Jersey Attorney General's assertion that Smith and VicodinES are separate.

Opic, another Codebreaker virus developer, has also been mentioned as a possible Smith alias. Opic has frequently named his virii after women, and he also seems to be about 30 years old, according to a *VDAT* interview. However, in that same interview Opic states that he doesn't use computers in his day job, which would seem to make the Opic/Smith connection more tenuous.

Still, given all the similarities between Smith and VicodinES, it's likely that even if they aren't the same person, they knew each other personally, rather than just electronically. And since it appears that Smith built Melissa on work previously done by VicodinES, that connection may be more than just casual.

You can see from the research in this case that the technical details of the virus combined with the media attention and communications between vzers are all used to build a case against an alleged virus writer. However, proving the guilt of these digital bad guys is tough. Arrests and prosecution rates for virus writers are obscenely low. That's one of the things that makes this type of crime so appealing for digital bad guys: The chances of getting caught are slim to none.

Keeping Your Computer Virus Free

Viruses are programs and, as with all programs, are bound by technological constraints. If a program written by the tech-support team at Dell can scan your system for misconfigured software, a virus written by a pissed-off 23-year-old coder can scan your computer for a copy of your tax return. In fact, both may require you to double-click and accept that a file is trying to install on your computer from the Internet. Learning what to double-click and what to cancel or throw out is one of the best defenses against computers. If you receive a file that seems fishy, be skeptical. When in doubt, throw it out. If you are asked on a weird website to download code that you don't understand, use your Back button and bail.

Recognizing a virus is getting harder with clever social engineering, and viruses change and evolve faster than we can write about them. You also now know how difficult it is for authorities to track down and prosecute virus writers. Using an AV program, updating your virus definitions often, and patching your software makes fighting viruses a lot easier, and will help you keep your computer safe.

Use an AV Program

If you're not using an AV program, how are you supposed to know that an email contains a virus? You can't. Without an AV program, no one can determine whether an email is safe, given that some viruses execute if a recipient just reads the email.

For this reason, everyone, even those of us who are in the security business and keep track of every single new virus, needs to run an AV program. It's not about being vigilant, it's about screening all incoming data to determine whether it fits the profile of a known virus.

Think of an AV program as an x-ray machine at the airport. Each file scanned as it enters your computer is like a carry-on bag. The AV program scans the file looking for known malicious files, just as a screener tries to identify explosives and weapons. At the airport, screeners are constantly updated on new weapons that may not be made of metal or that may be disguised as other items to get around the screening process. As authorities discover these new weapons, the word is spread to all screeners so that they can change their protocol. They look for new weapons as well as the old familiar guns and knives.

Antivirus programs work the same way. When you install Norton, McAfee, or Trend Micro, for example, the program starts with a working database of known viruses. The AV program protects you from existing malicious code or from any viruses that employ similar characteristics of known viruses. If the virus is new and has not been added to the AV database of viruses, however, the AV scanner presumes the file is safe until headquarters adds that new virus to the database.

Note

Not all AV programs work off of *signatures*, the qualities that identify them as viruses when the EXE or infecting file is scanned. For instance, Finjan's software (http://www.finjan.com/) works off of behavior rather than file signatures. The program kicks in when any Registry modification or file deletion is attempted and attributed to browsing or reading email. These are common signs that a virus has just been activated. The advantage to the Finjan approach is that if a virus is modified or mutates, it could be overlooked by the AV scanners described previously, but Finjan (in theory) is harder to thwart. Finjan's AV scanner is primarily geared toward large companies and networks, so it's not a great program for home users. However, the concept points the way other, more traditional AV scanners may evolve their defensive strategies.

TechTV's Roundup of AV Programs

TechTV Labs, in conjunction with AV Test Labs and Joe Wells, an AV guru, tested the latest AV software from major companies to see which one offered the best overall deal.

The Contenders

We selected AV software from the three leading companies: Symantec's Norton AntiVirus, McAfee's VirusScan 6.02, and Micro Trend's PC-cillin. Prices varied, but only slightly. Norton AntiVirus and McAfee VirusScan 6.02 each costs $49.95; PC-cillin will set you back $39.95. All three packages are geared toward home users and small businesses.

Testing Methodology

To see how well each package detected viruses, we asked Wells to test each product. Wells is also the founder of the WildList Foundation, a volunteer organization that publishes a monthly web-based list of currently circulating viruses.

Wells put the three applications through a battery of tests that checked for 287 samples of 190 different file-based viruses and worms. These viruses and worms represent infections users are likely to encounter. Wells also conducted tests on each application's capability to handle a PC already infected with a Sircam worm. Other tests included one that calculated each application's speed when scanning for viruses, as well as startup and shutdown times. To make sure the latest versions of each software package were tested, we downloaded updates, patches, and data files.

To complement the virus testing, TechTV Labs conducted hands-on evaluations of each product. We wanted to know how easy it might be for an average computer user to install and configure the software. We also took into consideration each program's additional features, such as bundled utilities. We also considered tech-support policies, because if software doesn't work properly users will likely call the company help lines for assistance. Nothing produces more frustration or annoyance than a non-functioning computer system.

Testing Results

The good news is that this crop of AV software detects infection very well. Keep in mind that no AV application will be 100 percent effective, because a new virus could hit at any time, requiring an update. All three applications detected our test viruses 100 percent of the time. That's good news for consumers looking for ways to protect their systems from damaging

continues

files. They also received high marks for returning zero false positives. (A file erroneously reported as being infected with a virus is a *false positive*. False positives may contain a small but ineffective strain of a virus.)

All applications have features we would recommend and features we wouldn't recommend. Which one should you buy? We like Norton AntiVirus for small businesses, but recommend McAfee's VirusScan for most home users. Although we like its price and ease of use, we found enough drawbacks in PC-cillin to recommend that you steer clear of it.

Common Features

Most AV applications offer the same features. For instance, each of the packages can scan both incoming and outgoing email. McAfee VirusScan and Norton AntiVirus enable users to schedule scans for specific dates and times; PC-cillin doesn't. PC-cillin and McAfee VirusScan offer a few extras, such as a firewall protection. McAfee VirusScan also throws in a basic backup utility. All offer automatic updates that run in the background and can update virus signature (DAT) files when they become available. Applications that run in the background are typically resource hungry and can slow system performance, especially if you have an older system.

In addition, each of the programs can scan floppy disks, email, and specific files for VBS (Visual Basic Script) viruses, such as the Anna Kournikova, which can be sent to everyone in an Outlook address book. Each of the programs can filter potentially harmful Java and ActiveX programs, which often reside in a web page's HTML code.

Both PC-cillin and McAfee VirusScan offer other security tools, such as a firewall utility. Although neither utility will give you as much information as you'll find in a program such as ZoneAlarm Pro 3.0, they do provide basic protection against possible intruders. Both firewalls were easy to set up and configure, but PC-cillin caused one of our test systems to crash. PC-cillin also offers an Internet-filtering tool. It's a standard-issue application and blocks sites that you specify, but specifying sites might be too time consuming for most people. McAfee VirusScan and PC-cillin provide additional protection for PDAs running Palm OS 3.0 and later. Due to the dearth of PDA viruses, this feature is likely to appeal only to those mobile users who use their devices heavily for mail transfers.

Installation

Aside from a few glitches, each package proved is easy to install. Norton AntiVirus required less overall work; installation was a matter of just following a series of Next prompts. We didn't have to reboot several times during the process, a problem that plagued previous versions of Norton AntiVirus.

In contrast, McAfee VirusScan needed more work as we had to reinstall the software a second time due to a program lockup during our initial installation. When we began the second installation, however, the process went smoothly.

PC-cillin is different from the other two. It's a download available at the company's website. A retail box version is also available. It provided the least appealing installation of the three tested. PC-cillin detected a version of Norton AntiVirus and required that we remove it before continuing. It also detected ZoneAlarm Pro 3.0 (firewall software) and suggested that we remove it in favor of the one PC-cillin offered. PC-cillin also requires that you register with the company to receive information about updated virus definitions, technical support, and product updates, which to us seems unduly restrictive.

Setup

In our hands-on testing, we found each of the programs relatively easy to set up. Both Norton AntiVirus and PC-cillin get high marks for having well-organized and easy-to-follow interfaces. PC-cillin features two modes for setting up your computer: Simple and Standard. Simple mode enables you to perform relatively easy and common tasks, such as viewing the tools you've enabled and scanning all drives. Standard mode features more advanced functions, such as selective scanning of drives or folders.

Virus Detection

Although all the applications were equally good at detecting viruses, there are differences between how they perform in a *system scan*—an automatic feature that checks for viruses.

Our test for full scans in a test system (7,333 files in 436 folders) revealed big differences. For instance, McAfee VirusScan took the longest to scan our test system for viruses: 1 hour, 2 minutes, and 15 seconds. Norton AntiVirus came in second with a zippier scan time of only 12 minutes, 10 seconds. PC-cillin surpassed them both, scanning the system in an impressive 6 minutes, 30 seconds. Scan times can vary depending on your system. The more files you have, the longer the program will take to scan.

Infected Systems

What happens if your system is already infected with a virus? Can you install and use one of these programs after the damage has been done? Unfortunately, taking this common sense approach might cause more harm than good. Wells, our formal tester, designed a test for this scenario and came back with surprising results.

continues

Wells infected a test system with W32Sircam A, a worm that all three product websites list as being one of the 10 most common. Wells then installed each of the programs to see how the software would fight the infection.

Based on this test, none of the programs performed flawlessly, and in most cases average users need expert help to get their systems up and running. PC-cillin did not remove the worm or repair the Registry. Instead, it detected the worm and denied access to any program we tried to run.

Norton AntiVirus was equally ineffective. The software detected and deleted the worm, but without restoring the Registry, leaving the system nonfunctional.

McAfee VirusScan, on the other hand, was able to detect the worm and remove it successfully, although not during a typical installation.

When it comes to virus protection, the best defense is an aggressive offense: It's far better to have AV software installed on you system before you're infected.

Tech Support

Until recently, it wasn't uncommon for companies to staff large tech-support departments and offer toll-free support lines—at least for software. These days, part of that expense is being passed on to end users via toll charges as companies look for ways to pump up profit margins.

We evaluated tech-support policies because when a PC is infected with a virus, a user is likely to call tech support for help in restoring their systems to a clean state. All three companies charge a fee to speak with a tech-support person via telephone, but a few offer unique ways for end users to get their questions answered.

McAfee charges $2.95 a minute (the first 2 minutes are free) for tech support, which is billed to your phone bill. There's also a "per-incident" charge of $39.95 for complicated questions, such as how to fix a virus after you've been infected. It's also the only company to clearly state what fees it charges for phone support. Rounding out the tech-support options, the company provides help via an online chat with one of the company's tech-support reps. It's a good option for typical problems, such as installation failures, but it's not likely to be successful with complicated problems that might require several questions. Still, in our random test the chat session went well. The rep we chatted with was courteous and answered our questions and sent a link with detailed instructions on how to fix the problem. The link worked well. A 15-minute phone call would cost $39.35.

Norton AntiVirus doesn't offer as many choices as McAfee, but its per-incident option is cheaper by about $10. Like McAfee VirusScan, Norton AntiVirus provides a toll number that costs $2.95 per minute and is charged to your phone bill. We tried one number posted on the site, but decided to hang up after 10 minutes of waiting. Given that the company charges more for its software, we would like to see less costly phone support. Still, many problems could be solved through the company's "knowledge tree," a system of questions and answers for common problems; try there first before racking up toll charges. A 15-minute toll call would set you back a whopping $44.95. That's on a par with Cleo's Psychic Hotline.

PC-cillin offers the best overall deal when it comes to tech support. It doesn't provide a one-time charge option. It has toll-free support, although it might not be the quickest route; a disclaimer on the website informs you of this. If you want an answer to your question quickly, you can call a priority number. Trend Micro charges $2.50 the first minute and $1 per minute thereafter, billable to your phone carrier. A typical 15-minute call would cost $16.50. Tech support is available Monday through Friday from 8 a.m. to 5 p.m (pacific daylight time).

You have an alternative to these and other $30 to $40 AV programs: AVG from Grisoft is a free AV scanner. Here's a TechTV review of its capabilities.

AVG 6.0 Anti-Virus System has a clean, easy-to-use interface and a nice set of customizable features, you'll be amazed Grisoft is giving it away.

Features

AVG performs the same functions as other antivirus programs:

- Manually scan your drives.
- Scan removable media.
- Schedule automatic tests.
- Check files on bootup.
- The most useful feature of all: Scan your email attachments.

An AV program is only effective if it updates its virus definitions regularly. The Grisoft website says free virus updates are offered at least once a month and AVG has a built-in update feature.

Using the Heuristic Protection Feature

AVG also offers heuristic AV protection to help protect your system against new viruses. This is great in a world where new viruses are being released into the wild every day.

continues

The feature looks for activity of malicious code that doesn't match known virus definitions. This type of active surveillance requires some computing power, reducing computer performance. AVG has a great resource explaining heuristics that's freely available for everyone to read.

```
http://www.grisoft.com/unique/wpheur.doc
```

How Well Does It Work?

To test this software, we clicked several email messages containing attachments in our inbox. AVG instantly popped up a screen warning that several messages contained a virus. It detected both the Klez.H worm and Nimda.

What do you lose by using AVG rather than a program such as Norton? AVG offers no technical support for its free version. If you're having problems with it, you may be out of luck.

You can download AVG from Download.com (`http://www.download.com`).

Scheduling Virus Definition Updates

No matter what AV program you decide on, you have to keep the database of viruses current. As a user, you have to schedule your AV program to check in with headquarters regularly so that you can keep your database up to date. AV companies know that the value of their service is not in the software as much as the updates. They charge a subscription fee to allow users access to the current virus definitions. Without these updated virus definitions, your AV software is mostly useless.

A key part of your defensive strategy is automating the process of updating your virus definitions. I recommend once a week, but if a really big worm or virus breaks, you should manually run the update as soon as you hear about it. Each AV program has a different method for automating the virus definitions update process, so look in the Options section of your program and find the automation tools. If you are on a cable or DSL modem, the updates will take place automatically, so you won't even notice they are happening. For dial-up users, your computer will instruct the modem to dial in to your ISP and then connect to the AV company. You may need to configure your AV program to launch the correct Internet connection. You may use EarthLink now, but perhaps used AOL before and configured your computer to use AOL as the default ISP. The first time you schedule your AV program to update definitions, watch the process to make sure it's okay.

Following are the steps for doing this in Norton and McAfee.

If you are using Norton, follow these steps:

1. Click the LiveUpdate setting.
2. Choose the General tab.
3. Select Express Mode.
4. Select the I Want LiveUpdate to Start Automatically option.

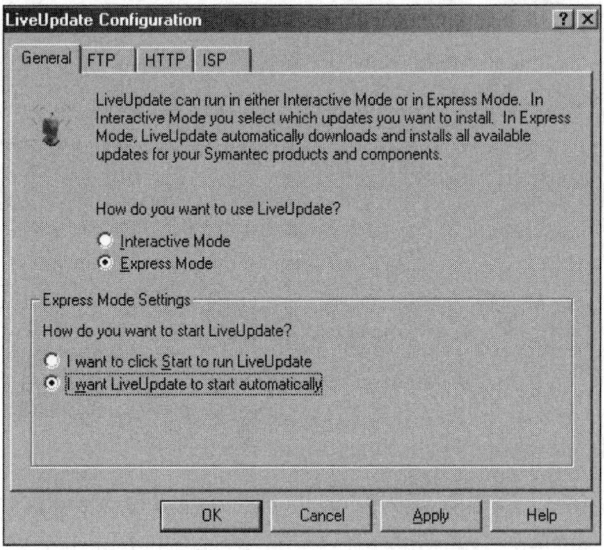

Figure 4.3

If you are using Norton as your AV software, use LiveUpdate to schedule virus definition updates.

If you are using McAfee, follow these steps:

1. Find the McAfee VirusScan icon in the system tray of your Windows taskbar and double-click it.

2. Click the Pick a Task button.

3. Select Change My VirusScan Settings.

4. Select Configure Instant Updater.

5. Choose Auto Update.

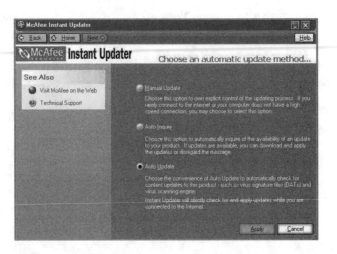

Figure 4.4

If you are using McAfee as your AV software, use McAfee's Instant Updater to set your virus definition updates to update automatically.

Computer Slowdowns and AV Programs

AV programs can slow down your machine. Back to our airport analogy, just as you line up to put your bags through security in airports, data lines up to be scanned before gaining entry to your PC. However, the real slow-down of AV programs comes from resource allocation. Suppose there were no security at your local airport—you breeze in and out of the gates with no barriers. Suddenly the FAA mandates airport screeners and tells the airlines they have to provide a third of their counter staff to serve as bag screeners.

Check-in lines would go into snake-like mazes, and the whole process of checking in would take longer. Resources have been diverted for security.

The same thing happens with security programs running on your computer. Scanning data holds up incoming data, scanning files on the hard drive takes up CPU cycles that could be applied to other computer tasks, and downloading new virus definitions takes up bandwidth and slows other incoming data.

Resource Meter

If you want to see how an AV program affects the efficiency of your computer, run the Windows Resource Meter. To launch this tool, click Start, Programs, Accessories, System Tools, and finally Resource Meter. Click OK on the dialog box that pops open, and then the resource meter will appear in your *system tray*, the set of icons in the lower-right corner of the desktop.

When the meter is green, you have lots of spare memory; when it turns yellow or red, you are low on resources.

Get a baseline of the resource allocation of your PC before you install an AV program or when the program is not running, and then compare that to system performance when the AV program is active. You can pare down some of the functions of your AV program if you take a significant PC performance hit, but this will mandate more vigilance and user intervention on your part to keep your computer safe.

AV Programs and Shutdown Hangs

Another, very common problem associated with AV programs for Windows users is called a *shutdown hang*. You use the Start button to properly shut down the computer, but it stalls in the "Windows is shutting down" screen. This can occur for a number of reasons, but one of the main reasons this happens is that an AV program tries to scan the computer's floppy drive at shutdown. Try disabling this floppy scanning feature in your AV program, if you have a shutdown problem. If that doesn't help, it's not your AV software; now you need to go to Microsoft for help (sorry).

Update Your Software

Virus writers know the weaknesses and flaws of most pieces of available software. Mainly, they are interested in PC software, not Mac-ware. One of my top tips for fighting viruses, is "Buy a MAC." But regardless of your OS (operating system), updating critical software, specifically Windows software, is a key to protecting your system and data. If you keep your software updated, you have fewer weaknesses the bad guys can exploit.

Software companies try to find these vulnerabilities before the release of a program, but holes that aren't found are often discovered after the software is in our hands. When a hole is found, software companies post security patches on their websites. It's up to you to find those patches and install them.

After you have installed a patch, it rewrites the portions of code that caused the vulnerabilities in the first place. This shouldn't change the behavior of your software. Sometimes other upgrades or updates are included in these patches, but all are intended to be beneficial. Updates are free, and you should get into the habit of updating your operating system software (Windows) three or four times a year or whenever you hear of a vulnerability and a new patch.

Code Red Wiggles Through Internet Information Services Hole

A big hole in a Microsoft Web Server program allowed vxers to create viruses that exploited the hole, specifically Code Red and Nimda. The bad guys wrote these worms, and watched as they spread. No other human had to interact with the code, the worms just exploited the software hole and ran wild.

Lots of the media coverage of viruses in 2001 focused on the Code Red and Nimda worms. Both attacked higher-end corporate computers running a web page server program from Microsoft called *Internet Information Services* (IIS). A flaw in the program was discovered and made public by Microsoft on June 18th, 2001. Just 28 days later, a virus writer released the Code Red worm, which crawled from network to network exploiting the IIS flaw. (The worm was named after the highly caffeinated spinoff beverage from the makers of Mountain Dew, a cherry-flavored soda called Code Red.)

Estimates from the Carnegie Mellon Computer Response Center (CERT) put the number of computers infected by Code Red at near 350,000. The Internet traffic it generated as infected computers scanned for new victims put a significant dent in the Internet's overall speed.

The intended payload of Code Red was to use all the computers it infected to launch a distributed denial-of-service (DDOS) attack against the Whitehouse.gov website. In a DDOS, many computers flood one website, network, or computer *IP address* (its unique Internet identifier number) with data, attempting to overload the target to the point that it's completely frozen.

The Code Red worm had the power of thousands of computers in its planned DDOS attack, but the virus writer made a tactical error. Instead of programming all those computers to attack Whitehouse.gov, they were instructed to attack the IP address of the White House's site. The threat of shutting down the largely promotional site of the White House was not a national-security issue, but it would have been a pretty big accomplishment for the virus writer. The web masters at the White House site apparently took the threat seriously and found a way to thwart the whole DDOS attack.

Changing a static IP address is a task that normally takes weeks if not months. In a short 24-hour period, however, the Whitehouse.gov webmasters had their IP address changed with no effect on users trying to find the site. Whitehouse.gov redirected to another IP address, one not targeted by the Code Red DDOS attack.

Updating Microsoft Software

Although Code Red affected corporate computers, its spread underscores the need for Windows OS updates

Microsoft funnels its users to the Windows Update site (`http://www.windowsupdate.com`), where a diagnostic tool queries a user's system to determine which operating system the user's computer is running (Windows 95, 98, Me, 2000, NT, or XP) and when, if ever, it was last updated. Based on the finding of that automatic survey, the site offers the user a choice of updates.

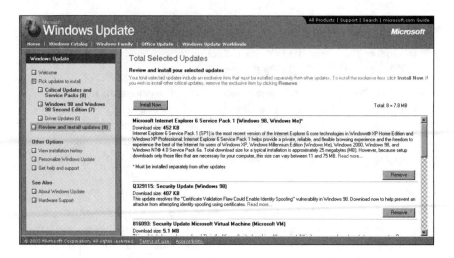

Figure 4.5

To protect your computer from viruses that operate through holes in your software, use Windows Update to update your Windows operating system.

> **Note**
>
> Microsoft takes great pains to note that no private information is being gathered or distributed. Their site says, "This scan is done on your computer to ensure the safety and privacy of your system information. None of this information is sent to Microsoft or over the Internet."

Because bandwidth is precious, Microsoft doesn't want you to continually keep downloading updates you already have. After your system is inventoried, you'll find a list of updates. Some are deemed critical updates, meaning they are necessary for fixing security holes, performance bugs, or any known flaw. The rest are optional, meant to optimize performance or add niche performance benefits. If you want more technical information about any of the updates, you can click the Read This First link. That link leads you to details such as a more detailed description of the component, how to begin using the component, instructions for uninstalling, and the support policy.

We recommend you update your Windows operating system at least once a month, or when a big virus hits:

1. Close all programs except your browser.
2. Make sure you are online.
3. Go to www.windowsupdate.com.
4. Click Product Updates.
5. Accept the system evaluation; click Yes when asked if you want to download and install the Microsoft Updater.
6. Both critical and optional updates display. Click the Critical Update box.
7. In the upper-right corner, click the gray Download box.
8. Click Start Download.
9. Accept any other options.
10. After all components have downloaded, restart your computer.

These instructions may vary depending on your operating system, but the process is similar in all versions of Windows.

In the Sea

Author William S. Burroughs said, "Language is a virus from outer space." The mini-programs called viruses and worms are no different from the huge number of programs we run every day. Our computer is not a closed box—it gets updates, we share files and programs, and we exchange lesser viruses (such as bad Internet humor).

Viruses can be easily stopped, but to do so we must realize that we are afloat in a vast sea of data. The purpose of this book is to remind you again and again that you are in the sea. We hope that you are whale watching most of the time, but sometimes you should look out for sharks.

Web-Based Viruses

Browsing the web has become more and more dynamic. Advances in web programming languages have enabled creative web-masters to program miniature movies, animations, and interactive programs that we can view and play on the web. Unfortunately, bad guys have used these languages to create web-based viruses. The threat is that you will visit a malicious website that has disguised a virus as a component that's normally used for enhancing web browsing. That virus might have the capability to download to your machine even if your computer is running an updated anti-virus program.

To address this concern, Microsoft has created security levels you can set in Internet Explorer. Your options are Low, Medium-Low, Medium, and High—with Low being the most security lax and High being the most security conscious. The problem with setting your browser to High is that you will be constantly interrupted during your web browsing because the security controls will prohibit legitimate web components from downloading. The High setting will block images, animations, and cookies to the extent that your surfing might be greatly compromised. The Medium setting will protect your computer from most malicious code, but to be really safe and minimally inconvenienced, I suggest customizing the security settings:

1. Click Tools and choose Internet Options.
2. Go to the Security tab and click the Custom Level button.

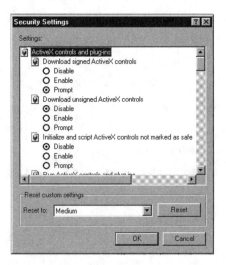

Figure 4.6

By customizing your web browser's security settings, you can choose where you want higher levels of security.

Following are the settings I suggest for each option (your mileage may vary). Customizing the settings is trial and error on each computer, so use this as a starting point and if any one control seems too prohibitive while you are browsing the web, you can go back and change the setting. If you hear of any new viruses exploiting a particular feature you can change its setting back to a more secure state. Generally, if you keep ActiveX and Java on high security settings, you should be safe.

- Download signed ActiveX controls: Prompt
- Download unsigned ActiveX controls: Disable
- Initialize and script ActiveX controls not marked as safe: Disable
- Run ActiveX controls and plug-ins: Enable
- Script ActiveX controls marked safe for scripting: Enable
- Downloads: Enable
- Font download: Enable (set to Disable for more protection)
- Java Permissions: High safety
- Access data sources across domains: Disable
- Allow META REFRESH: Enable (set to Disable for more protection)
- Display mixed content: Enable (set to Prompt for more protection)
- Don't prompt for client certificate selection when no certificates or only one certificate exists: Disable
- Drag and drop or copy and paste files: Enable (set to Prompt for more protection)
- Installation of desktop items: Prompt
- Launching programs and files in an IFRAME: Prompt
- Navigate sub-frames across different domains: Prompt
- Software channel permissions: Medium safety
- Submit nonencrypted form data: Enable (set to Prompt for more protection)
- Userdata persistence: Enable (set to Disable for more protection)
- Active scripting: Enable (set to Prompt for more protection)
- Allow paste operations via script: Enable (set to Prompt for more protection)

- Scripting of Java applets: Enable (set to Prompt for more protection)
- Logon: Automatic logon only in Intranet zone (set to Prompt for more protection)

Hoaxes, Virus Myths, and Scams

Bananas shipped from Costa Rica are infected with flesh-eating bacteria. A sick child desperately needs your help. The government wants to tax email service. Your computer has been infected with a virus that will erase your hard drive and the hard drives of everyone in your address book. There are millions of dollars waiting, unclaimed, in a foreign bank account, and your signature is all that's needed to claim them.

Sound startling? These warnings and promises would be, if they were true. But they're not; they are actually email hoaxes—digital messages passed from person to person that warn readers about everything from fatal illnesses to computer viruses to what will happen to you if you don't immediately forward the message to 10 friends.

Hoax emails are the ingrown toenails on the stinky foot of the web. They are the web's version of prank phone calls, only more damaging, and sometimes truly dangerous. Forwarded by gullible newbies, and even more gullible teenagers, a quality email hoax can spread across the globe in days and linger for years. They can tie up Internet service providers (ISPs) or convince people to purge their computers of fake viruses. In the very worst cases, people have died because they fell for Internet scams perpetuated by true criminals.

The hoax writer is trying to target an unsuspecting audience. Why? He thinks he's smarter than you. The classic hoaxes are urban legends, threats of looming government action, requests for prayers offered up on behalf of a sick child, or the lure of free money if you "just forward this email to everyone you know." They're dumb jokes perpetuated by malicious practical jokers. Virus hoaxes fall into a similar category: They're the emails that claim that something terrible is attacking your computer. When you forward those letters, you waste your friends' time and slow down company networks. But email untruths get seriously dangerous with scams: attempts to bilk you out of money. The Nigerian letter scam, for example, detailed later in this chapter, promises extreme wealth, but has led gullible victims to kidnapping, bankruptcy, torture, and even death.

Hundreds of Hoaxes

Hoaxes can be a powerful force on the Internet. Suppose you get the famous "Bill Gates wants to give you thousands of dollars for forwarding this email" hoax. You decide to forward it with the line "I don't know if this is true, but it's worth trying." I received hundreds of such emails from friends. I stopped debunking the myth after copy 47 arrived at my inbox.

Suppose, however, that you decide that it really can't hurt, so you forward it to 5 friends. One of them is savvy enough not to continue the chain, but two of the others forward it to another 5 friends, one forwards it to 10 more people, and the last is totally unsuspecting and sends it on to the 30 people in his address book. In total, 56 people have been affected so far (including you). Now they have to make the same choice you made: Depending on their decisions—and the size of their address books—the email could easily reach another 500 to 5000 people before the end of the day. Before the end of the week, the number could be closer to 5 million or 50 million. That many emails means lost bandwidth, slowed email servers, and a colossal waste of time for everyone who receives the hoax, reads it, and sends it on.

And the number of hoaxes just keeps growing. "In the last 5 years, we've seen hundreds…of hoaxes," says William Orvis, a security specialist at the U.S. Department of Energy. Orvis and his team investigate hoax emails for the government, as part of a group called the Computer Incident Advisory Capability (CIAC). Their website (www.ciac.org/ciac/) warns consumers about fake emails, and lists many of the most popular. They break email hoaxes down into several types:

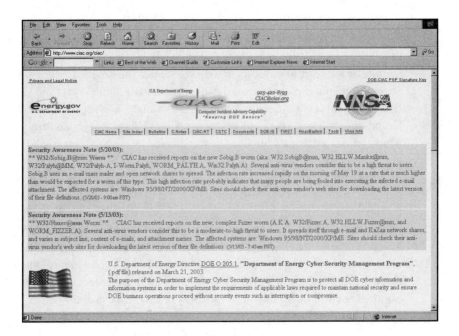

Figure 5.1

The CIAC's website warns consumers about email hoaxes and scams, and lists many of the more popular ones.

- **Malicious code (virus and Trojan horse) warnings.** These hoaxes come in two flavors. One arrives as an email that suggests that a file on your computer is a virus, such as sulfnbk.exe. The other warns of a coming threat so bad that we must all be on alert for its devastating presence. The first is the more common of the two.

- **Urban myths.** HIV-laced syringes on gas pumps, prospective gang members hiding in the backseats of cars at gas pumps, gas pumps turn into man-eating snakes and eat your spleen.... If it sounds like a story you heard once at band camp or sitting around a fire on a cold and dark night, it's a hoax.

- **Giveaways.** The Gap will send you a pair of cargo pants for every email you forward. IBM will send you computer equipment. Microsoft will send you money. Miller Brewing will send you beer. Nope. Big companies do not give away big bucks when you send emails to your friends.

- **Inconsequential warnings.** Cell phones at gas pumps, exploding gel candles, hot water in the microwave—these are warnings of things that might have some truth to them, but are statistically unlikely.

- **Sympathy letters and requests to help someone.** The American Cancer Society will donate 3 cents toward cancer research to fulfill 7-year-old cancer patient Jessica Mydek's dying wish. The Make-a-Wish Foundation will pay 7 cents toward the hospital bills of 7-year-old Amy Bruce, who is suffering from lung cancer caused by secondhand smoke and a large brain tumor caused by repeated beatings. BCC Software will donate 5 cents to help with 7-year-old Kalin Relek's operation for internal bleeding, as result of being struck by a car. Does this imply that doctors are standing by the bleeding boy until you forward this plea and get BCC Software to fund the operation? They're not. However, both the American Cancer Society and the Make-a-Wish Foundation received so many questions about those particular hoaxes that they had to post disclaimers on their websites. The Make-a-Wish foundation says it gets hundreds of inquiries a day—not the most productive use of the organization's time and energy.

- **Traditional chain letters, threat chains, scam chains, and scare chains.** Good luck, bad luck, send a dollar, send information, a class is working on a project to see how far their email can travel: You know these. They're not much different from traditional chain letters, although some are nastier and some—the scam chains—have the potential to get you into real trouble. Whenever an email tells you to pass it along to 10 people or to everyone you know, be wary. The chances that you're passing along a lie are high.

- **Hacked history and misplaced political activism.** Hillary Clinton got Black Panthers off for murder (nope); the female members of Congress staged a walkout for peace (nope); Oliver North was afraid of Osama bin Laden 15 years ago (nope). These stories are just that, stories. They're sent around the Internet as truth, presumably by people with their own political agendas.

Another type of hoax in the hacked history category is the misplaced political activism. Helping Afghani women is a great idea, but it's not going to be accomplished via an Internet petition. As far as I can tell, Internet petitions are good for one thing and one thing only: They give spammers lists of active email addresses to which they can send junk email.

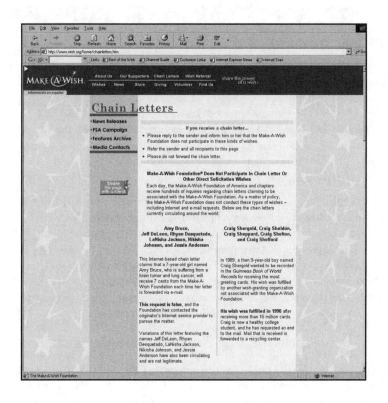

Figure 5.2

Many email hoaxes claim to be associated with the Make-a-Wish Foundation. The foundation received so many inquiries about the hoaxes that they now list disclaimers on their website.

techlive

The Embarrassment of Bill 602P

In the really embarrassing department, this one takes the cake. In 2000 millions of people were outraged to learn about proposed Bill 602P. It would have permitted the Federal Government to tack a 5-cent surcharge onto every email delivered. Forwarded emails about this bill spammed everyone and their mom. It was one of the biggest Internet hoaxes to date. Worse, it gained temporary legitimacy in 2000 when two New York Senate candidates found themselves debating the merits of the nonexistent congressional bill.

During a debate sponsored by WCBS-TV, Democratic nominee Hillary Rodham Clinton and her Republican rival Representative Rick Lazio were asked where they stood on "Federal Bill 602P." Both candidates were strongly opposed to the measure, which would purportedly levy a 5-cent surcharge on every email communication. Neither had much reason to worry. The bill, like its backer, "Congressman Schnell," does not exist. Bill 602P is a long-running web hoax that has prompted repeated denials from Congress and the United States Postal Service.

"The fact of the matter is that there is no such congressman, and bills are not named in this fashion," Representative Billy Tauzin, a Louisiana Republican who sits on the House Commerce Committee, warns readers on his congressional website. "Officials with the U.S. Postal Service have stated that they would never contemplate such legislation, nor would they support this legislation."

In fact, the House, perhaps seeking to lay the rumors of an email tax to rest, passed a bill in May that prohibits federal fees on Internet access. The bill is pending in the Senate. So how did this fake Bill 602P become the very real topic of a Senate campaign debate? According to WCBS-TV, the hoax was one of several thousand questions submitted online by voters before the debate.

"The debate's moderator, Marcia Kramer, was not aware that there is no such bill," the station said in a prepared statement to the press.

Apparently, Clinton and Lazio were equally clueless, although both expressed disdain for the notion of email taxation. Clinton, who was forthright in admitting she knew nothing of the bill, said the bill sounded "burdensome and not justifiable." "I have been a supporter of the moratorium on taxation on the Internet. I think that we do have to let loose this extraordinary communication device and see how far it can go in connecting people up," she said. Lazio was also averse to the idea. "I am absolutely opposed to this. This is an example of the government's greedy hand and trying to take money from taxpayers that, frankly, it has no right to. We need to keep the government's hands off the Internet."

- **Jokes and true legends.** Should these qualify as hoaxes? Some of the jokes are actually funny, and many of the true legends are actually stories that a lot of people simply found interesting and then forwarded to a lot of friends. Yes, Outback Steakhouse really did go to Afghanistan and feed steak to 6700 troops. Yes, the Oregon Highway Authority really did explode a whale—and it was as bad an idea as it sounds! But true or not, when you send these stories to all your friends and family, you tie up bandwidth and slow down the Internet.

Web Hoaxes

Not all hoaxes come direct to your inbox: Some live on the web. One that threw even the FBI for a loop was BonsaiKitten.com. The site claims to be "dedicated to preserving the long lost art of body modification in house pets." It shows pictures of kittens squeezed into glass containers. Never mind that the photos were massively altered in Photoshop. The descriptions of how to prevent the animal from spoiling the pristine glass environment with its bodily waste were scientifically impossible, not to mention utterly ridiculous. However, the intended humor in the site's inane premise was lost on many of the millions of people who flocked to the page. A clever invention by an anonymous MIT student, the site made the Sophos security firm's top-five list of hoaxes in early 2003. I heard the morning DJs on one San Francisco radio station going berserk over the injustice and the cruelty. People called in ready to go to war over the kitty abuse, but it was all a ruse.

Unfortunately, this site—however implausible it was—became a hoax when presumably well-meaning writers wrote letters warning of the horror of science and giving the link. The incensed user, full of righteous indignation, visits the site, sees kitties in jars, and then forwards the original message to all of his kitty-loving friends. Lo and behold, an email hoax is born.

As you can see, the vast majority of these hoaxes are harmless—to you, at least, if not to the companies, businesses, and public individuals whose reputations may be at stake. Does this mean you shouldn't worry about them? Let's take closer looks at two types of hoax: malicious virus warnings and scams.

Malicious Virus Warnings

A coworker, Jocelyn, called me with a question I hear a lot: "Do I have a virus?" She told me a friend had emailed her in a panic with this message:

```
I have some bad news. I was just informed that my address
book has been infected with a virus. As a result, so has
yours because your address is in my book. The virus is
called jdbgmgr.exe. It cannot be detected by Norton or
McAfee antivirus programs. It sits quietly for about 14 days
before damaging the system. It is sent automatically by
Messenger and Address Book, whether or not you send email.
The good news is that it is easy to get rid of!

Just follow these simple steps and you should have no
problem.

1. Go to Start, and then Find or Search.
2. In files/folders, write the name jdbgmgr.exe.
3. Be sure to search in you C: drive.
4. Click Find or Search.
5. The virus has a teddy bear logo with the name jdbgmgr.exe
   Do not open!
6. Right-click and delete it.
7. Go to the Recycle Bin and delete it there also.

If you find the virus, you must contact everyone in your
address book.

Sorry for the trouble, but this is something I had no con-
trol over. I received it from someone else's address book.
```

Jocelyn followed the email instructions to look for the jdbgmgr.exe file, and sure enough it was right where the warning said it would be. She stopped short of deleting the file, however, and instead called me for advice.

"Do I have a virus? I have this file called J-D-B...." I interrupted her "G-M-G-R, right?" She was worried: It must be a bad virus, if I had heard of it.

"Not to worry," I said. "J-D-B-G-M-G-R is a part of the Windows operating system that helps it compile Java script. It comes included with Windows."

She was relieved. This warning was nothing but a hoax, a trick to get unsuspecting computer users to remove a part of the Windows operating system from their computer. Luckily, the deletion of jdbgmgr.exe has very little impact on the functionality of the Windows operating system, unless you debug Java—a task most of us need not face.

For the author of the hoax, I can only guess that this was a trick to see how many people he could scare into a harmless dismantling of Windows—a power trip that says, "Hey all you computer users who are freaked out by this big beige box, I know more about computers than you do, and I can prove it."

Jocelyn broke the virus hoax chain when she called me to check that jdbgmgr.exe really was a virus. For more information, I directed her to an article I had written and a link to Symantec's website that detailed the hoax. She relayed that information back to her friends and stopped that strain of the hoax in its tracks.

Where's the Danger?

Virus hoaxes eat up bandwidth on the Internet and tie up email servers, and although this is annoying, it's not truly dangerous. However, that's not the only damage virus hoaxes do.

"[People] are frightened that they're going to ruin their computer if they read this email," said Rose Miller, the security specialist who handles the CIAC hotline. "Something bad is going to happen if they don't forward this on to all their friends, everybody they know. They panic. They literally panic out there."

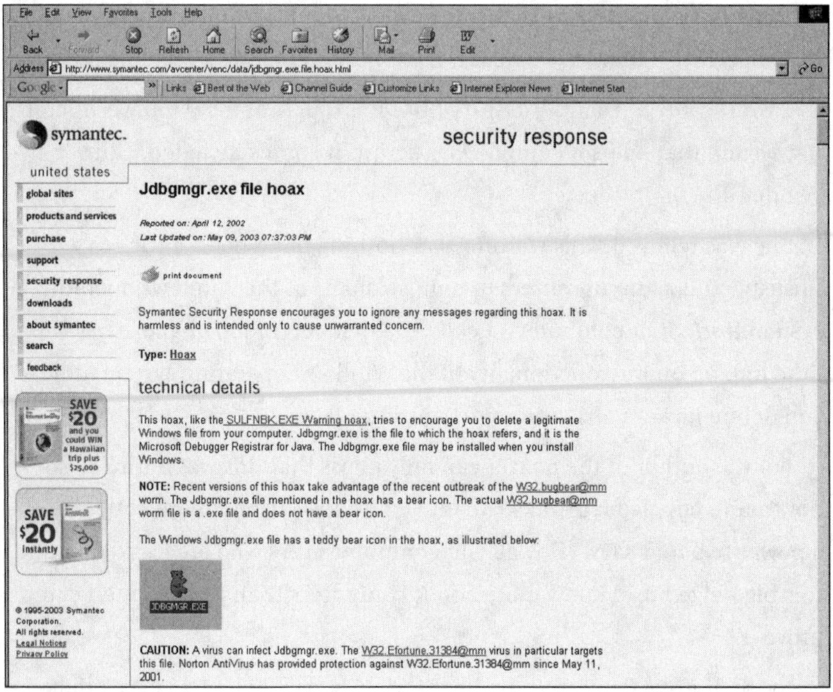

Figure 5.3

The jdbgmgr.exe virus hoax convinced a lot of people to delete a perfectly safe file from their operating system. Symantec's website was one of many to warn people about the hoax.

"A virus hoax [may say] there's a new virus spreading, and it can scare the IT manager, and he may shut down his mail servers. And we have actually had cases where a company has shut down mail servers," Motoaki Yamamura, an analyst at antivirus firm Symantec, said. "Later on, they found out it was a hoax and they lost a full day's worth of productivity."

And then there's the embarrassment. When a friend sent out a warning that a killer virus called sulfnbk.exe was on the loose, I had to send back the hoax alert to all on the mass-mailing email. Sulfnbk.exe is a real file distributed in the Windows operating system, and the alert email had thousands of people deleting it to purge their systems. My friend was embarrassed: She had been trying to do the right thing and felt guilty about infecting all those people; I felt bad that I had embarrassed her. Another negative effect of virus hoaxes is that they perpetuate confusion about how we should really protect ourselves from malicious code. The success of virus hoaxes stems from the very fears that caused you to buy this book: You feel like you need to know more about protecting your computer, but aren't sure what that really means. Is an antivirus scanner enough or do I need to manually delete bad programs off my computer? The short answer: There are tens of thousands of viruses, and no one could manually scan their entire computer filename by filename.

Virus hoaxes play upon our intentions to do the right thing, to try and help. When users receive an email, such as Jocelynn's, and scan their computer and actually find a copy of jdbgmgr.exe, it's like they've figured something out. They think they are part of the solution in fighting viruses—they're just trying to be active in protecting their computers and data from viruses. Deleting jdbgmgr.exe is billed as a way to rid your computer of a foreign devil, and warning your friends is a way to protect them and make sure they are equally proactive.

Recognizing a Virus Hoax

Sure we all want to help stomp out viruses. Without recognizing a virus threat as a hoax, however, we're really just contributing to the problem. Hopefully from reading this book, you'll learn to spot a hoax from a mile away. Maybe you can even become a connoisseur of the virus hoax.

Techno-babble is a giveaway that the virus threat isn't real. Hoax writers often play off of the idea that you know very little about computers, and so they use made-up terms, or techno-babble, to make the email sound as frightening as possible. If you don't understand the jargon, or the message is warning you about files in your computer you've never heard of, chances are it's a hoax.

In 1994 when most, if not all Internet users were newbies, the Good Times virus warning played upon all the fears and inadequacies modern viruses do, but with little of the current finesse. Good Times didn't need to be sophisticated because the Internet population was generally new to computers and overwhelmed by technology. Good Times still pops up from time to time today. It reads like this:

```
The FCC released a warning last Wednesday concerning a
matter of major importance to any regular user of the
Internet. Apparently, a new computer virus has been
engineered by a user of America Online that is unparal-
leled in its destructive capability. Other, more well-
known viruses such as Stoned, Airwolf, and Michaelangelo
pale in comparison to the prospects of this newest cre-
ation by a warped mentality.

What makes this virus so terrifying, said the FCC, is
the fact that no program needs to be exchanged for a new
computer to be infected. It can be spread through the
existing email systems of the Internet. Once a computer
is infected, one of several things can happen. If the
computer contains a hard drive, that will most likely be
destroyed. If the program is not stopped, the computer's
processor will be placed in a nth-complexity infinite
binary loop—which can severely damage the processor if
left running that way too long. Unfortunately, most
novice computer users will not realize what is happening
until it is far too late.
```

Techno-babble is rampant in the Good Times virus. "nth-complexity infinite binary loop." What is that? It means nothing, but then there's the added reinforcement that you must be too dumb to understand it.

I should admit that I actually forwarded this email in 1996 to a few friends warning them of the horrors. I thought I was really doing a service to humanity and showing off that I knew a lot about computers and would save the day by preventing them from infecting themselves. A more savvy friend debunked the hoax, and that was the last virus warning I ever sent out via email.

A really nasty version of Good Times came with the subject line "Good Times," causing users to think they had actually downloaded the terrible email (and perhaps sent it on) and that doom was imminent.

The Good Times Parody

Having admitted to falling for the Good Times hoax back in the day, I can't resist this parody. It still gives me a chuckle. (According to the CIAC, this was written by Patrick J Rothfuss; if true, kudos to Mr. Rothfuss.)

```
December 1996

Read this:

Good Times will rewrite your hard drive. Not only that,
but it will scramble any disks that are even close to your
computer. It will recalibrate your refrigerator's coolness
setting so all your ice cream goes melty. It will demagne-
tize the strips on all your credit cards, screw up the
tracking on your television, and use subspace field har-
monics to scratch any CDs you try to play.

It will give your ex-girlfriend your new phone number. It
will mix Kool-Aid into your fish tank. It will drink all
your beer and leave its socks out on the coffee table when
there's company coming over. It will put a dead kitten in
the back pocket of your good suit pants and hide your car
keys when you are late for work.

Good Times will make you fall in love with a penguin. It
will give you nightmares about circus midgets. It will
pour sugar in your gas tank and shave off both your eye-
brows while dating your girlfriend behind your back and
billing the dinner and hotel room to your Discover card.

It will seduce your grandmother. It does not matter if she
is dead, such is the power of Good Times; it reaches out
beyond the grave to sully those things we hold most dear.

It moves your car randomly around parking lots so you
can't find it. It will kick your dog. It will leave
libidinous messages on your boss's voice mail in your
voice! It is insidious and subtle. It is dangerous and
terrifying to behold. It is also a rather interesting
shade of mauve.

Good Times will give you Dutch Elm disease. It will leave
the toilet seat up. It will make a batch of methamphetamine
in your bathtub and then leave bacon cooking on the stove
```

continues

> while it goes out to chase grade-schoolers with your new snow blower.
>
> Listen to me. Good Times does not exist.
>
> It cannot do anything to you. But I can. I am sending this message to everyone in the world. Tell your friends, tell your family. If anyone else sends me another e-mail about this fake Good Times virus, I will turn hating them into a religion. I will do things to them that would make a horse head in your bed look like Easter Sunday brunch.

In 2000, another virus hoax made the rounds, called Virtual Card for You. Using a lot of techno-babble in its explanation of impending doom, it preyed upon that same computer inferiority described earlier, but without the technical sophistication of the jdbgmgr.exe hoax that sent you to find a file that was supposed to be there in the first place.

The Virtual Card email read as follows:

> A new virus has just been discovered that has been classi-fied by Microsoft (www.microsoft.com) and by McAfee (www.mcafee.com) as the most destructive ever! This virus acts in the following manner: It sends itself automatically to all contacts on your list with the title "A Virtual Card for You." As soon as the supposed virtual card is opened, the computer freezes so that the user has to reboot. When the Ctrl+Alt+Del keys or the Reset button are pressed, the virus destroys Sector Zero, thus permanently destroying the hard disk.
>
> Please distribute this message to the greatest number of people possible. Yesterday, in just a few hours, this virus caused panic in New York, according to a news broadcast by CNN (www.cnn.com).

The techno-speak "Sector Zero" is an attempt to make you feel like you are out of your depths. Bottom line: If you don't understand the language in anything you read about your computer, don't assume it's true. Find a reli-able source that can explain the concept in plain English or debunk the warning as a myth.

> **Note**
>
> What is Sector Zero? Great question. The writer of the email might be referring to the master boot record, an essential part of your computer. If the master boot record were to be destroyed, your data would be impossible to find without intervention from your local computer doctor.

Another feature of this email that should let you know that it's a hoax is this line: Yesterday in just a few hours, this virus caused panic in New York, according to a news broadcast by CNN (www.cnn.com). This is the hoax writer trying to lure you in. When did a computer virus ever cause "panic," let alone cause panic in New York City? On the one hand, the use of CNN or any credible news organization lends authenticity to the story. On the other hand, that same referenced source provides a great way for a skeptical reader to check the facts of the warning...in a hurry.

All credible news organizations—ABC, NBC, CNN, TechTV—put much of the content they air on TV on their websites as well, and thus provide you with another source to research virus threats. These websites are especially heavy on technology-based content. If CNN covers a computer virus on air, you can bet that it's also all over the Technology section of their website. If it's not there or in their archives, that's a good tip that the virus never existed.

The Nigerian Letter Scam

Hoaxes and fake virus warnings are annoying, but the scary stuff comes from scams. The Big Daddy of Internet schemes is the Nigerian letter scam. The FBI says millions of dollars have been scammed from unsuspecting investors, but the real number is purported to be in the hundreds of millions; many who are bilked feel too ashamed to report their losses. However, this scam isn't just about losing a fortune: A government agency, the National Archives and Records Administration, says at least 17 people have been killed because they fell for the Nigerian letter scam.

Suppose that you've just received an email asking for your help in freeing an enormous sum of money currently stashed inside a foreign country, and your reward will be a percentage that may reach into the millions. All the desperate contact asks for in exchange is that you allow the money to be transferred to a bank account in your name. Sound too good to be true? That's because it is! However, a surprising number of people still fall for such scams each year.

Despite having been around for years, the fraud—also known as the 419 Scam (named for the African nation's penal code regarding this type of crime)—continues to attract victims with the lure of quick riches. According to the website of the Secret Service, the Financial Crimes Division of the Secret Service receives "approximately 100 telephone calls from victims/potential victims and 300–500 pieces of related correspondence per day." The fraud's transition from hard copy to the Internet has allowed the con men involved to quicken the pace of the ruse while still maintaining its difficult-to-trace nature.

After your interest has been piqued by the tale of a wealthy businessman or government official who managed to squirrel away money from contract overpayments before his untimely demise, all that remains is to pick out the color of your yacht, right? Not so fast. Bank transfer fees will suddenly arise, and officials will of course have to be bribed. Numerous other charges—each coming out of your own pocket—will start to mount, along with the excuses from overseas as to why the transfer of funds has yet to occur.

What's thousands of dollars compared to the millions you'll be making? Realistic documents seem to back claims that the money is *almost* yours. If at this point you realize that you've been conned, you'll be poorer and embarrassed, but hopefully wiser. You should also consider yourself lucky to get out now rather than later.

Continuing to fall for the scheme may result in a trip to Nigeria (or some other far-flung destination), where you'll be at the mercy of the scam artists. They'll bribe a customs official to get you into the country without a passport. Bad idea. This then means they'll be free to extort the rest of your money by threatening to turn you in to the police. Even that would be a better fate than turning up dead or missing, something that has happened numerous times, according to the United States Secret Service. Read `http://www.secretservice.gov/alert419.shtml` for more information.

If you do make it out unharmed, one small consolation is that you weren't alone in being duped. The 419 Coalition, a group dedicated to combating this scam, says reports place the scam anywhere between the third and fifth largest industry in Nigeria. Think you would never fall for a ruse like this? The National Archives and Records Administration says recipients respond to 10 percent of all Nigerian scam emails. Of those respondents, 1 percent become seriously involved.

If you're like most people, you've probably found more than one Nigerian scam email in your inbox. The details vary, but the theme is the same. For a great overview of the last couple of years, including dollar amounts and country of origin, read `http://www.tip.net.au/spam/Nigerian-419-Scam.html`.

techlive

The Scam Turns Deadly

Juergen Ahlmann is an entrepreneur in Southern California. In January 2001, he and a business partner were looking for ways to get some extra cash to launch their new catfish importing and exporting company.

In an interview with TechTV, Ahlmann says he was aware of 419 scams, but the origin of the messages played a big role in his decision to answer one he received.

"I did not have any concerns," Ahlmann said of his first impression. "If it had been Nigeria, perhaps it would have been a different story. I never heard of anything coming out of Kenya." The man who contacted Ahlmann said his name was Mike Otieno and that he was from Nairobi, Kenya. Otieno claimed he was a business promoter who had a client who was willing to invest in Ahlmann's project.

Juergen negotiated with the "investors" for nearly 4 months before they insisted that he and his associate, Jim Harrel, fly to Nairobi to sign some papers. But shortly after the two businessmen arrived in Kenya, their negotiations took a turn for the worse when the "investors" found out the two did not have as much money as they thought.

That's when Ahlmann and Harrel became instant hostages to the men who had lured them to Kenya. "We were chained around the ankles and around the wrists," Ahlmann said. "The window [of the room they were held in] was covered with a piece of plywood so there was no daylight coming in." Their kidnappers demanded that a sum of $30,000 be paid for their release.

While in captivity, Ahlmann and Harrel met another American, Reverend William Danny Marrow, a native of Norfolk, Virginia, who runs an international import and export company.

Marrow says he was also lured to Kenya via an Internet message. He says Otieno sent him an email saying he had raw diamonds worth more than $9 million. He flew to Nairobi to close a deal for the diamonds.

The 60-year-old says he was physically tortured with burns to his feet and genitals after being taken hostage in January 2001. Ahlmann says he was also subject to mental torment by the kidnappers. They threatened to hang him and his business partner upside-down and kill them if their wives could not come up with the ransom money. Most of the threats were made by a man guarding the Americans. Juergen says the others called this man "Fat Boy." Fat Boy apparently drank a lot and made lots of threats, Juergen says, but he also promised Juergen a beer if his friends decided to release him.

After receiving an unusual email from her husband, Sheila Ahlmann knew something had gone wrong in Kenya and quickly contacted the FBI. FBI agents in San Diego worked with Sheila Ahlmann as she agreed to send a ransom of $7,000 to a Western Union office in Nairobi.

Agents from the FBI's San Diego field office contacted the bureau's office in Nairobi about the kidnapping. With the help of Kenyan police, authorities arrested Otieno, whose actual name is Augustine Nwanga, when he arrived at the location to pick up the ransom. Shortly after the arrest, Nwanga phoned his cohorts and the three American hostages were released.

"I think they're extremely lucky," said FBI Special Agent William Peterson, who works out of the bureau's San Diego field office. "Had it not been for FBI representation overseas, this would have turned out differently." Nwanga, who is Nigerian, was tried and convicted of kidnapping and is now serving a 9-year prison sentence in Kenya. Reports from Kenya indicate that two of Nwanga 's accomplices, Johnson Obasi and Felix Ansoike, fled after making bail.

The whereabouts of the one called Fat Boy are still unknown. Authorities believe he fled shortly after the hostages were released. This doesn't mean the heavy-drinking guard wasn't good on his word. Just before his release, Fat Boy approached Ahlmann and said, "I promised you I would buy a beer at the airport when you are free. I cannot come to the airport. Here are 200 shillings. That is enough for 2 beers."

> **Note**
>
> On a more playful note, several Americans have started their own project to scam the scammers. Called the Chaos Project, they have even been able to pry small amounts of money away from the conmen. Check out their antics at `http://ecobank.customerservice.inbox.as/`.

Avoiding the Scam

The best advice I can give you about email or Internet-based investment opportunities is this: "Don't do it!" The Nigerian scam is just the tip of the iceberg. A friend of mine had a heart-breaking experience trying to help her 76-year-old father who lost 50 percent of his retirement to an Internet scam. If you want to find a good investment, get a good money manager or find a reputable brokerage, real estate, or investment firm. Warren Buffett isn't looking for great spam-solicited investment opportunities.

In the past few years, the number of scam sites trying to bilk Internet users out of their money has grown dramatically. Because the Securities and Exchange Commission (SEC) considers it is such a plague on the investment industry, they have set up fake investment opportunity sites to educate the public about scam investment ruses (`http://www.mcwhortle.com/` and `http://www.growthventure.com/parsons`). They first take you through all the hype and marketing. Then, if you click the Invest Now link, a page displays the warning "You could have been scammed." The SEC claims it received more than 150,000 hits in the first 3 days that the McWhortle site was online.

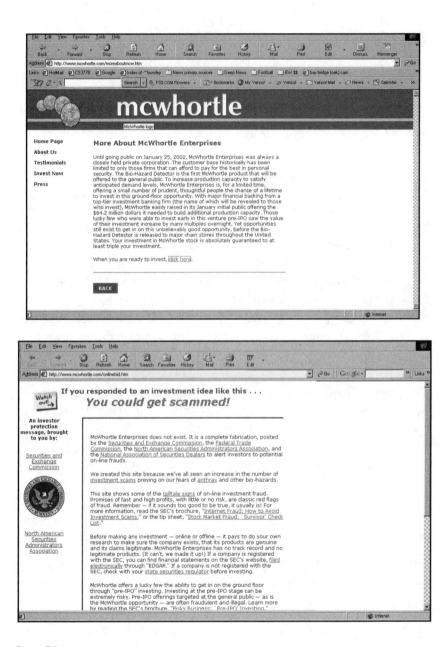

Figure 5.4

The SEC's fake McWhortle Enterprises investment site was designed to show consumers the dangers of online investment scams.

Protecting Yourself—And the Rest of Us, Too

If hoaxes and scams such as the email taxation bill, JDBGMRE, or the Nigerian 419 letter, gets so much credibility, how are you supposed to spot a hoax in your inbox? Most hoaxes are unimaginative, following very predictable patterns that you can spot from a mile away. Here are hints to identify the basic hoaxes:

- **Subject line.** As Thomas Jefferson said, an email hoax is only as good as its subject line. (That's a test: Did Thomas Jefferson ever utter those profound words? Skepticism my friends, bring on the skepticism.) Amateur hoax writers usually settle for hackneyed ALL CAP exclamations such as "IMPORTANT!! TRILLIONS OF DOLLARS FOR YOU!!!! OPEN NOW!!" A more believable hoax would begin with something more personal, yet broadly applicable, such as, "I know you hate your grind of a job."

- **If it looks too good to be true, it is.** Ted Turner, Paul Allen, the Prince of Brunei, or Disney want to give you $5,000. Please forward. Don't believe it. There's no such thing as a free lunch. Any email that's offering you something for nothing is likely to be false.

- **If it sounds too bad to be true, it probably is.** Some horror scenarios sent via email may be true, but I don't know of one. Men trying to kidnap women using ether in perfume bottles, tortured kittens, poison in Diet Coke—if it sounds incredible, it's probably not true.

- **Crime doesn't pay.** If someone is asking you to do something clearly illegal—for example, steal money from a foreign government or lie about your identity to a bank—don't do it!

If you get an email that has any of these characteristics, break the chain. How? Look it up! Sites that debunk email and online hoaxes abound on the Internet. The best are Vmyths.com, Hoaxes A-Z, and Snopes.com. In addition, CIAC's hoax website (www.ciac.org/ciac) lists hundreds of the most popular email hoaxes.

If the email is about a virus, go straight to the websites for antivirus companies, such as McAfee or Symantec, to see whether their databases list the virus. "There are hundreds and hundreds of hoaxes. And we've only kept track of the virus hoaxes, and I would say there are a few hundred virus hoaxes," insisted Motoaki Yamamura, an analyst at the antivirus firm

Symantec. On these websites, you can search for the content from the email warning. Your search will return information that tells you whether the email describes a real virus or will debunk it as a hoax.

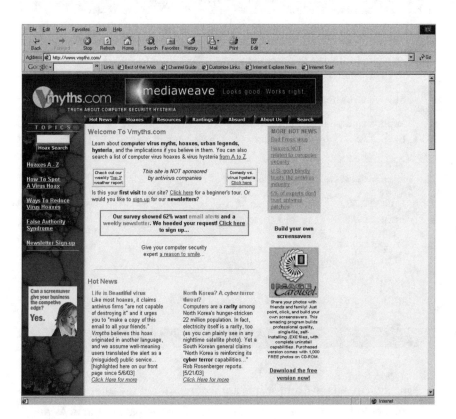

Figure 5.5

Vmyths.com is one of the best online resources for debunking email and Internet hoaxes and scams.

Another option is to research the topic at a reputable media outlet. Of course, TechTV will have information about any Internet-based phenomenon, as will the *New York Times*, the *Washington Post*, Reuters, and most other reputable news organizations. Don't trust Billy Bob's website at

`www.Tripod.members.billybobzadoc.23465ewiuhufdemaliary973245r.html`.

Find a trustworthy news source and work from there to validate anything you read in email or online.

Where to Look

Before you panic and forward any emails, check the following websites:

Symantec antivirus resource center
`http://securityresponse.symantec.com/`

McAfee virus hoax center `http://vil.nai.com/VIL/hoaxes.asp`

Sophos.com hoax center
`http://www.cert.org/other_sources/viruses.html`

Vmyths.com
`http://www.vmyths.com/index.cfm`

Hoaxes A-Z
`http://www.vmyths.com/hoax.cfm`

Snopes.com
`http://www.snopes.com/`

CIAC
`http://www.ciac.org/ciac/`

Hoaxes, virus myths, and scams are scourges upon the Internet. Do your part to identify, debunk, and resist the urge to participate in them. As my mother would say, "You're better than that." Hoaxes are all about ego—the author throws a pebble into the pond of the Internet to see how far the ripples will travel. Harmless but annoying? Not really. In some cases, scams can be deadly; more commonly, scams are costly. The loss of your life's savings or even your life should keep you from *ever* replying to these "investment opportunities." Share what you know about these hoaxes with the people you fear may be vulnerable.

Safe and Sane Online Interactions

Safe and sane online relationships result when you conduct yourself with the understanding that privacy and honesty are different in the digital world. You are also less likely to come to grief if you understand that online connections do not map surely to those in real life. When we talk about connections, interactions, or relationships, we aren't limiting ourselves to romantic endeavors. People meet and interact online by the millions each day and only a small percentage of those encounters are romantic. Applying the tenets of this chapter to your online interactions—amorous or not—will lead to better encounters offline in the real world.

Privacy Online

Scott McNealy, CEO of computer manufacturer Sun Microsystems, once said, "You've got no privacy anyway. Get over it." He was referring to the fact that because so much personal information about you has been collected and observed by so many entities, both public and private, it's naive to pretend otherwise. He was also referring to the way that websites can retain all kinds of information about our web-cruising habits...without our permission.

It's not just credit bureaus, government agencies, telemarketers, and e-commerce websites that may have diminished your privacy by gathering information about you without permission: Another kind of privacy loss is self-inflicted. It can happen anytime you send an email or post anything anywhere online. When whatever it is leaves your computer, it has gone into the public domain forever—and as such, always has the potential to resurface and do damage.

What You Say Might Come Back to Haunt You

Laurie Garrett, the Pulitzer prize–winning journalist, is a science writer for *Newsday* and wrote the book *The Coming Plague*. She sent an informal email to a few of her friends laying out her thoughts and impressions from her week spent at the 2003 World Economic Forum at Davos, an annual invitation-only confab of many of the richest, most powerful, and most influential people in the world. Garrett's email was forwarded to the wife of a friend, who sent it to two of her sisters, who sent it to a coworker, who then released it into the global information sea, where it was posted and enjoyed and discussed widely.

Garrett had a professional reputation to protect—as did her employers and publishers—and had no intention of "publishing" such informal and subjective work. What's more, libel is always a concern for any professional writer, and her email had plenty to say about folks both famous and infamous. Because she makes her living as a writer, she also wants control over and payment for her written work. Garrett made public on various Internet forums her understandable displeasure with the realization that all email, no matter how originally intentioned, can become public.

Web Logs Aren't Private

Heather Armstrong is a Utah web designer who kept a blog (web log; that is, an online diary) in which she had rough things to say about her Mormon upbringing, and in which she also vented about her work life. No surprise, her brother eventually came across her blog, and word reached both her parents and her employer. This precipitated a family crisis as severe as that which had taken place when her parents had gotten divorced 20 years before. In addition, Armstrong's employer fired her.

People Read What You Publish Online

Fiona (name changed at her request) had lived in the San Francisco Bay Area most of her adult life, where she fell in love with the blues. The Bay Area has long had a tradition of cultural and musical diversity: black and white musicians and their fans have famously commingled for years. John Lee Hooker owns a blues club in a vibrant, racially mixed San Francisco neighborhood, attended by all—and Fiona, a white woman, had never felt uncomfortable going to clubs and boogying down with the music. When Fiona's children had finally gone off to college, she realized she could clear an enormous profit from selling her house for a typically astronomical Bay Area price (she had bought her place for little in the early 1960s), and retire with the resulting enhanced bank balance to a small town in southern Mississippi famous for its annual blues festival.

The blues festival was the main source of income (tourists!) for the small town, and was run by a nonprofit African American organization that used the proceeds from the event to fund scholarships for local kids to attend traditionally black colleges. The festival had originally started when a blues musician who had made good after he moved up North came back home on a summer weekend to celebrate and to give back to the community he had sprung from. Because he felt liberated by the enthusiastic response he'd received in the North and in Europe, he started the 1-day festival on the weekend after June 10, which commemorates the Emancipation Proclamation. The festival featured a star headliner, attracting people from all over the South. The festival thrived commercially because it came along after June weddings and graduations, so people were free to travel to it.

Fiona made her big move in March, only a few months before the festival was due to make its annual appearance. People in this small town didn't know her yet, and Fiona, coming from the famously liberal Bay Area, hadn't yet gotten the hang of living in a community with a long and painful history of racial divisiveness. After the festival, Fiona wrote an amusing, hyperbolic rant about how it was just too damned hot to have an outdoor music festival with dancing in late June, no matter how great the music, and posted it on a local blues-fan *zine* (that is, an underground, do-it-your-self online publication). The piece then spread throughout the entire blues community, all over the world, and caused her no end of grief at home.

The festival organizers thought she was racist, because it appeared that she was sabotaging their annual fundraiser. After all, she had gone on at great length about how no sane person would be able to abide a blues festi-val in Mississippi in mid-summer! The black club owners began to be ner-vous about her, wondering whether she was trying to stir up trouble—a white woman attending black blues clubs by herself. Suppose a black man who knew of her rant started giving her grief and then she called the cops? Bad memories were being triggered here.

For Fiona, the backlash was in full force. Aside from filleting catfish or picking cotton, there were not a lot of jobs for which Fiona was qualified in that small town. Every time one of these scarce jobs in town opened up, such as writing press releases and brochures for the chamber of commerce or working as a library assistant, she wasn't even given an interview. Fiona had poisoned the well in the community that she loved—and whose trust she has since had to painstakingly regain.

Tangible harm, way beyond what these people experienced, can result from things written or sent online. Electronic "speech" acts can have adverse consequences in the world outside cyberspace, sometimes for years to come.

There Is No Privacy Online

It is always risky to assume that you have security through obscurity. That is, do not assume that just because you are living in a time of info-glut, when so much email is sent and received and so much material is made available online, that your writings online will be ignored. In some new form of Murphy's law, the very people whom you would never want reading something potentially explosive you wrote are the very same peo-ple who will stumble upon it and freak out.

Even remarks posted to private email lists may make their way into the public domain. If that list is archived in such a way that search engine spiders can crawl it, scan it, and enter its data into their database, it can be read. In addition, comments made in private forums can always be grabbed and forwarded to places they were never intended to arrive.

Mail List/List Serve Mail lists, or list serves, are online email groups to which members post messages or write emails that are sent out to all the people on the list. They are meant as forums for group discussion in email form.

Ronald (name changed at his request) is a scientist who participates in an elite private email list with other people who are experts in his same field. Ronald has successfully held executive positions in various high-tech companies, and has been able to hire folks he likes and respects. Ronald noticed when Toby (name changed for obvious reasons)—a new, young, and smart addition—joined the list.

Ronald initially championed Toby because of the young man's smarts and technical expertise. He also considered creating a position for him at the company where he held a C-level position. After observing over time that Toby's posts to the professional group were brash, confrontational, and inclined toward making accusations not necessarily grounded in fact, Ronald decided that not only would he never hire Toby, he would also recommend against anyone else hiring Toby. Toby will probably never realize that his behavior on a private email list will dog his professional career for years to come.

Confidential in the Eye of the Beholder

Toni (name changed at her request) is a freelance journalist who often reports on controversial topics, people, and enterprises. After she had finished working on an exposé of a high-profile business, one of her sources inside the organization who had been very helpful and informative both online and on the phone invited her to lunch. The informant suggested meeting Toni at a satellite campus of the company, the site where he actually worked, a few miles away from the corporate headquarters. Because Toni was sociable—and always interested in cultivating good sources—she agreed. When she showed up at her source's workplace, he was indeed friendly, in fact too friendly.

He insisted on showing her his collection of online pornography and began to exhibit himself to her. The satellite campus was isolated, and Toni felt very scared and violated. She was able to extricate herself from the situation without any physical harm, but she did feel shaken up. A few weeks later, a sympathetic woman friend to whom Toni confided her story—the source turned creepy—suggested that Toni write about her experience in a private online women's forum, perhaps as a way to warn other women away from this low-grade sexual predator. Members of this online community swore confidentiality and were not to repeat anything said within the community to anyone outside the forum.

Within 48 hours of posting her tale of woe, Toni was contacted by the head of human resources at the creepy source's place of business; 24 hours after that, the CEO of the enterprise contacted her. This was particularly awkward for Toni, because she had written an unflattering story about the place and hadn't been visiting the "source" on official business. More importantly, however, Toni realized that there was no such thing as online privacy.

In most cases, we inadvertently leak our own information. The possibility that hackers or network support people are monitoring our email is remote, but it does happen.

The Snooping System Administrator

Jenna and Patrice (names changed at their request) were both well known in their local arts community. During the time they were dating, they habitually sent each other instant messages filled with double entendres. One night when Patrice was by herself, she received a whispered phone call from someone purporting to be Jenna. The caller said that she was at that very moment participating in an orgy with the theater troupe she managed, describing in graphic detail what she was doing and with whom. Upset, Patrice called Jenna first thing the next morning. It turned out that Jenna had not made any phone calls the night before and hadn't ever had group sex with the performers she managed...or with anyone else, for that matter.

It took a fair amount of time and reassurance before Patrice believed Jenna. A few days later, Jenna received a suggestive email from the system administrator of her local Internet service provider, suggestive in a way similar to Patrice's description of her obscene phone call. At that point, Jenna realized that the system administrator must have been voyeuristically enjoying the instant messages she and Patrice had been sending—and that he, disguising his voice, had probably been the bad guy a few nights back.

Making the Internet More Private

With regard to interpersonal communications you consider truly sensitive, your best defense against privacy invasion is **not** to send it electronically. If you must send it electronically, however, you should securely encrypt the communications. Encryption software programs scramble data in such a way that it cannot be unscrambled without complementary descrambling software. Although encryption programs can be somewhat complex for ordinary people to implement, they are definitely worth it if you routinely communicate matters that you want to keep private. Ordinary use of passwords and user IDs is not enough to keep sensitive communications secure.

PGP (Pretty Good Privacy) is the most common encryption software, and is available both in free and commercial versions. You pay for the commercial version, but you get support and manuals and updates.

An example of something that should have been encrypted but wasn't was a disk containing detailed information about the Republican party's strategy in preparation for the 2002 elections. A Democratic party staffer found the disk in Washington, D.C.'s Lafayette Park.

Although all work-related communications are not so critical as to demand encryption, they still have to be handled mindfully. Computer scientist Martin Minow once said, "Don't put anything in **any** email to anyone you don't want stapled to your resumé."

Just as important, do not use the email system provided by your employer for personal matters.

The courts have ruled repeatedly that email created, sent, and received under an employer's auspices is not personal or private, and belongs to the enterprise paying the bills. Further, employees cannot take it with them when they leave the company. Such email is almost always archived and subject to subpoena.

Threatening the Company Image

Websites such as www.fuckedcompany.com and www.InternalMemos.com are eager to report on corporate shenanigans of all kinds—even when they might seem personal to the participants. There are places where no employer would ever want anything written by an employee to be published.

Peter Chung was a young man on the rise in the financial world. He got a plum job in Korea after living in New York. Using the corporate email system of his employer, The Carlyle Group, a high-end financial organization, Chung sent a broadcast brag to his friends boasting about women he had already bedded in Seoul—and the hordes more with whom he was planning to score.

The email originated from the Carlyle domain, and ended with Chung's email signature file (data automatically attached to outgoing email that includes work phone, fax, email, and postal mail information). His tale of once-and-future sexual prowess very quickly got into general circulation on the Internet, and was posted prominently on the website `www.fucked company.com`.

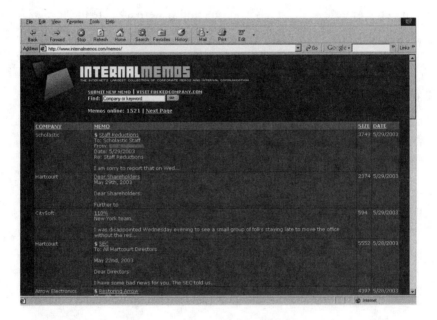

Figure 6.1

Websites such as InternalMemos.com and www.fuckedcompany.com are eager to expose the shortcomings of corporate employees. InternalMemos.com is devoted to exposing sensitive email messages.

Chung's comments, which might have been merely amusing to his friends or mildly distasteful to strangers, were now publicly connected to The Carlyle Group, a global financial powerhouse, and as result became irresistible, worldwide public reading matter.

Discretion is what people in the finance community count on, and Chung didn't demonstrate much. Very soon after his boasts of bedroom conquests went public, Chung was fired/forced to resign from his cushy job.

Along similar lines, Bradley Chait, a British lawyer who worked with the London firm of Norton Rose, forwarded an exchange with his girlfriend that had positive (and explicit) things to say about oral sex. This, too, ended up flying all over the world, and it got Chait in talks with his employer over disciplinary actions and breaches of contract.

Jacqueline Kim worked in the Major Gifts and Planned Giving department of the American Heart Association's midwestern affiliate in Chicago. She sent a blow-by-blow description of a first date with Chicago day trader Casey O'Brien to several of her friends, using the AHA's email system, and clearly identifying her AHA institutional affiliation. The email made her appear to be remarkably materialistic, self-important, vain, and not all that bright. She was not portraying herself as the fine ambassador for AHA's mission of good works.

To make matters worse, the email included details of her falling asleep drunk on the young man's couch, and contained the remark that the young man couldn't expect to get any further with her unless he "cut his hair and gave me gifts." This email flew around the Internet, and also ended up being posted on the `www.internalmemos.com` website,

O'Brien had been planning to continue his courtship, but that plan came to an abrupt halt after Kim's email was published worldwide.

InternalMemos.com also posted the response Kim made to people who emailed her about her high assessment of her own looks and her date's capacities as a walking ATM machine. Among other things, she wrote in her response is that "email is a powerful tool. I've learned my lesson."

The effects can spread far beyond what happens to a single individual because of electronic comments made at work: Personal communications at work on personal topics can have negative business implications.

Dangerous Consequences

Radu (name changed at his request) was born in an Asian country where free speech and human rights are not very highly respected. Years after he had become a U.S. citizen, living and working in the United States, he began working for a large U.S. company with many offices overseas. On the company's internal employee message board housed in a server in the company's U.S. headquarters, he posted a personal comment expressing concern over how his uncle, and his uncle's lawyer, had been thrown in jail in his Asian homeland.

What happened next was a panicked response from one of Radu's fellow employees, who was working in the company's Asian office, in the very country where Radu was born. The frightened employee was rightfully worried that the company would be thrown out of the Asian country (the regime there had done similar things to other companies for seemingly equally minor offenses), or that he would himself be jailed if he didn't act to get Radu's posting squelched.

Radu was horrified to realize that even from a distance of thousands of miles away, and merely in the electronic equivalent of a comment made around the water cooler, he had not only placed his employer (and by extension, his own livelihood) in jeopardy, but had also placed a coworker in danger.

In addition to email, *instant messaging* (IM) used in the workplace is often archived by the employer, and can be used as evidence.

IM at work with intimates and family should not be about highly personal topics: Senders of IM have no way of knowing who else, aside from the beloved intended recipient, may be staring at a computer screen at any given moment. Do you really want your sweetie's boss to know what you two did with the feather duster last night?

techlive

Instant Messaging Ban

Investment banking firm Thomas Weisel Partners banned instant messaging in the summer of 2001 amid worries the informal communication system could one day prove a legal liability.

"People were not happy when we blocked IM," said Pamela Housley, the firm's director of compliance. "People want to use this and they don't necessarily see the ramifications of using it improperly."

But Housley later reinstated IM—along with special software allowing the company to archive and review every message. It was important, she says, because federal regulations require that all corporate-client communications be archived for auditing.

"We'll be able to look at all of our instant messaging every day and probably look at 70 percent of [the messages] and make sure that nothing is problematic," Housley said.

Nationwide, employers are taking a good look at how employees use the Internet—and then taking steps to regulate workers' online behavior.

The goal is to block hacker attacks and boost productivity while preventing lawsuits stemming from inappropriate emails or Internet usage. Employers are installing software aimed at doing everything from filtering spam to monitoring whether workers are shopping online when they should be working.

"They want to know what employees are doing when they're sitting at their desks, when they're in their cubicles, when they're supposed to be conducting business," said Nancy Flynn, executive director of the ePolicy Institute. "When you sit down at your company computer workstation, don't assume that your activity is confidential. It's not. Your boss is probably keeping an eye on you."

> Digital civil liberties advocates dislike "blanket" monitoring in the workplace, but admit employers are acting within their rights. The federal Electronic Communications Privacy Act of 2000 allows employers to monitor all email and Net activity that takes place on corporate computers.
>
> "If an employer is suspicious of someone," said Lee Tien, senior staff attorney for the Electronic Frontier Foundation, "that's a very different situation from, y'know, 'We're just gonna watch and listen to and track everyone who might do something wrong.'"
>
> Still, Tien said, "As long as you give notice and make reasonable disclosure to employees, you can engage in a great deal of monitoring. And employers would be crazy not to actually take advantage of that."

Choose the right time, computer, and online venue for personal interaction. Use your personal computer at home for the really personal stuff. If you have to conduct personal business while at work, use a web-based email account and keep it to a minimum. As for IM with friends while you're at work, I can't recommend it. It's a time drain and a network-resource drain. Use a lot of discretion and assume you are being monitored.

Online Interactions

After you've chosen the vehicle for your interaction, you have to choose the right sites and services for doing what it is you want to do while online. The place for personal online relationships is on sites and in electronic communities that have been voluntarily chosen for such. Entire books have been written about the love, support, connection, and communities people have found online. People can find sympathy and support while coping with colon cancer, for example, and organize around preventing the spraying of pesticides near local elementary schools. People have discovered soul mates, with entire websites devoted to helping find romantic interests, or have simply found other people from around the world who share their interests in Lotus cars or Abyssinian cats.

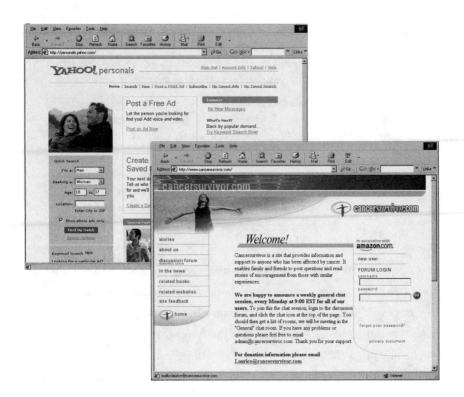

Figure 6.2

People can find all kinds of support online, from finding romance to coping with cancer.

However, people online are no better or worse than people offline: Dishonesty and nastiness and the capacity to hurt others lurk online, too.

Following are some rules of thumb for posting messages online safely:

- Use an email address that doesn't reveal gender, age, geographic location, or anything else that can obviously be associated with you. Be sure that any information used in a "sig" (the trailer at the bottom of your email) reveals no personal information.

- Use an email address that's disposable: Spammers have become viciously efficient at harvesting email addresses from all kinds of sources, so it's best to use an email address that you would be ready to kill in 6 months or a year if the volume of spam becomes too great. This is also helpful if you become the victim of online harassment: Your friends will continue to know where to find you, but your harasser won't.

- It's usually preferable to hang out in moderated forums—that is, online spaces where someone is charged with watching out for bad behavior and bad actors. It's a sad thing, but sometimes a Big Boss is necessary to ensure civility, because self-governance doesn't always work.

- Be aware that a peculiarity of online communication is that it tends to magnify the negative. No one really knows why, but Ph.D. theses have been written documenting how common it is that something written online that was meant to be sardonic will come across as nasty; something meant to be merely factual will come across as combative; and statements that might seem merely direct or forceful in print or in person can be read online as acts of aggression. Sarcasm and irony can be lost, just coming across as mean. Be very judicious in how you phrase things, screening for language that may unintentionally convey hostility. Keeping yourself safe online means protecting yourself from unintentionally provoking fights and ill will.

Cyberstalking

According to the May 2001 "Stalking and Domestic Violence" report from the Department of Justice to Congress, women are twice as likely to be stalked as men, and 8 times as likely to be stalked by those with whom they've been intimate. The Los Angeles District Attorney's office says that 20 percent of all stalking cases involve electronic devices.

Although cyberstalking is a fairly new phenomenon, its effects can be devastating. Consider the case of Amy Boyer, who was killed by a man who had stalked her online for more than two years without her knowledge.

techlive

How Online Obsession Led to Murder

"Amy had so much going for her," Tim Remsburg said of his stepdaughter. "She had so many plans."

Those plans would have included graduation from dental school and a 21st birthday party last year. But Amy Boyer's life was cut drastically short when a young man's obsession turned to murder.

On October 15, 1999, Boyer was shot and killed outside the dentist's office where she worked in Nashua, New Hampshire. Her killer, 21-year-old Liam Youens, then killed himself.

But Boyer's murder really began on the Internet, years before the brutal killing.

Maniacal Stalking

"This was an obsession that this man had, where he went on the Internet and went into detail about how he was going to kill this young woman," Seargent Frank Paison told TechTV. Paison, a detective with the Nashua police department, investigated Boyer's murder.

Her killer may have silenced himself, but he left behind a telling, disturbing website that included the words, "I wish I could have killed her."

"Once we opened the entire website, it explained to us what this was," Paison said. "This was almost maniacal stalking done by this man against Amy Boyer. It was a horrifying thing that detailed his plans to kill this young woman."

From High School to Death

Youens' infatuation with Boyer began in high school, but according to Remsburg, Boyer never even knew Youens.

"He mentions in the website that he was in her algebra class in the 10th grade and that's where the obsession began," Remsburg said. "The teacher said her name, he looked up and said 'Amy,' and he looked over and that was the Amy that he remembered."

"From that point on, he followed her around school, watched her in the hallways, watched her on the bus, paid attention to everything she did," Remsburg continued. "But she never had any idea this kid was out there."

All the while Youens was stalking Boyer, methodically, both off- and online. He was also stockpiling a cache of weapons in his bedroom, including AR-15s, semiautomatic rifles.

"[The AR-15] shoots a projectile or a round that travels at 3,200 feet per second," Paison said. "That weapon was made to kill people. It is not a hunting rifle; it is not a target-shooting rifle. The only purpose that it serves is an anti-personnel and anti-human being weapon."

Youens' website proudly displayed the weapons, including the gun that was ultimately used to kill Boyer. A photo of it was posted alongside chilling details of his fixation. He wrote, "God I love her…" and "Why don't I kill her too?" on the site.

The website also details the killer's stalking patterns. He wrote that he planned to kill her outside her home. However, he ultimately decided upon a different location because, during several surveillance sessions, he saw her father's truck parked outside the house. He assumed the family was on to him.

"He wrote in his website, 'I cannot do this here,'" Paison recounted. "'I must find somewhere else.' He then put a search out for her employer's address. All these research companies came back with, 'Can't find. Not enough paper trail on this young woman. We need more information.'"

Desperate to find out where Boyer was working, Youens went online and bought her Social Security number for less than $50, which ultimately led to her location.

"After several weeks of logging her hours [and] learning her schedule, on the 15th of October he was there waiting for her when she got out," Remsburg said. "And that was the day she died. And what upsets me is these companies just sell all this personal, private information. They sell Amy Boyer's Social Security number, and they have no idea who the man is they're selling it to."

Remsburg is also upset that no one, including the Nashua police department, knew about the killer's website prior to the murder, even though it was live on the Internet for years.

continues

"No one in Nashua knew it, most certainly the police didn't know it, the Remsburgs didn't know it," Paison said. "Possibly he communicated with people out there. We know he did have a conversation with [someone] in Europe who may have actually seen this website, but didn't take it seriously. But no one in this area had ever seen this website."

"When this first happened and the police called us to the station the night of the murder and told us what they found in his room and they found these websites, I was, I was just so angry," Remsburg said. "How could this information have been out there for two and a half years and nobody made a phone call, no one's responsible for this?"

Could Online Clues Have Saved Amy?

Would there have been a different ending if the family and police had known about the website before Boyer's murder?

"If someone had told us this website existed, or [told] the Remsburgs, I think we would have been able to save this poor woman's life," Paison said.

That is cold comfort for Tim and Helen Remsburg.

"I just wake up every day and try to function," said Helen Remsburg, Amy's mother. "I personally feel like our life is ruined. You know, some days I get up and I can make it through the day and other days I get up and I can't do anything. I don't know how you get through it. Hopefully, time will help."

The couple says that time, however, will never help them understand why no one saw it coming.

"We would never have sat back and watched this unfold if we knew this was going to happen," said Tim Remsburg. "Amy would have been taken down to Pennsylvania to her grandmother's retirement apartment, she would have been living down there in...silence until this thing was taken care of."

But Tim couldn't fight a battle he didn't know existed. Although it's impossible to say definitely, those close to the case, including law enforcement, agree Boyer's murder might have been prevented.

"If the police had known about this website, I really believe this murder would have been preventable," said Paison. "We would have been able to seize these weapons. We would have been able to arrest him and charge him for the threats he made against this woman."

Threats were made in black and white, on the Internet, including such explanations as, "Why am I killing her."

Blame the Internet Service Provider?

While Youens was the person most immediately responsible for the murder, he ended his own life immediately. Paison, who investigated Boyer's murder, says some of the burden should be shouldered by the Internet service provider (ISP).

"I think absolutely, these Internet service providers are responsible for what they carry on the Internet," Paison said. "They're making a fortune. It's a billion-dollar industry. There should be some federal or governmental regulation as to what you have to do or the approvals you have to meet, before you can put something on the Internet."

Yet, the Communications Decency Act states that ISPs, like Yahoo's GeoCities, which hosted Youens' site, cannot be held accountable for the postings of third parties. And while Tim Remsburg has a clear understanding of the law, he says morally, it's a different story.

"That's the hardest thing," he said. "Knowing how easy this thing could have been avoided and how unfair it was that I wasn't notified. No one let me know that I'm in this, this war with this kid. You know, these companies said there were at least 50 hits on the site, you know? Most were probably him creating the site, we don't know. But I'm sure some weren't."

Trudy Gregorie, director of training at the National Center for Victims of Crime, believes that something could have been done before the murder.

"If indeed she had known that she was being cyberstalked, that there were pages that described what her murder would be like, then indeed she could have taken some actions that maybe could have given her measures of protection," Gregorie said.

"Certainly the Internet service providers who were allowing these types of home pages to exist on their service could have removed those home pages."

A Cry for Help

It's not clear whether the ISP even knew what was on Youens' webpages. However, according to the Remsburgs, they should have. His website was a cry for help that went unanswered.

"I know how sick he was to do something like this," Gregorie said. "This was on the Internet for [more than two] years, and he was begging for help. I think it got to the point that when nobody helped him, you know, that just, you know, made him want to do it even more. I really think he was begging for help."

continues

Gregorie offers advice to other families for preventing this from happening to them.

"We suggest you put your children's names, your children's friends' names, your children's school into the computer on a regular basis, looking to see who might be out there targeting them," Gregorie said. "I mean if we had put Amy Boyer's name in there, she'd be here now."

"My question is when do we do that? How many does it take? Is it going to take a brainiac kid from school that can figure out how to build a bomb and blows up the entire school? And leave a note somewhere that says, 'Check out www...you should have looked at my dot com.' I mean, what's it going to take?"

Unfortunately, it might take just that. In January of 2001, the 106th Congress removed the Amy Boyer Bill from the Omnibus Consolidated Appropriations Act. The proposed law, sponsored by New Hamshire Republican Judd Gregg and first introduced in May of 2000, would have limited the sale of Social Security numbers online.

In rare cases the Internet is used to commit horrible crimes. These incidents are not the norm. This true story is not meant to scare you away from computing, but rather to raise your awareness of real-world crimes that cross over into the digital realm. If you are to take anything away form Amy's story: Know what information is posted online about you.

Cyberstalking involves threatening behavior or unwanted advances from someone using the Internet or other electronic communications. Stalkers tend to target their victims through chat rooms, message boards, discussion forums, and email.

When it remains online, it can be a traumatizing experience. Online harassment can take the form of threatening or obscene email, spamming, chat-room harassment or flaming, improper or threatening messages posted to message boards, and even electronic identity theft.

However, if the stalking ventures off-line—as it does in many cases—it can result in repeated and abusive phone calls, vandalism, trespassing, and physical assault.

An Angry Cyberstalker

Stephanie Brail ran into trouble through her postings on Usenet, the Internet's early collection of online discussion forums. In a newsgroup devoted to zines, several men nastily attacked a woman who wanted to talk about post-feminist, post-punk Riot Grrl bands and zines. After the young woman defended herself, and was further verbally attacked, Brail stepped in to protest the misogyny and contempt expressed by these Usenet posters.

Brail herself, alas, became the target of an angry cyberstalker from the Usenet forum, who for weeks sent her emails containing scary porno-graphic images full of violence, and posted bogus messages purportedly from her in other Usenet discussion areas, including those devoted to bondage. Even months after his email attacks slowed, Brail's stalker was able to send her chilling email to a **new** email address she had acquired—and his email indicated that he knew that she lived in Los Angeles. The system administrators of the time didn't or wouldn't help her. Only after she was finally able, with some fairly technical Internet sleuthing, to figure out her harasser's home email address and true name—and send him a warning email there—did the harassment stop.

Prevention

Although it is not always possible to prevent yourself from becoming the target of a stalker online, there are some steps you can take to reduce the risk, according to Internet safety organization CyberAngels (www.cyberangels.org):

- Use prudence when identifying yourself online. Don't use screen names that have sexual connotations, as that may encourage flirtatious solicitations.
- Women are more likely to be stalked than men, so choose a gender-neutral handle.
- Consider using an anonymous remailer, a tool allowing you to send an email message without revealing your personal email address.
- When chatting, do not reveal any personal information that you wouldn't want a stranger to have access to, such as name, address, or other identifying information.

If you or someone you know fears he or she is being targeted by a cyber-stalker, there are a few things you can do, according to the National Center for Victims of Crime (www.ncvc.org):

- If you know the offender, send the stalker a written warning, making it clear that the contact is unwanted. Ask the perpetrator to cease sending all communications. Then, no matter the response, never communicate with the stalker again.
- If the harassment continues, file a complaint with the stalker's Internet service provider, as well as with your own. Many ISPs offer filters that can block communications from specific individuals.
- Call your local police or FBI office.
- Collect all evidence and document all contact made by the stalker. Save all email, postings, or other communications. Record the dates and times of any contact with the offender.
- If you are being continually harassed, consider changing your email address, Internet service provider, and home phone number.
- Finally, under no circumstances should victims agree to meet with the perpetrator to "talk" or "work it out." Doing so can be dangerous.

For more information, visit the National Center for Victims of Crime cyberstalking page (www.ncvc.org/special/cyber_stk.htm), CyberAngels Online Guide, or call 1.800.FYI.CALL, 8:30 a.m. to 8:30 p.m., Monday through Friday, Eastern Time.

These websites might also be helpful:

- www.haltabuse.org
- www.antistalking.com
- www.cyber-stalking.net
- www.onlineharassmnet.com.

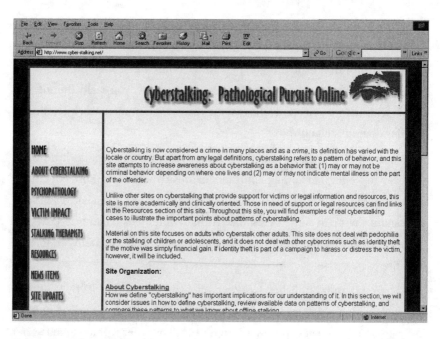

Figure 6.3

Cyber-stalking.net is one of several websites that help deal with the problem of cyberstalking.

Online Relationships

Be aware of the more subtle dangers to guard against in online relationships. Some people find it easier to express themselves emotionally and intellectually online than they do in person. Writer Philip Lopate once called this compelling but potentially duplicitous aspect of online communication the "pseudo-intimacy of the online world."

Confusing someone's online presence and real persona is a bit like confusing a work of art with its creator, or actors with the roles they play. There may be a correspondence between the two, or there may not be.

It's no coincidence that the first cartoon the *New Yorker* magazine ever published on the subject of the Internet showed a dog sitting staring at a computer monitor, explaining to his animal companion that "on the Internet, no one knows you're a dog." In other words, you really **do not know** with whom you are dealing when your sole connection with another sentient being is electronic.

Emotionally damaging situations can occur from this pseudo-intimacy. It's easy to forget that some people can express themselves more effectively and attractively online than in real life, and hence, find it easier to connect and seduce with, in some cases, unfortunate outcomes. Their attractive, intimate qualities may not necessarily map to similar personality traits in real life.

The first fiction published by *Wired* magazine was a novella by Paulina Borsook, which illustrated how a woman was seduced by a man's wonderfully personal and evocative love letters—until another woman emailed her to tell her that she, too, was one of the guy's love-thing correspondents.

Following are some rules of thumb for developing online relationships safely:

- If someone seems too good to be true, she/he probably is.
- Don't give out any identifying information: true name, phone number, street address, workplace, your habitual email address, or anything else that tracks to your real-world identity.
- When you get to the point of wanting to talk on the phone, block your phone number or use a calling card from a payphone.
- A dynamic tension exists with regard to safety in terms of deciding when to actually meet in person. You neither want be pushed to meet before you feel comfortable doing so, nor do you want to waste your time with someone who just enjoys flirting and cannot/will not engage in real life.
- When you are ready to meet in person and you have decided to exchange your true names, consider doing a web search on your date. Think about other ways to fact check the information you've been given. (For example, marital status is, sadly, a much-lied-about data point.)

The Cybercad

Carl Bailey Jones became notorious in Internet culture as the cybercad. He was written up in *Time* magazine after he carried on multiple simultaneous cyberspace-initiated affairs with several different women on The Well, a pioneering online community based in the San Francisco Bay Area. He pursued each of these women with psychologically entrancing email, followed by terrific phone contact (both emotionally and erotically satisfying), followed in some cases by an in-person meeting and sex—at which point, each woman was dropped.

With some of the women, he took advantage of their good natures and told them sob stories of needing cash for dental work, flights to visit them, and so on. In these cases, the checks were cashed, but Jones never showed. It also turned out he had been engaging with several women on a daily basis (on the phone or in email), and each had been led to believe that she had a sole, true-heart union with him.

Part of why the women trusted him is that he seemed like a good guy, in general, when posting in public chat spaces, emailing, or talking in person—and with each woman. This is a mark of a true psychopath. He was good at keying into what each woman wanted to hear. When Jones was ousted by the hurt and outraged women, he said, "I didn't think that the same concerns about fidelity I apply reflexively in physical relationships applied in cyberspace."

- On the first meeting, bring your own transportation, stay sober, and meet in a public place. Even then, limit the amount of personal information you give out. The last thing you want is a jilted suitor showing up outside your front door at 2 a.m. drunk, leaving unpleasant messages on your voicemail, or giving you baleful looks across the parking lot every time you leave your office to go home. Let a friend know your dating itinerary; even better, arrange to meet up with a friend afterward— and let your date know in advance that you have other plans afterward. This has many advantages: It gives you a graceful out if things start seeming scary or icky, it lessens the awkwardness of a first date because it makes it finite, and it serves as a reminder to you and your date that you have a life outside your dating interests. Being less needy is so much more attractive.

- If you are meeting someone new, cell phones really are your friend. If the situation becomes frightening, call for help.

- If you travel to another city to meet someone, arrange for your own lodging and transportation, and don't disclose the details of these (such as the license number and make/color of your rental car) to your date.

- At every point in the process (screening online profiles, entering into email dialogues, talking on the phone, going on an actual date), pay attention to your intuition. If someone seems hectoring, pushy, angry, evasive, inconsistent, or threatening, back off! Be wary both of folks who seem to become too intimate too fast, or who expect the same from you. You are trying to establish context, develop familiarity, and create safety; these things take time.

- Although photos can be a good thing, remember the obvious: They can also lie. Of all the tips and tricks offered here, they are all worthless if you are so infatuated with a person's photo that you don't listen to your instincts or to your friends and family. If you/they start to see red flags, proceed with caution or don't proceed at all.

Most people's partners consider flirting online and cybersex as infidelities. To pretend otherwise is disingenuous.

If you feel your partner is devoting more attention to what's appearing on his or her computer screen than to you, the problem is real—and as such, use of the Internet has become less safe for you both.

Internet Addiction

A brief comment about Internet addiction: Yes, it can happen. People can become addicted to web surfing and chat rooms, as well as to online gaming, gambling, auctions, and pornography, just as they can become addicted to gambling and drug use and overwork in the real world. If online activities begin to affect work or school performance, cut into school or family or social life, have deleterious effects financially, use of the Internet may have become an addiction—and needs to be treated like any other addiction or destructive compulsive behavior. About 5 percent of Internet users become addicted to the Internet, similar to rates of addiction in the real world with destructive behaviors, such as alcoholism or gambling.

The EverQuest Addiction

Who'd have thought technology would ruin Valentine's Day? But for Joy Barnes, the fantasy role-playing game EverQuest put a serious damper on romance. In fact, she says it killed her marriage.

Her husband was addicted to the game, she says, playing up to 16 hours a day. And when it came down to choosing between their marriage and the game, Barnes says her husband chose the digital fantasy world and his crowd of virtual friends.

"In a non-technological universe, he might have been at a bar," Barnes said. "But this was something he could roll out of bed and go into the other room to [do], and [he could] talk to all of his friends 24 hours a day. It's different from a bar; that has to close sometime."

But Barnes says she doesn't want to misrepresent the game. She's a gamer herself. She even took up EverQuest to play with her husband and hopefully find some common ground. She says the game is great, but she never had the desire to play for hours on end.

She eventually divorced her husband.

The game does lend itself to long hours of play. EverQuest is an online role-playing game in which players become mythical warriors who battle evil with the help of online friends. A lot of endless chatting goes on, and many complex social relationships evolve. And the game is truly endless—there's no big pay-off where you come to the end of the experience.

Clinical psychologist Richard Sherman says the game can take on a prominent role in the player's life.

"A person gets so hooked on these games that they would rather spend time with the game, which becomes in a sense their new lover, than with their own partner," he said.

continues

Barnes says she felt abandoned because her husband would rather spend time with EverQuest than with her. Unfortunately, she's not alone.

The "EverQuest widow" phenomenon has spawned online support groups like Spouses Against EverQuest and EverQuest Widow(er)s.

Grace Kim and her boyfriend, Steve Chow, are both members of EverQuest Widow(er)s. Chow spent 4 or 5 hours a day playing the game until he realized it was an addiction.

"It was kind of like smoking, in a way," Chow said.

"You kind of know you should stop, or maybe that it's not good for you if you're waking up in the morning, playing this game a couple of hours, and then going to work," he said.

Chow eventually quit altogether, although now he does play some PlayStation 2 games on a regular basis.

Psychologists say obsessive gaming is a symptom of bigger problems. Sherman says you must look at other things to identify the root of the gamer's addiction.

"The more a person is feeling good and secure and happy and positive with their partners, they don't have this need, this urge to withdraw and escape," he said.

Barnes agrees. An avid gamer herself, she says EverQuest was only making existing problems in her marriage worse.

"I would tell the widow it's not EverQuest," she said. "It's something else in the relationship that's not working."

The connectivity of the Internet and the power of computing has opened doors and introduced us to people who in the past we never could have met. The opportunities are endless, the dangers myriad, and the solution obvious. Common sense and uncommon courtesy go a long way online. Don't be a jerk, and don't put up with jerks online or in real life. If only it were that simple, right?

Protecting the Family

Parents' reactions to the Internet run the gamut, from "it's too dangerous, my child is never getting near it," to "Wow, what a great educational
tool." Kids are far more unequivocal: The Internet is fun! And for teens,
especially, the Internet is a way of life: It's how they communicate with
their friends, do their homework, and find out about the world.

But the Internet can be a dangerous place. Most computer-savvy parents
are already aware of some of the dangers. Pedophiles and pornography
being the most serious dangers, this chapter discusses them in more depth.
Pornography isn't the only thing you might not want your kids to be watching, however, and pedophiles aren't the only people you might not want
your kids to meet. From revisionist history to cyberbullies, the Internet is
full of ideas and people who your children need help avoiding or understanding.

The Images They See

How old were you when you saw your first *Playboy*? Your first *Penthouse*?
Your first X-rated movie? For some of us, the answer may be that we still
haven't. Others might have a reminiscent smile as we remember being 12,
with the next-door neighbor kid showing us his dad's secret stash. For our
kids, however, the answer to that question might be more ambiguous.

Wendy, mother to a 7-year-old boy, describes this experience. "I was working at home when a coworker forwarded me an email from an irate customer. One of the books I'd worked on, an instructional book on a software product, had a list of online links as additional resources. The customer was furious that one of the links was to a porn site. Well, I'd checked all those links personally, so I knew she was wrong. Without even thinking twice, I typed the site's address in my browser. Unfortunately, she wasn't wrong...and my son was in the room." In the year since the book had been published, the site had gone from being an online resource for software users to being an extremely graphic porn site, featuring young girls performing oral sex on older men.

This is not an isolated example. While hosting TechTV's Call for Help once, I meant to go to the Whitehouse.gov site, but instead, on live television, typed in Whitehouse.com; big mistake. Boobs, skin, and smut. Our director had to make a fast cut, and it took me a good 60 seconds to close all the pop-up ads and get out of the vortex of porn. I knew Whitehouse.com was a porn site. It's incredibly well known, but for one fateful moment I forgot.

In other cases, it's bait and switch. You click a link advertising a George Foreman Grill, and next thing you know, you are transported onto Billy-Joe's Barnyard fantasy site. And stumbling across porn happens to web surfers of every age and Internet proficiency.

In one study, done by the Kaiser Family Foundation in 2001 to determine whether young people were using the Internet to access health information, 70 percent of 15 to 17 year olds said that they had accidentally stumbled across pornography online. Of that number, a sizable minority (45 percent) said that they were upset or very upset by it. Another study produced slightly better numbers: The Youth Internet Safety Survey, conducted by the Crimes Against Children Research Center at the University of New Hampshire, interviewed 1,501 children aged 10 to 17 who used the Internet regularly. In that survey, 25 percent of the respondents reported having encountered sexual material, ranging from nudity to graphic sex, on the Internet.

Does early exposure to pornography damage children? Despite the long-raging debate about pornography in this country, no one truly seems to have determined whether it damages anyone. And yet there's a general consensus that it's not good for young minds; even the kids themselves think so. In the Kaiser study, 57 percent of the 15 to 17 year olds agreed that "being exposed to pornography could have a serious impact on those under 18." A majority agreed that it would cause kids to have sex before they're ready.

How They Get There

Unfortunately, it's hard to avoid pornography online. Web searches can provide unexpected results: A kid searching for toys can easily find the kind of toys that consenting adults might better understand. In the Youth Internet Safety Survey, 47 percent of the kids who'd seen something unexpected had gotten there from a web search gone bad.

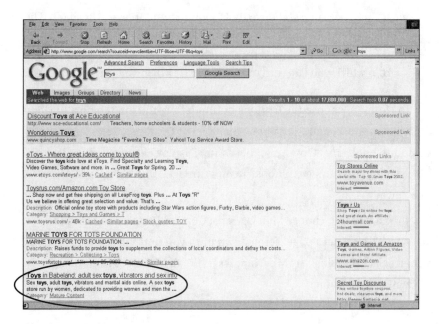

Figure 7.1

Even with a respected search engine, such as Google, chances of finding inappropriate material is high when performing searches.

If it doesn't come via a web search, it's likely just to appear in an email inbox. "End of the week fun," "Confirmation," "Save money," "Enhance your sex life"—okay, the last one was kind of obvious, but the others were either links to pornographic sites or ads that included graphic images that appeared in my email just this morning. A child can easily innocently click the "Hi, it's me" email that appeared in his or her email list and get a quick and unexpected introduction to the human body.

One way you can prevent email messages from inundating you and your family with porn is to turn off HTML. Email messages that are formatted in HTML allow the author to include backgrounds, formatting, fancy fonts, and images. Unfortunately, porn spammers sending out smut in HTML form expose kids to graphic images when they merely open an email.

If you turn off HTML in your email program or tell web-based email programs not to display images until prompted, you can reduce exposure to porn images sent in spam.

- In Outlook Express, choose Tools, Options, and then the Read tab. Then select Read All Messages in Plain Text.
- In web-based email programs, you have to find the Preferences tab, from which you can turn off images or HTML formatting.

In Hotmail, choose the Options button (along the top tab next to Home, Inbox, Compose, and Contacts). When on the Options page, in the third column, Additional Options, choose Mail Display Settings. Where it says Display Internet Images, choose Remove Images Until Messages Are Reviewed.

In Yahoo! Mail, choose Mail Options, General Preferences. On the General Preferences page, scroll down until you find the Security section. Then select the Block HTML Graphics in Email Messages from Being Downloaded option.

What Else Is Out There?

Of course, it's not just pornography that parents need to worry about: The Internet contains thousands of sites that may be even more harmful. Sites espousing racial bigotry, terrorism, and hatred aren't uncommon. In fact, the Hate Directory contains 97 pages of links to sites that advocate violence and hatred. (The 98th page is a list of organizations battling hatred.)

Think that's not a problem? Imagine this: Your child is doing a report on the Holocaust for his history class. As he researches the subject on the web, he enters a white-supremacist site that claims the Holocaust never took place, and goes on to make racist, violent statements. Apart from the fact that your kid may get an F on his history paper, he may also wind up believing what he's read online.

The Internet was quickly blamed when Dylan Klebold and Eric Harris went on a killing spree in Littleton, Colorado. It was also blamed in the case of Kip Kinkel, who shot 26 people, including his parents, in Oregon. He was widely reported to have found information about guns, ammunition, and bomb making on the Internet. Michael Carneal, age 14, killed 3 girls at a student prayer meeting in Paducah, Kentucky, in December 1997. The parents of the 3 girls filed suit in federal court against 25 media companies, including Meow Media, producers of a pornographic website.

Maybe it's not fair to blame the Internet in these cases: Certainly, the web has never put a gun into a kid's hand. However, some of the most violent, racist sites have been accused of using rock music and high-end designs to attract impressionable children and teenagers. On one site, the World Church of the Creator, a kid's page offered children under 12 the opportunity to play racist games.

According to "Children, Violence, and the Media," a 1999 report by the Senate Judiciary Committee, more than 1,000 studies on the effects of media violence have been done over the past 40 years, and, "The existing research shows beyond a doubt that media violence is linked to youth violence." Although there are no specific studies on the effects of Internet violence, it's likely to be even more harmful than television violence for one reason: Some of it is interactive. No study may currently provide evidence for this, but any parent has to guess that actually pretending to shoot people online is more likely to lead to violence than watching someone else shoot. Other online violence lacks context; most television draws a clear distinction between the good guys and the bad, but on the Internet (as with movies) that distinction can be a lot less clear.

> **Note**
>
> **Sex, Violence, Hate...What Else?** There are a number of "pro-anorexia" sites on the Internet—sites that provided support and information for readers interested in starving themselves, including lists of "suggested" over-the-counter drugs. I don't have a teenage daughter, but if I did, I would be appalled to discover that she had encountered these sites. I would much rather she knew that without intervention, anorexia has the highest fatality rate in the American Psychiatric Association's *Diagnostic and Statistical Manual of Mental Disorders*.

What Can a Parent Do?

You may be surprised at my first suggestion: Although software that filters offensive sites is available, I don't recommend you use it.

Filtering software, commonly called *nannyware*, works in many different ways. Some filtering software maintains "blacklists"—lists of sites that are specifically not approved. Other software maintains "whitelists"—sites that are approved. Some software uses textual analysis, some uses image analysis, and others use labels or addresses.

The fact is, however, none of that software is perfect. It is guaranteed to filter large quantities of useful information, while at the same time missing stuff that may strike you as highly objectionable. In May 2002, the National Academies' National Research Council released a report on children on the Internet in which the writers warn, "Technology solutions seem to offer quick and inexpensive fixes that allow adult caregivers to believe that the problem has been addressed."

Filters are too reassuring. They make us believe that the problem is solved, when in fact it's not. In addition, it's important to understand that a web filter does its job using values and criteria that someone has chosen—and that person isn't you. The company that creates the filter determines what content should be blocked, and most of the companies keep those criteria secret. Parents who choose to use filtering software don't get to know the values that the filter applies. They're placing their trust in strangers.

Of course, it's not the end of the world if you do use filtering software. Plenty of people do, and it does help—although you should be aware that a smart kid can always find a way around it. Filtering software is not a solution, however, and you shouldn't believe that it's the cure.

Note

If you do decide to include filtering or monitoring software in your protection plan, how do you choose which to use? Try `http://www.getnetwise.org/tools/`. They offer a comprehensive checklist of options that enable you to find the right solution for your family.

Here's what I recommend:

- **Talk to your children.** Yes, I know it's embarrassing. Yes, I know you don't want to be the one to explain oral sex to your child. But if not you, who? Nothing you can say is likely to prepare your kids for the worst stuff that they could encounter on the web—from bestiality to child pornography—and I don't recommend you try. It's much better for you to be the person who explains the basics. However, you should be the person who explains the basics.

- **Move the computer to a public space in your home.** Yes, it may be annoying to have to listen to the beep, beep, beep of video games while you relax on the couch, but do it anyway. Cyberangels.org, an organization dedicated to the online safety of children, says, "You wouldn't allow a stranger in the bedroom with your child, don't allow them in via computer either!"

- **Spend time with your kid online.** The best way to know the sites your children are spending time at is to be sitting right there with them while they surf. The best way to know whom your children are talking to is to see the instant message coming in and ask.

- **Teach your children to lie.** Did this one catch your attention? It's probably an unusual recommendation, and yet, there's a time and place for lying. Specifically, the best way for your children to avoid spam is for them to never give out their real email address. Some guidelines suggest that parents tell children never to give out their information: Perhaps it's cynical of me, but I suspect that won't work. If a child wants to use a site that requires her to register, encourage her to use a different, made-up email address. Remember, those sites don't generally test the address. There's no reason for you to tell the truth online, and there's no reason for your children to do so either.

> **Note**
>
> **COPPA**   Laws are in place to protect childen's privacy: specifically, the *Children's Online Privacy Protection Act* (COPPA) requires websites to obtain verifiable parental consent before collecting information that might identify children under the age of 13. However, some sites ask anyway, or don't consider an email address a violation, and even some mainstream sites have gotten in trouble with this law. In April 2003, for example, Amazon.com was accused of violating the law, for allowing children to publicly post their names, email addresses, and locations with product reviews. For more about COPPA, and how it has succeeded and failed, see Chapter 8, "Privacy." The section "Children's Online Privacy Protection Act" has full details.

- **Look for kid-friendly search engines and tools.** Ask Jeeves Kids and Yahooligans are two of the most well known. These search engines limit their search responses to pre-approved, family friendly sites. Ask Jeeves Kids includes only "G-rated" pages and pages written specifically for children and is primarily an educational site, although with some fun and games. Yahooligans is a little more fun, but has advertising.

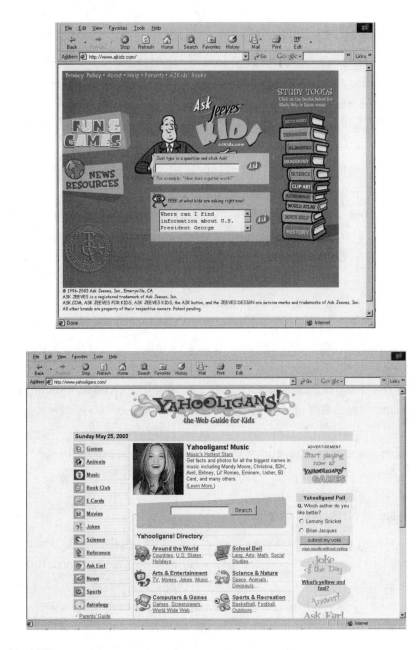

Figure 7.2

Search engines Ask Jeeves Kids and Yahooligans limit search responses to pre-approved, family friendly sites.

The People They Might Meet

Not much is known about 13-year-old Kacie Woody's interactions with David Fuller. The police think that they met in an Internet chat room. They believe that the two corresponded for about a month. They suspect that Fuller might have convinced Kacie that he was a teenager like her. What they do know for sure, however, is that on December 4, 2002, he abducted her from her home, killed her, and then killed himself.

Chat rooms, support boards, instant messaging—since the dawn of the Internet, one of the things that people have most loved about life online is the sense of community. Unlike other forms of entertainment, the Internet isn't passive: One of the great pleasures is that you can interact with other people.

For teens especially, these interactions have become a big part of online life. According to psychologists, teenagers have a developmental imperative to form relationships; maybe that explains why they're using the Internet far more than adults to create and sustain relationships. One study showed that 16 percent of teenagers had made a close online friend within the past year. A 2001 report from the Pew Internet and American Life Project suggested that close to 13 million teenagers use instant messaging as a means of communication—sometimes with friends, and sometimes with strangers.

Beware of Strangers

In October 2002, parents of a child in Miami reported a situation to the *National Council for Missing & Exploited Children* (NCMEC): A man their daughter had met over the Internet was calling and sending her mail. Turns out the 71-year-old man was already under investigation by the FBI. He had been communicating with 150 different children online—and 8 of them had already become his victims. In February 2003, he was arrested on 13 felony counts of child molestation, attempted child molestation, and attempted manufacturing of child pornography.

How big a problem is this? In Louisville, Kentucky, an agent working with the Louisville Innocent Images Task Force posed online as a 14-year-old girl. In an 18-month period, they arrested 9 men, ranging in age from 23 to 53, on charges of surfing the Internet to find and lure minors for sex. The CyberTipline (`cybertipline.org`), an online hotline for reporting crimes against children, had more than 7,500 reports of online solicitation of children for sex by January 2003.

In the Youth Internet Safety Survey, almost 1 in 5 of the children surveyed had received a sexual solicitation or approach over the Internet in the past year. In fact, it's a practice so common it has a name: *cybering*, being solicited for online, sexually suggestive talk by strangers. For 1 child in 33, however, that solicitation was defined as aggressive: The person asked to meet them; called them on the telephone; and/or sent them regular email, money, or gifts. With numbers like that, it's almost guaranteed that a child you know has had this experience. Would she or he know how to respond?

How Pedophiles Work

To protect your children, it's important to understand how pedophiles work, especially online. A sexual predator who targets children online seduces his targets. Some predators may openly proposition minors, but the more dangerous ones start by befriending them.

A successful online predator builds a relationship with a child. He listens, sympathizes, encourages, and pretends to understand. As the relationship grows, he becomes more affectionate and friendly, and sex may creep into their conversations, usually in ways that seem innocuous or innocent. Eventually, their online conversations may become more explicit. The sexual predator's goal is to encourage your child to meet him.

In 1999, the NCMEC identified 785 cases in which a child or adult traveled to meet a person met online. In some of these cases, the relationship may be innocent. In one story that received national attention, a 15 year old from Massachusetts—an honor student and gifted musician—went to Rome (the one in Italy) with a 21 year old she'd met on the Internet. Despite the difference in age, the girl returned home safely, and no charges were filed against her male traveling companion. However, other cases end more tragically, and it's important for parents and children to be wary.

Creeps Caught Online

A housewife becomes a crusader as she tracks down pedophiles preying on children who surf the net.

He arrived at a fast-food restaurant in suburban Denver, expecting to see the underage girl he met on the Internet. But the only date 36-year-old Thomas Ormsby got was one with the law.

Ormsby is one of dozens of potential child molesters a Colorado housewife has helped put behind bars over the past few years. Lafayette, Colorado, homemaker, Julie Posey, is a self-proclaimed cybercrime fighter.

Thomas Ormsby met Posey, after she responded to one of his 49 newsgroup messages expressing his desire to have sex with a preteen. Posey, pretending to be a 13-year-old girl named "Kendra," agreed to meet Ormsby for sex.

Critics argue that private citizens chasing pedophiles can amount to police entrapment and at the very least is unnecessary. "I don't see the need for private citizens stirring up these cases, luring people into conversations that may seem illicit, and may seem illegal, and then turning it over to the police," defense attorney Stefani Goldin told TechTV in an interview. Goldin represented one of the defendants targeted by Posey. "I just don't think that need is there."

"I am not a vigilante," said Posey. "I let police do their work, I make contact with these people or they make contact with me, then they solicit me, then I turn that information over to the police."

Posey is a licensed private investigator in Colorado and spends most of her time helping police rid cyberspace of pedophiles. The 37-year-old mother of a 13-year-old daughter, is herself a sexual assault victim. "The thing that seemed so important to me is that there are literally tens of thousands of these child predators online. They are looking to meet a kid and they do meet kids in rare instances. I've been through being raped, and, I would never want that to happen to anybody."

186

When Posey finds a potential pedophile, she often turns her research over to husband-and-wife team Mike and Cassandra Harris, investigators with the Jefferson County Prosecutor's "Crimes Against Children Unit."

One of Posey's most notable cases took place in April 2000. In that case, Posey, pretending to be 13-year-old "Kendra," went undercover in an Internet chat room called "Older Guys for Younger Girls," and met 34-year-old Jeff Beebe.

"He asked me how old I was, and I said, 'I'm 13,' and he says, 'I'm 34, is that okay?' And I said, 'Well if you don't mind that I'm 13, then, yeah, that's okay.' And he said, 'Oh, I love young girls.'" Posey said of their initial conversation.

Once Beebe began making sexual advances, she turned the chat logs over to the Harrises, who assumed Kendra's role. The explicit conversations went on for several more months; then, on July 9, Beebe traveled from Loveland, Colorado, to Jefferson County intending to meet and have sex with 13-year-old Kendra. Beebe was arrested at the motel room where they had arranged to meet.

Beebe pled guilty to attempted sexual assault on a child and enticement of a child, and is now serving a 3-years-to-life term in a Colorado State prison.

Investigators remain grateful to Posey. "Julie is very good," said Mike Harris. "She understands the vulnerabilities that sex offenders look for in children. She understands what makes sex offenders tick."

Along with Posey's investigative work in Internet chat rooms, she also runs a website called Pedowatch.org (`http://www.pedowatch.org/pedowatch/`), which is designed to enable parents and other concerned adults to report child pornography and exploitation.

What to Watch Out For

If you have any reason to feel uncomfortable about your child's interactions online, be proactive.

- Check your computer for downloads from email or online sources.
- Get caller ID put on your phone line.
- Find out what other computers your child has access to.

This is not invading your child's privacy, although it might feel like it. A successful online predator will convince your child that he is a friend. That's why it's important that you be the grown-up and take responsibility for knowing what your child is doing and with whom your child is talking.

Remember, however, you're not the bad guy, and neither is your child. Your children need to trust you: If they've had uncomfortable experiences online, they need to feel that they are able to come to you for help. If your response is to punish them or withdraw privileges, you'll never know the next time it happens.

Trying to set rules such as "don't make friends with people you don't know," or "don't make friends with adults online," is unlikely to work, especially for teenagers. It's unrealistic. Telling your kids to tell you about their Internet friends is more likely to work, but with some teens this is still not going to happen. Realistically, the best approach is to still to talk to your kids: Remind them that not everyone they meet is telling the truth, not everyone is a good guy, and some people have ulterior motives for what they say and do.

If your child wants to meet someone he or she met over the Internet, don't go ballistic: Instead, go with them. Meet in a safe, public, supervised place and make sure that others know you're meeting there.

Cyberbullying

Not all online dangers come from strangers. A growing problem in cyberspace has a new name: *cyberbullying*.

Before the Internet, rumors and nasty comments could hurt kids, but their exposure was limited. Not anymore! One website, Schoolscandals.com, boasted more than 30,000 subscribers able to read comments about teens who were described as "racist, obscene, and malicious."

One Boston teenager described her response to a nasty website profile: "I became physically sick. I vomited early in the morning. I didn't want to go to school. I was shaking. Sometimes at night I would lock my door and

just cry. Or put the music up so that way my mom wouldn't hear me cry."
(ABCNews.com, May 6, 2003.)

Harassment is another problem: In "Online Victimization, A Report on
the Nation's Youth," 6 percent of the teenagers surveyed had been harassed
via computer within the past year. Harassment was defined as including
threats to hurt the respondent and the respondent's friends, family, or
property, as well as efforts to humiliate or embarrass the respondent.

It's not just online harassment. Cell phones equipped with text messaging have been a new means for technically gifted bullies to attack others.
Calling with threats or texting aggressive messages allow the bully
inescapable access to their victims. Often given to children as a safety
device, their cell phones are always with them, always on, and may at any
point become the means by which another child harasses them.

One important component of harassment is that the perpetrators,
although they may be unknown to the victim, know information that
indicates that they are nearby. This makes the threats more compelling to
the victims. More than 30 percent of the victimized teenagers showed
symptoms of stress after the harassment and described themselves as upset
or afraid.

Unfortunately, as with other forms of bullying, your options as a parent
are limited. I can't give you a prescription for a cure or for prevention. The
best advice I can offer is to fight back—not by fighting fire with fire!—but by
looking for legal options. School administrators and parents managed to
get Schoolscandals.com shut down; and in a noteworthy case in
Massachusetts, a teenage boy's probation agreement prohibited him from
engaging in "unsupervised" instant messaging, after he was charged with
harassment.

Kids face dangers in our world, and technology introduces a whole new
set of those dangers to worried parents. The computer is not a babysitter,
and it's not an educational panacea. However, letting kids explore and learn
online is a vital part of growing up in the 21st century. As a parent, you *can*

do something to protect them, without depriving them access to the web. As with the ads fighting teen drug use, asking questions and being a vital (if not always welcome) part of your child's Internet experience is the key. What you don't know about their web surfing and communications online can hurt you both. Get involved and stay involved.

Privacy

What you do is your business. It's a keystone of the American system of beliefs. So long as you aren't breaking laws, you deserve to be left alone, right? Fears of a police state or of corporations keeping tabs on us have made the privacy issue a hot topic, but how much truth lies in our fears?

Companies use complicated legal agreements that hide the fact that their software reports back to the marketing department about what sites you surf and what you buy online. Cookies track how often you visit a website. Keyloggers on public computers can record your account names and passwords. Pop-up ads tell you that your IP address is being broadcast to the world. The federal government is using Trojan horse programs with keyloggers to collect evidence on suspected mobsters....

If a company is going to collect information about me, I want to know when, why, and how they will eventually use the information. I control the information I release about myself online: I don't give anyone my home address, I use dummy names as much as I can, and I limit the details I disclose in chat rooms and in posts to message boards. I want to protect my identity, and I don't need anyone to know the details of my life. As for the government, legal search and seizure are tenets of our constitution. The Internet and new technology should have no bearing on those tenets, and watchdog groups, such as the *Electronic Privacy Information Center* (EPIC), are constantly working to make sure actual law-enforcement techniques using new technology are in line with the intent of the constitution.

All that said, you and I both have to take steps to protect our privacy or at least be aware of how technology helps snoopers track us. This chapter shows you how to do just that.

Let's begin by looking at the benign invasion of cookies.

Cookies

When it comes to the web, cookies are not the tasty treats delivered each spring by Girl Scouts. Nor are they the demon spawn of webmasters intent on spying on your browsing habits. Netscape, the company that invented cookies, calls them "persistent client-side state information." If that's the kind of language that rings your chimes, you can visit the preliminary cookies spec site at `http://wp.netscape.com/newsret/std/cookie_spec.html`. If you would prefer a plain-English explanation of cookies, however, and what you can do about them, read on.

What Are Cookies?

Part of the problem with cookies is their name. Some think it's based on an old UNIX program called Cookie Monster. The monster would ask for a cookie every time you logged on. Netscape says the name means nothing. What cookies mean to you depends on how privacy sensitive you are. Both the Netscape Navigator browser and the Microsoft Internet Explorer browser allow websites to send and retrieve information about your visit. These information crumbs are called *cookies*.

Websites such as the *New York Times* (`http://www.newyorktimes.com`) use cookies to save your ID and password—not for any nefarious reason, just to speed up your login. Other websites use cookies to keep track of your visits. They commonly log the visit frequency and the pages and areas visited. A shopping site might record your purchases. Cookies can be helpful, saving you the trouble of retyping a user ID and password, but they can also be used to collect market research.

Cookies are like preference files. Just as programs such as Microsoft Word use preferences to keep track of how you like your windows arranged, what fonts you prefer, and which language you speak, websites can use cookies to keep track of how you like things to be online. Suppose you make a reservation at an airline site: A cookie allows the site to greet you by name the next time you return and prominently display your itinerary.

Some privacy advocates fear that cookies invade your personal space, but remember that a website only knows what you tell it, and all cookies are stored on your hard drive. A cookie contains very little text, but it provides your user identity when you revisit the website from which it came.

Figure 8.1

If you open a cookie file in a text program, you'll see that there is very little text, but there is enough information for a website to recognize you from your previous visits.

If someone were snooping around on your computer, the only "personal" information they could glean from cookies is what sites you visit and the alphanumeric string that identifies you. However, the site that originally placed the cookie on your hard drive can figure out all the things you've previously done on their site. When I go back to Amazon.com, it grabs my cookie, runs the alphanumeric identifier through its database, and pulls up my file. At Amazon.com, I like this treatment. They recommend new albums from artists I've purchased in the past or show me sale items that they think I might like.

This could become a problem if sites were able to read the cookies stored by other sites—and in the early days of cookies, they could. Thanks to privacy advocates, however, sites today can only read their own cookies, and there are limitations on the quantity and kinds of information sites can store. If you are using the Netscape browser, for example, any given site can store only 20 cookies at any one time on your hard drive. With Internet Explorer, each domain can save only 1 cookie per page you view.

What You Can Do About Cookies

So, now you know how cookies are used; nothing previously mentioned seems like too great an invasion of privacy to me, but it does to some. I say live with cookies: If they help sites do a better job targeting their products, they will sell more, achieve higher profit margins, and hopefully pass a cost savings down to the consumer—you. If they really bug you, however, here is how to fight back against cookies:

- **Delete cookies.** You can safely delete cookies already created. Netscape Navigator users can erase the cookies.txt file stored in the Netscape folder. (If you can't find it, use the Windows File Find feature to search for "cookies.txt.") Explorer users will find their cookies stored in a folder called Cookies inside the Windows folder. Deleting these files (after you've exited your browser) causes no harm. You don't have to go looking for the Cookies folder to delete cookies, however. Explorer and Navigator provide an easy process for deleting cookies from the browser window:

  If you are using Internet Explorer, follow these steps:

  1. Open Internet Explorer.
  2. Choose Tools, Internet Options.

     You should now be on the General tab.
  3. Under Temporary Internet files, click the Delete Cookies button, and then click the Delete Files button to erase the entire Temp folder.
  5. Under History, click Clear History.
  6. Click OK.

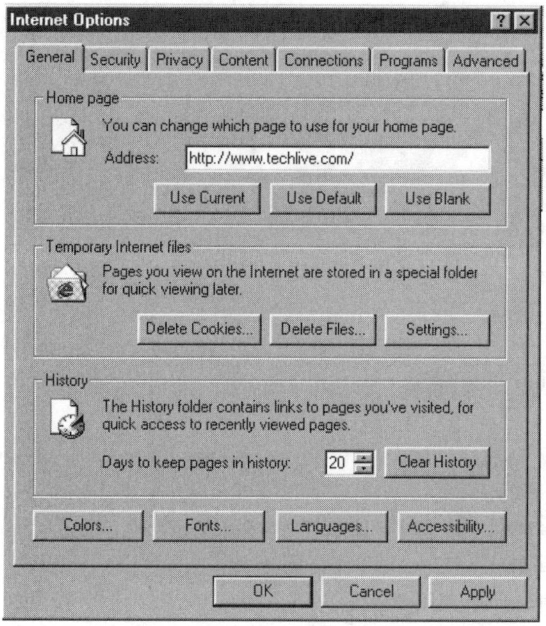

Figure 8.2

From the Internet Options, General tab, you can delete the cookies on your hard drive and clear your History folder.

If you are using Netscape, follow these steps:

1. Choose Preferences from the Edit menu.

2. Click Navigator, History, and then click the Clear History button.

- **Set cookie warning level.** Explorer users can select the Options item from the View menu. Click the Advanced tab at the top of the Options dialog box. You'll see a setting to Warn Before Accepting Cookies. Netscape Navigator users can select Network Preferences from the Options menu. Click the Protocols tab in the Preferences dialog box to find the Show an Alert Before Accepting Cookies setting. Be warned, however: So many sites use cookies that the warnings may get annoying quickly.

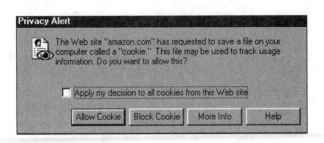

Figure 8.3

You can set up your browser preferences to alert you when a website is attempting to give you a cookie.

- **Use anticookie software.** Users searching for more sophisticated cookie management can turn to a variety of downloadable programs such as Limit Software's Cookie Crusher or RealTime Cookie Cleaner for the PC or Mac, or Washer for the Mac. These are free to download and try at www.download.com; if you decide to keep the trial-ware, however, you have to pay for the upgrade. These programs make the process of hiding your tracks and managing cookies easier, but they don't do anything special that you couldn't do manually to control cookies.

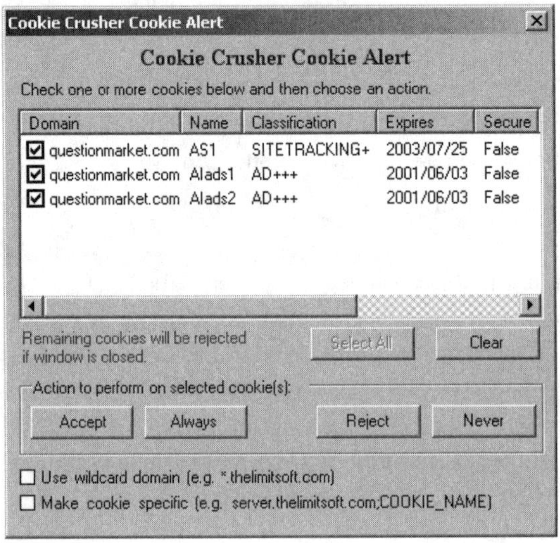

Figure 8.4

Limit Software's Cookie Crusher is one of several programs that provide you with more control over the cookies on your computer.

196

Cookies on Your Hard Drive

TechTV uber-geek, Leo Laporte, makes the analogy that cookies are like post-it notes that a website sticks on you, the customer. Imagine you are getting a coffee from virtual cafe, Barista.com. You order a double latte with 2-percent milk. The Barista writes your order on a Post-it note, sticks it to you, and you leave with your latte. Next time you show up, she asks, "Would you like another double latte with 2 percent?" She has read your post-it note. While you were gone, she didn't keep the post-it note. If you were to go to Starbucks.com, they couldn't read the virtual Barista.com post-it note. The same is true of cookies. They are placed on your hard drive by the websites you visit. You are in possession of them at all times, and other websites can't read them when you visit their sites.

Looking toward the future, groups such as the *Internet Engineering Task Force* (IETF, http://www.ietf.org/) and the *World Wide Web Consortium* (W3C, http://www.w3.org/) are working to develop standards for websites and browsers that offer greater privacy protections. Since 2001, Microsoft has voluntarily released versions of Internet Explorer that incorporate cookie controls stipulated in the *platform for privacy preferences* (P3P) under development by the W3C. The problem now is getting websites to adopt the same use of the W3C standards. Giving users control over the information-tracking tools used online will require cooperation from both sides of the exchange: browsers and websites.

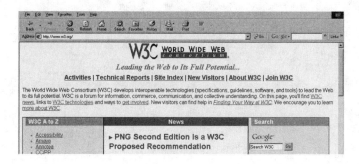

Figure 8.5

The W3C is working to create privacy standards for the Internet.

Covering Your Tracks

Preventing websites from logging your habits isn't the only privacy issue about which you should be concerned.

Most of us share a computer with someone else. For whatever reason, you want your web habits private. The obvious motivation: You're looking up images or data that's a little embarrassing or you're trying to plan a surprise and don't want the recipient to find out. People want privacy for a million different reasons; sometimes it's even a life-or-death issue.

The website Brokenspirits.com helps victims of abuse and incest get information online. They have a detailed explainer on how and why abuse victims should cover their tracks. The site reads, "Often times in abusive relationships, jealousy and paranoia are two of the most common symptoms. This can lead to suspicion, which can turn into your worst enemy. In protecting yourself it is best not to view content on the topic of abuse from a mutual location. Instead visit a public library, a friend's house, a school computer, or a work computer if available. Never underestimate your abuser. They will search for reasons for their actions."

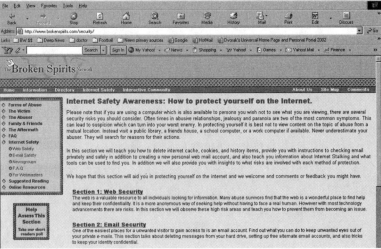

Figure 8.6

Brokenspirits.com helps victims of abuse find online support and offers advice to cover their tracks online.

The site does, however, go on to explain how one can and should erase any history of their online research.

The point I raise is many people have reason to keep their web history private on shared computers: Sometimes for less-than-honorable purposes, other times it's a critical step toward self-preservation. Motivation aside, here's what you need to know.

Your machine keeps a log of where you've been online. Cookies are part of the machine's intended or unintended tracking; the files for cookies are actually kept on your hard drive. They are kept in a file called Temporary Internet Files (usually at C:\Windows\Temporary Internet Files). In this same file, you can find image/graphic files, HTML files, and web scripts. All of these items are saved or cached so that you can go back to the originating websites and not have to download all the content again. They speed up your surfing and are meant to be timesavers. Intentionally or unintentionally, they end up providing a record of your online activity. Opening one of these cached files will offer a glimpse of what you've seen and where you've been.

Cached files, also known as *temp files*, can be deleted in one of two ways. In an easy sweep, you can delete all of them in Internet Explorer by clicking Tools, Options. Click Delete Files, and you will get rid of all the cached data files.

However, that's not the only record of where you've been. Your history file is even easier to use as a tracking tool. In Internet Explorer, click the View button, then click Explorer Bar, and then History. A side panel will open in your browser listing all the sites you've visited in the past few weeks. It's meant to help you retrace your steps. If you forget where you accessed a piece of data, look at the day you think you searched for it and you'll see where you were. (I use this feature all the time and value it over protecting my privacy, but for many it's an invasive tracking tool, especially on shared computers.)

You can delete history files manually by right-clicking each file/URL in the side panel or you can clear them all simultaneously. For the clean sweep, choose Tools, Internet Options. Then at the bottom of the window that pops up, choose Clear History. You can set the history to 0, but it will still record your history for 24 hours. Covering your tracks on the Internet needs to occur directly after you've decided your Internet session is finished. The History folder records every web address you've ever visited during a set period of time. Unless you clear the history before you leave your computer, all those web addresses you just visited remain in the log.

Covering your tracks can be a full-time job, and the tricks listed are just the most obvious ways to keep your doings private. Anyone with the right amount of time, access, and skills could track you in many other ways. There are breadcrumbs all over your hard drive that a forensic computer analyst or hardcore geek could uncover. Don't think that following these steps completely erases everything you do. They will, however, keep your habits private from 99 percent of the snooping public.

Spyware

As pointed out throughout this book, everyone wants your data. Privacy is your right—not just because it makes you safe from identity theft and scams, but because it is part of your human dignity. If someone plans to collect data about you, you should know and consent. In an effort to create new revenue streams, however, many software products have looked past that tenet, or at least fudged it a little.

In the "nothing's ever free" department, companies offering "free" software available for download online make money by selling data about users' surfing habits and preferences. They collect that data from mini-programs called *spyware* (a program that reports your Internet habits to companies gathering demographic information) embedded in the larger programs you download. And they claim users consent to the spyware, by agreeing to the *end user license agreement* (EULA) where the spyware is mentioned—in tiny print somewhere in that morass of legalese. However, don't think it's just free software that can contain spyware.

techlive

A Run In with Spyware

A few years ago I realized, much to my chagrin, that I had a secret Trojan horse program running on my three desktop computers and my notebook. I didn't install it and have no idea where it came from, but it sits there, running in the background, monitoring my every move. It's so secret, I couldn't even find it by looking at a task list of running programs. But luckily my firewall alerted me to the fact that some program was sending data out from my computer without my consent.

This program runs in the background and monitors my Internet surfing habits. It keeps a log of everywhere I go and everything I do and periodically uploads that log to its servers. Once there, it uses information about me to send me targeted ads.

It's almost impossible to get rid of this unwelcome intruder. Even when you uninstall the host application that brought this parasite down to your system, the parasite remains. There's virtually no way to know that you've installed it, and no way to remove it once it's installed. Yes, this miserable little creep of a program just sits in the background, collecting information on me and sending it to a server somewhere on the Net.

The program comes from a company called Aureate Media Corporation. Even though its privacy statement claims that the information is collected "anonymously," the fact that this application is downloaded in secret, runs in the background, and is almost impossible to detect, makes me suspicious of claims of even minimal protection. This is one nasty piece of software.

Programmer Steve Gibson calls Aureate's program "spyware." It's as good a term as any. Thanks to Steve, I now know that this insidious creep of a program is running all over my systems. I also know that Aureate's not the only spyware out there. At least one of my systems is running equally nasty programs from Timesink and Comet Cursor. I certainly don't want these spyware programs following me around the Internet and reporting on my surfing habits. Frankly, I'd rather no one knew about some of the places I inadvertently end up.

In 2000, Mattel Toys put communication functionality into hundreds of its interactive titles. The program, called Brodcast, sent data back to Mattel, including what products had been installed and when. The company said they were not engaging in data harvesting, but privacy watchdogs kept an eye on Mattel Interactive to make sure. The company eventually posted a download that enabled parents to remove Brodcast, but the precedent had been set.

It's not just spyware that's installed on your PC with these downloadable and purchased programs. Adware will hammer you with more pop-up ads than you could ever imagine. Some adware underlines key words on any page you're reading online and links to sponsors who have paid to buy those words. Another adware program creeps up when you install the peer-to-peer file-sharing service KaZaA. The defaults will have you installing an adware program called SaveNow that pops up ads on an all-too-regular basis; even worse, it is incredibly difficult to remove.

Some Downloadable Spyware and Adware Products

The following are just **some** of the known downloadable programs that include spyware or adware:

Abe's FTP client	IMesh
Admiral virus scanner	KaZaA
Audio Galaxy	Limewire
BearShare	MailAlert
Bonzi Buddy	Morpheus
Comet Cursor	Odigo
Copernic	PCDJ
CuteFTP	Spam Buster
Flyswat	Timesink
Gator	Web Coupon
Go!zilla	Webcelerator
Gohip	Win3000
Grokster	

That said, I know that quite a few programs I use contain spyware or adware. Instead of buying the product, I am trading my personal information for it. I'm sure they are not taking copies of my taxes, but they may log when and how long I use their product, what the settings are on my computer, and what type of connection I have. Or, they are choosing when and how to interrupt my tasks to advertise products to me.

The problem is I have to trust some remote marketing guy to show some restraint—to limit what he tells the spyware harvest and how often he tells the adware to pop up an ad. It's a gamble and an annoyance, but in some cases, I am willing to take the chance to use these programs. With adware, I can stand the occasional pop up; incessant, invasive intrusions really bug me, however, so I remove the over-the-top adware products and look for others that are less invasive. For example, I won't stand for a Bonzi Buddy, but Limewire or KaZaA I can handle; you will have to make those decisions for yourself.

techlive

I discovered one company using spyware in an unbelievably under-handed way, iWon.com. iWon.com offers prize money to web surfers who visit the site and make it their home page. However, the installation of its iWonPlus subscriber package installs a malicious, hidden Trojan program that sends data to the iWon.com servers long after you've followed directions to uninstall the program.

Especially disturbing is that iWon.com is a TRUSTe company, meaning it promises to publish a privacy policy and live by its tenets. Nowhere in the iWon.com privacy policy does it state that the spyware program hides itself and continues transmission after you attempt to remove it.

continues

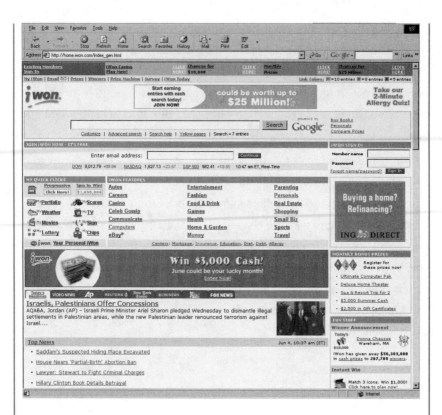

Figure 8.7

iWon.com delivered a Trojan horse program to subscribers of its iWonPlus package.

A viewer tipped us to the fact that the extra software needed to participate in many of the iWon.com programs installs a nasty piece of spyware
called aornum.exe. Aornum tracks user web-browsing habits and sends
that data back to iWon.com. This practice is clearly noted in the
iWon.com privacy policy: "iWon Software Products automatically communicate over the Internet with iWon's servers and, in order to provide
you with information or services, may convey to iWon certain information regarding your activities, including, for example, the URL of sites
you visit."

iWon.com says it collects user data and shares it with third-party
marketing organizations unless users have opted out of such information sharing. iWon.com says it also uses the personal data to send
"targeted email" to users.

Deleting Spyware Is No Easy Task

Many who find the aornum spyware program opt to remove the entire iWon package to prevent the data leakage. The instructions at iWon.com's site advise using the Add/Remove Programs function in Windows for a full uninstall.

After performing an add/remove and rebooting one of our machines, however, a spyware scan still found traces of the aornum program. Aornum renamed some of its files "ornum," and hid the aornum program deeper on the computer. Within minutes, the program was attempting to send data. Our firewall logged the series of requests, noting aornum.exe as the offending malware. (*Malware* is evil software; from Latin *malus*, meaning bad or evil.)

To see whether the aornum software is as insidious as our tipster proposed, we set up a test machine.

We took a newly imaged Windows XP desktop, installed two free spyware-detection programs, Ad-aware and Spybot (discussed later), and then scanned the machine with both programs. Neither one detected any spyware associated with aornum or iWon.com.

We installed the free consumer version of the Zone Alarm firewall and set it to detect and alert us to all outgoing traffic.

We then visited the iWon.com site and signed up for its services. We discovered that playing online bingo doesn't install the spyware, but can become habit forming.

We rescanned our computer with the two spyware detectors and still found no alerts for aornum.

We then downloaded the iWon.com chat program to qualify for "more winning opportunities" and began browsing the Internet and playing the iWon.com slot-machine games (also habit forming). It was then that our firewall gave its first warning. Aornum was attempting to send data.

A scan with Ad-aware didn't detect aornum, but Spybot picked up multiple entries.

We followed the iWon.com removal instructions to rid our PC of aornum and discovered that our only recourse was to uninstall all the iWon.com software using the Add/Remove function in our Control Panel. Once removed, all the previous iWon.com gaming, chat, and prize functionality was gone.

continues

After a reboot, we scanned our computer with Spybot and found aornum entries. There were fewer of them, and their locations and Registry modifications had changed. We began accessing the Internet and again our firewall popped up, alerting us that aornum was attempting to send an outgoing data transmission.

The iWon.com removal instructions left the spyware on our computer. That means aornum is a Trojan horse, or malicious hidden program. Aornum is not just spyware.

To truly rid our PC of the spyware/Trojan, we used the "search and destroy" function in Spybot, rebooted the computer in Safe mode, searched the entire computer for "aornum," deleted all references to the Trojan, emptied our Recycle Bin, and rebooted the machine normally. A subsequent Spybot scan gave our computer a clean bill of health. So far, there have been no additional alerts from our firewall. This is the best removal advice we can offer. It keeps you from having to do a Registry edit, and you can do it for free.

Shortly after I published reports of the iWon.com spyware, the company offered a public apology and promised to change its practices. iWon.com chief privacy officer, Mark Stein, called me to say that the company removed all the software's spyware communication functionality.

"We will remove all components that relate to this issue," he said in a telephone interview. He added "even though the company's privacy policy states we may collect personal data such as browsing habits, we've never actually collected any data from users."

Stein said the new version of the software will no longer contact iWon.com servers with surfer data. Stein insisted that iWon.com would never knowingly distribute software that violated the company's own privacy policy. He added that iWon.com could include the communications-reporting tool in future downloads, but not until the company comes up with a "complete uninstall solution to make sure users are 100 percent satisfied."

The iWon.com example was an anomaly—they took the spyware out. When you install free software programs downloaded from the Internet, you should assume they contain spyware. Most file-sharing programs such as KaZaA or Morpheus are riddled with the stuff. There's no way to disengage the spyware from the peer-to-peer programs. You wanna share music, you're gonna have to share information about your habits. The companies that use spyware in their programs say that's the only way they can offer the software for free.

Eliminating Spyware with SpyBot S&D

SpyBot Search and Destroy (SpyBot S&D) is my favorite program for eliminating spyware, because of its many features. In addition to adware and spyware, it also does the following:

- Detects some Trojans (programs that put backdoors into a computer)
- Detects Internet dialers (programs that make your computer call in)
- Detects browser hijackers (programs that direct your web browser to sites of their choice)
- Finds and fixes invalid Registry entries

As if that weren't enough, SpyBot S&D also cleans your tracks. I'm not just talking about the usual Internet browser stuff, either. Sure, it'll let you clear cookies, URL history, and temp files, but it'll also let you clear stuff within individual programs, including lists of recently viewed photos in your favorite imaging program and text in Word.

Spybot is my favorite program for ridding the PC of adware and spyware, an opinion I share with May 2003 *PC Magazine*, which gave Spybot its Editor's Choice award for spyware-removal tools. You can download a free version of Spybot at www.download.com. Spybot is not the only program that does these things, however. Another really good program is SpyCop, but it costs $50. (You learn more about SpyCop a little later in this chapter.)

Keylogging

Traveling in London a few years ago, I stopped at an Internet cafe to check my web-based email. The World Wide Web was really feeling truly worldwide, but there were things I didn't feel comfortable doing on this public Internet terminal: checking my bank balances, using my online bill-paying service, or making sure my automatic deposits were being made into my 401K account. Public computers pose a host of security problems because anyone can install spying hardware or software to steal data from unsuspecting users.

These data recorders are called *keyloggers*. They are usually software programs that can record the exact keystrokes, everything typed on a keyboard, so that all your account numbers, passwords, IM text, and work information, for example, is accessible in a log. You can see the security risk any public computer poses. Library computers, Internet cafe computers, school computers, business kiosks in airports, even shared work stations in your office can have programs installed that record data.

They also often take screen grabs and store them for use by computer security professionals. Chats, email, letters, and instant messages are stored for the installer of the keylogging program to look at later. That data can be encrypted in a hidden file on the hard drive or emailed out through an SMTP engine, a stealthy email program designed to leave no trace of what has been sent. For identity and credit card thieves, public computers are a treasure trove of opportunities. Some of the most popular keylogging programs are eBlaster and Spector from SpectorSoft, and the Starr keylogger from Lopus.

Keyloggers report your actions in a few different ways:

- They keep a report on your computer that the observer can access at a later time.
- They send an email version of the report to the observer at a remote location.
- If you are on a corporate network, the log file from a keystroke monitor may be saved on a network drive, without you ever seeing the file on your hard drive and nothing being emailed out to a network administrator.

Using one of the keylogging programs we tried, WinWhatWhere, I sent logs to a remote email account. The program has its own email client, so no record of these logs being sent out is traceable in any email client on my computer.

Keylogging as Good Parenting

Jonathan Dias is 18 and under surveillance. "It really sucks because you feel like you're being confined or you have no leeway of what you can do or your life or whatever. You're always being watched." So who is Jonathan's so-called big brother? His computer—actually it's a software program on his computer that was installed by his father, Mark Dias.

Jonathon's take, "My dad calls it 'monitoring,' but I say it's spying."

Dad's take, "He calls it spying. I call it public domain."

Mark gets an email every hour and a half when his son is online at home. It has a full transcript of every email, chat, and website Jonathan's checked out. Mark has no qualms about this all-access pass to his son's online activities. "In my opinion, teenagers don't have the rights that an adult has. They don't have the knowledge, they don't have the maturity, so I monitor him."

Mark installed a copy of the eBlaster keylogging program called Spyware (www.spywaredirectory.com/eblaster.asp), and Jonathon knows it's there. His dad told him it was in place, and even though Jonathon doesn't like it, there's nothing he can do about it.

eBlaster calls this good parenting. Doug Fowler, a spokesperson from SpectorSoft, the makers of eBlaster, is in favor of using the monitoring program this way: "Just in the same way that it's important for parents to know that their child is going outside the home to a neighbor's house or to the movies or to school, it's important for them to know where they're going on the Internet. I think its more of an issue of making sure that you're bringing your child up the right way and making sure you're keeping them honest."

In the case of the Dias family, all parties knew the monitoring software was in place. In most cases, however, the software is installed secretly and the programs work in stealth mode. They're not listed in the program file, they make untraceable modifications to your Registry, and you can only launch the program to generate reports by using obscure commands. For example, you could designate hotkeys such as Ctrl+Shift+Spacebar to open WinWhatWhere, a popular keylogger.

Alternatively, you could access another keylogging program called Starr by typing **starrcmd** in the Run dialog box.

techlive

Undercover Devices: KeyKatcher

Not all keyloggers are software based. Our labs reviewed the KeyKatcher and this is how they described the $99 device.

The KeyKatcher (www.keykatcher.com/) is an interesting little security gadget that monitors the keystrokes on a computer by saving them on a nonvolatile microprocessor within the dongle-like device itself. You can later access the info using a text reader like Notepad or Word. The interesting thing about it is that there's no software or drivers to install to get it to work. The KeyKatcher is pure plug and play.

The KeyKatcher looks like a keyboard plug without the keyboard. On one end is a space to plug your keyboard into, the other end fixes into the socket on your computer. To run it, just plug it in. You won't know it, but as soon as you plug it in, it starts recording the keystrokes you type. The 32KB version we reviewed can store about 16 pages of data. KeyKatcher is also available in 8KB and 64KB versions

It's advertised as a way parents can keep track of their children's online activities, but because of its simple installation and the fact that it doesn't leave any fingerprints on the computer used, it can actually be used by anyone who wants to do a little spying. All you need to do is hook up the device between someone's keyboard and his or her computer. Then when the person is finished typing, you can take it off, hook it up to your own computer, and read what your subject typed. To read the keystrokes, you open Notepad or Word for Windows and type **keykatcher** without any backspaces. A small menu appears on the screen, providing you with options to view the stored keystrokes, search for strings, change the password, and erase the keystrokes saved.

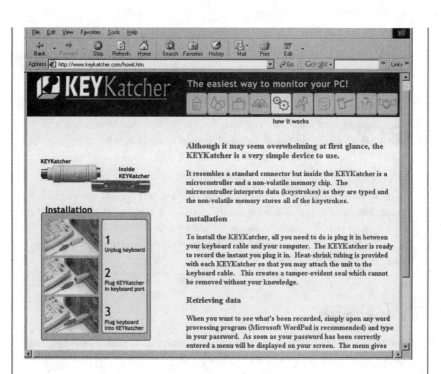

Figure 8.8

The KeyKatcher is a plug-and-play device that records keystrokes within its embedded microprocessor.

Before we tried using it, we were a little reticent about the KeyKatcher, but after recording many different typing sessions from a number of different computers, we are definitely converts. Ethical issues aside, the KeyKatcher did everything it said it would. It may go beyond ethical issues. It's probably okay for a parent to snoop on his child, but an employer might not have the right to do so, or any angry spouse—any more than they would have the right to tap a phone. Some interesting court cases will come from this technology to say the least.

That's not to say the device is all golden. Besides the fact that it works, the best thing is that you don't have to install any software. But because there's no software, there are also a limited number of options and settings for retrieving information. Another problem we found is that it takes a lot of time to transcribe and display everything the person typed. It's also difficult to switch between applications. As soon as you switch, it

continues

tries to write the text into the active window. Additionally, once the KeyKatcher runs out of memory, it will stop recording. It will not begin recording again until the memory has been erased. (Memory is erased through menu options.)

Finally, so much of what happens on a computer these days is pointing and clicking with a mouse. While the KeyKatcher records keystrokes, and even has a special NetPatrol option that searches memory for occurrences of "http," "www," ".com," and ".net," it won't detect anything you do with a mouse.

One way around this for someone knowing it's there is to use the built-in (with XP) mouse-controlled keyboard…it uses clicking to select letters but doesn't show up with keyloggers. It's slow to type this way, but can be used to get around some of these technologies. The smarter kid leaps over the slower technology.

FBI's Magic Lantern

Not just credit card thieves, protective parents, and suspicious spouses use keyloggers. Privacy watchdogs and homespun hackers alike were in an uproar when reports started surfacing about a secret keylogging program the FBI developed called *Magic Lantern*.

The Magic Lantern technology began as part of a broad FBI project called *Cyber Knight*—the same project that spawned the notorious email-monitoring device Carnivore. Magic Lantern goes much further than Carnivore, however. Magic Lantern is a Trojan horse program that—similar to a keylogging program—records all the keystrokes typed on the keyboard, steals passwords, reads encrypted messages, and then sends that information to a remote PC in front of an FBI hacker, all without the user ever knowing it was even installed on his computer.

Magic Lantern can not only record all keystrokes, it can also peer into files and even translate encrypted words into readable text. With many encryption programs available on the Internet, the FBI had been frustrated in efforts to break open encrypted messages, and officials were increasingly concerned about their ability to read encrypted messages in criminal or terrorist investigations.

Magic Lantern also resolves another important problem with the FBI's existing computer-monitoring technology: the "keylogger system." In the past, investigators had to break into a target's residence armed with a warrant and physically attach a device to a computer. Magic Lantern can be installed over the Internet by tricking a person into opening an email attachment. It is unclear whether Magic Lantern would transmit keystrokes it records back to the FBI over the Internet or store the information to be seized later in a raid.

Magic Lantern is essentially a Trojan horse program, a software application that sits on a computer and runs without the user knowing that it's there. Trojan programs usually come disguised as an email attachment or an innocuous software download. For example, one popular Trojan came hidden in a downloadable game called Whack a Mole.

Trojans thought to be similar to Magic Lantern include Netbus and Back Orifice. These Trojans enable other people to control your computer via the Internet. When you run a program that contains the Trojan, it copies itself to the Windows or Windows\System directory and adds itself to the system's Registry.

After the program has been completely installed onto a computer, it hides itself on the task list, and it doesn't show any icon or indication that it's running. Whoever is controlling your computer uses a program that enables him to record keystrokes, copy files, or basically do whatever he wants.

> **Note**
>
> **The Registry**   Think of the Registry as the very heart of Windows. The Registry is a database that stores critical system information and settings. Configuration data for your hardware, software, and user preferences is contained in the Registry. Anytime a program is added, deleted, or radically modified, the Registry reflects those changes.
>
> The Registry is usually referred to as a single file, but it's actually two files: System.dat and User.dat. Both of these files are stored as hidden files in the Windows folder. A third file, Policy.pol, is sometimes used in the Registry in corporate and networked environments.

Stopping Keyloggers

A few programs can detect software-based, keylogging programs successfully. Programs such as Anti-keylogger (http://www.anti-keyloggers.com/) or SpyCop (http://www.spycop.com/) alert you if you're being watched or logged.

SpyCop is a $50 program that has a frequently updated list of keylogger programs. Use the simple user interface to scan your computer for spy programs. Once scanned, SpyCop generates a clear report of programs and suspicious files. It even scrambles any screenshots of its interface that a monitoring program tries to capture. This keeps the presence of the antikeylogger secret from the monitoring software. As an added benefit, SpyCop also searches your computer for spyware.

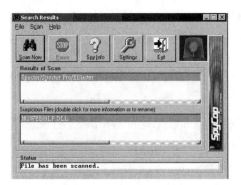

Figure 8.9
SpyCop alerts you to spyware and keyloogging programs on your computer.

Privacy Acts

Although the government hasn't offered a lot of help protecting our data in cyberspace, a few privacy acts have been passed—notably the *Children's Online Privacy Protection Act* (COPPA) in 1998, and the *Gramm-Leach-Bliley Act* (GLBA) in 1999.

Children's Online Privacy Protection Act

In March 1998, the Federal Trade Commission presented Congress with a report on the availability of data online about children. The impetus of that report eventually led to 105 H.R. 4328, a Department of Transportation appropriations bill, enacted by Congress and signed by President Clinton on October 21, 1998. COPPA became effective on April 21, 2000.

The act attempts to create guidelines for the operators of websites aimed at children, laying down a framework of rules on collecting data from those under the age of 13. The act defines personal information as children's first and last names, home addresses, email addresses, telephone numbers, Social Security numbers, and any other personal identifiers of the child or his/her parents, such as IP addresses or customer IDs in cookies. The act states that website operators must do the following:

- Post a privacy policy that clearly states who the operators are, what information they are collecting from children, and what they will do with that information (will it be sold to third parties?). A link to that privacy policy must be clearly displayed on the site.
- Obtain verifiable parental consent before collecting personal data from any child under 13.
- Allow parents an opportunity to review any information collected about their child. Parents should also be allowed to delete (but not alter) any information about their child that's collected.
- Refrain from mandating the collection of unnecessary data from a child for the sole purpose of participating in a game or contest.
- Protect the data that they collect online from children.

In 2002, the *Federal Trade Commission* (FTC) conducted an informal survey to assess compliance with the COPPA.

According to a release they published, roughly a quarter of the kids' sites visited provided a wide variety of children's content without collecting any personal information. Of the sites that did collect kids' personally identifiable information, however, roughly half appeared to have substantial compliance problems. Those sites received an email, which, in part, read as follows:

> Although the law requires that you take certain steps to protect the privacy of children online, your site appears to collect personally identifying information from children under 13 without providing a privacy policy, without giving notice to parents, and/or without getting parental consent. We recommend that you review your website with respect to information collection from children in light of the law's requirements. Be aware that the FTC will monitor websites to determine whether legal action is warranted.

Then in February 2003, the FTC announced that two sites were forced to pay the largest fines to date for COPPA infringements: Mrs. Fields Cookies and Hershey Foods Corporation.

- **Mrs. Fields Cookies.** Portions of Mrs. Fields websites—MrsFields.com, Pretzeltime.com, and Pretzelmaker.com—were directed at children. Birthday clubs for children 12 or under mandated the entry of a child's full name, home address, email address, and birth date. Although the website did not sell or share this data with third parties, it's alleged that more than 84,000 children submitted data without parental consent. The company paid $100,000 in fines for the infractions.

- **Hershey Foods Corporation.** Hershey has more than 30 websites, all candy related and many aimed at kids. According to the FTC, some of these sites obtained parental consent in a way that did not meet the stipulations of COPPA. The FTC alleges that Hershey collected data from children under 13 using a parental consent form online that had no measures in place to verify that a guardian saw or filled out the consent forms. The FTC further alleged that even if a supposed parent or guardian did not submit information on the consent form, the company proceeded to collect the child's personal data—including full name, home address, email address, and age. Hershey paid $85,000 in fines.

Aside from the obvious issue of companies selling information on minors to unknown third parties, one of the biggest problems with data collection from minors is that it blurs the line on information sharing. We tell our kids to never tell anyone online where they live or what school they go to, but then if they want to enter a contest to win a free packet of M&M's they should give up all details about themselves? It's confusing, and for that reason alone data mining from children is something companies should be very careful about.

Gramm-Leach-Bliley Act

The *Electronic Privacy Information Center* (EPIC) is a watchdog group that keeps tabs on government, corporate, and individual practices that infringe upon our privacy. Epic.org (`http://www.epic.org/`) is an incredible clearinghouse for information about privacy issues and the source of the following three stories that underscore why laws protecting our private information are so vital:

- In November 1997, Charter Pacific Bank of Agoura Hills, California, sold millions of credit card numbers to an adult website company, which then proceeded to bill customers for access to Internet porn sites and other services they did not request. Some of the customers billed did not even own a computer. The website company had set up numerous merchant accounts under different names to avoid detection. In September 2000, the FTC announced that it had won a $37.5 million judgment against the website company. Although the bank maintained that it did not do anything wrong, it has since stopped selling credit card numbers to merchants.

- In 1998, NationsBank (later merged with Bank of America) was fined millions for securities law violations because it shared customer information with its affiliate subsidiary Nations Securities. The subsidiary then convinced low-risk customers to buy high-risk investments. Many NationsBank customers lost large amounts, and many senior citizens lost large amounts of their life savings.

- In June 1999, the Minnesota Attorney General initiated a lawsuit against U.S. Bancorp for sharing customer information with third-party marketers in violation of its own policies without customer knowledge or authorization. The telemarketers then illicitly charged those customers. U.S. Bancorp eventually settled that case, along with those brought by 39 other state attorneys general. In April 2000, Minnesota settled with the third-party telemarketer, Memberworks, that U.S. Bancorp used. According to Memberworks's Securities and Exchange Commission filings, 19 out of the 25 largest banks in the United States had contracts with it. Other prominent banks, including Chase Manhattan and Citibank, have been involved in schemes where personal account information was sold to telemarketers.

In response to incidents such as these, the GLBA, which is also known as the *Financial Services Modernization Act of 1999*, was enacted. Its goal is to protect your financial data from misuse, and it has the following provisions:

- Banks, brokerage firms, and insurance companies must take adequate precautions to securely store your personal data.
- These financial institutions must advise you of how and with whom they are sharing/selling your personal data.
- You must be given the opportunity to opt out of their information-sharing practices.

Opting out of data sharing presents itself in a few different ways. If you get a mortgage on a house, for instance, you should receive a letter from your lender offering you the opportunity to opt out of data sharing. The customer service center for your bank should also be able to help you with an opt-out request over the phone, and there is also a centralized phone number where you can call to opt out of all pre-approved credit card offers (as discussed in Chapter 2, "Identity Theft: Who Owns Me Now?"), which are a result of data sales between financial institutions.

Misleading Email Circulating

Unfortunately, the GLBA has spawned confusion and its very own email hoax. I received this email from a viewer named Jeanette:

I received two different emails advising me that starting July 1, 2003, the four major credit bureaus will be allowed to release credit info, mailing addresses, phone numbers, etc. to anyone who requests it. If you do not want to be included in this release, call an 888 number. Do you know anything about this?

Here's the text of the email that's sending so many people into a panic:

Just wanted to let everyone know who hasn't already heard, the four major credit bureaus in the U.S. will be allowed, starting July 1, to release your credit info, mailing addresses, phone numbers ... to anyone who requests it. If you would like to "opt out" of this release of info, you can call 1-888-567-8688. It only takes a couple of minutes to do, and you can take care of anyone else in the household while making only one call, you'll just need their Social Security number.

This misleading email is full of half-truths. The FTC debunks the falsehoods and offers advice on its website (`http://www.ftc.gov`).

The Real Truth

Here's the FTC's information on this email hoax:

Credit bureaus can release your credit information only to people with a legitimate business need, as recognized by the *Fair Credit Reporting Act* (FCRA). For example, a company is allowed to get your report if you apply for credit, insurance, employment, or to rent an apartment.

In addition to the uses described above, lenders and insurers may use information in your credit file as a basis for sending you unsolicited offers. This is known as "prescreening." However, you have a right to opt out of these offers. The toll-free number—1-888-567-8688—is the "opt-out" line for the major credit bureaus for "prescreened" offers only.

The July 1 deadline relates to the Gramm-Leach-Bliley Act (GLB), which set July 1, 2001, as the deadline for financial institutions to give you notice of their privacy policies and a way for you to opt out of some of their information-sharing practices. The July 1 date is not a deadline for consumers to do anything. In fact, consumers can contact their financial institutions anytime to opt out under GLB.

Protecting Your Privacy

Lots of entities are trying to get information about you. Mostly this is for marketing purposes, but you should be able to control what information is exposed. The great irony of modern privacy is that we willingly give up more private information about ourselves than a hundred nefarious programs could ever harvest or process.

Here are a few general tips for keeping your personal information private:

- Remember, what you post on a newsgroup or mailing list can imply a great deal about you.
- Minimize the information that you put in your mail signature files.
- Carefully consider what you put on your personal web pages.
- Consider what information you give out to websites.
- Periodically delete your browser's history and cache files.
- Do an ego search on the people locators and search engines to find out what sites list your personal information. Type "your name" into Google and you never know what you might find. Don't forget to search the Groups and Images categories of Google as well.

Data-Submission Forms

How many times a day do you have to "sign up" for something online? You find a cheap airline flight through a new service and you need to become a member. The article you want to read is in a members-only section of the *New York Times*. Your soccer team is using the group service at Yahoo!, and you need to become a member.

For every sign up, you need to fill in myriad data fields: name, birth date, address, email address, phone number (daytime and nighttime), job description, income level, mother's maiden name, favorite pet's name. This is a lot of personal data—data you lose control of the second you submit the form. You can mitigate the amount of data released about your life and identity with just a few steps:

- **Assess the site.** First off, assess whether the site you are using is reputable. If Bobby Joe's web link page requires an elaborate sign on, forget it. Get the information somewhere else. On the other hand, if a reputable organization is asking for your personal data and they are the only source of the information you need, you'll probably have to fill in some information to proceed.

Assessing a Site

Consider the following four factors when assessing a website:

- **Subjective.** This is most important, yet hardest to quantify. Does the site "ring true" to you? Does it promise you things that seem to be to good to be true? Does it defy your common sense? Do you find it at odds with things you know about the world?

- **Quality.** Does the site seem hastily thrown together? Is there a combination of "Take advantage of this deal today" come-ons and many typos? Does it point you to parts of the site that don't work (particularly legal documents such as disclaimers)?

- **Congruence.** Does the site have the same information as other sites on the same subject, or does it lack in basic concepts? Does the site plagiarize large sections of other sites? These may signal that a site was established for the wrong reasons. Does the information make you want to visit the site again?

- **Harmony.** Does the material on the site fit the mission of the site? (In other words, does a site about athlete's foot have a long essay about politics on it?) Do its links relate to the topic at hand, or send you off to other sites about unrelated products/services (especially those with "buy right now" themes).

- **Only fill in required data fields.** On most forms, you only have to fill in the required fields to move on to the next step. Look for an asterisk next to each field to assess whether you must input text.

- **Lie.** You don't have to put the correct data into every web form, but this exercise requires some critical thinking.

Suppose, for instance, you find a great fare for a plane ticket at Cheapestfaresonearth.com. You have to first register to buy the ticket. They want your name, address, phone number, and email address, along with your mother's maiden name, Social Security number, and occupation. All fields are required.

First, is Cheapestfaresonearth.com legit? Do a little homework when dealing with a peripheral e-commerce company—it's not always worth the $20 bucks you save on the fare, especially if they have bad customer service (or worse, they wind up being a phony company).

Now you have to decide what fields you have to fill in honestly. Does the airline need your real, full name? Yes. Phone number? They have these services that call you if there's been a time change on your flight, so yes. Email address? They are going to send you a confirmation, so yes. Street address? Often e-commerce sites check your address against the address tied to your credit card. It's a way to make sure that you're not using a stolen credit card or number. So the address you use in the form should match the address where you receive your credit card bills. Mother's maiden name? Maybe this is their hint for reclaiming your password if you forget it; often they have other choices that don't put your credit or identity in danger, however, so choose something else or decide that your mother's maiden name from now on is always Smith (or Worley). Does the airline need your Social Security number to process your ticket? Nope, so I would enter 111-11-1111 as my Social Security number.

At sites where you aren't buying anything, you can enter anything you want for name, age, address, and email address. Most sites won't check that your email address is real, they just need to see a string of text in front of an @ symbol and then text.com, .net, .edu, or .gov. So you could enter jane@fakeemailaddress.gov and still move through the web form with no problems. On the other hand, if a site is sending your password via email, you need to provide a working email address so that you can receive the password.

Keeping Your Email Address Private

A great way to protect the privacy of your email account is to have multiple email addresses. I have five personal email accounts, but three will do the job—one for each type of correspondence:

- **Sign ups and spams.** This is for signups that require a working email address. (They want to send you a password for confirmation, for example.) After they send you the password for your account, the spam will start rolling in. They'll sell your email address to hundreds of other spammers, and you will then be a popular target for junk email. (I use the address bwspamaccount@hotmail.com for most signup forms online.)

- **Newsletters.** I like to get alerts from various companies about new products or security developments. I also subscribe to newsletters from a couple of different media sources. I use my bwnewsletters@ yahoo.com account so that these periodicals don't overwhelm my personal account. I also know that many newsletters will spam you or trade/sell their email list to spammers, so these accounts will fill up pretty fast. I also use this address when I post to newsletters or in any articles I post online. I hope I get interesting email in this account, but the reality is I end up wading through spam to find real emails here.

- **Personal account.** I guard this address fiercely. It is only for friends and family, not to be used in any way that would allow spammers to get hold of it.

Know Your Rights

If you are using a corporate network, your company is probably keeping at least some record of what you do online. Many firms are required either by the Securities and Exchange Commission or their own legal policies to log all employee communications. When network-based monitoring programs are in place, no software or hardware need be installed on your personal machine; it can all be done from the server side, not the client side.

The best policy for understanding what level of privacy you can expect at work is to ask your boss, your IT administrator, or the human resources manager. They should be able to provide you with a company policy about electronic monitoring of computers, phones, and faxes.

Privacy is a right that took years of philosophy and law to recognize. It is our duty to maintain that right. We can't sit idly by and hope that someone will do that job for us. We have to find the tools and use them, as well as exercise our rights as citizens to stop encroachment in privacy issues. People want to know what we think, what we type, what we look at. Let's disappoint them!

Protected Not Paranoid

I've spent eight chapters trying to inform, entertain, and educate you. Along the way, I may have scared you. That's because some of the stuff happening out there *is* scary. People lose time dealing with spam, hoaxes, and viruses. Some people lose money to scams, identity theft, and fraudulent online merchants. In some circumstances, people are even physically threatened, hurt, or killed as a result of digital crimes.

True-crime books will scare the pants off you. Although most people won't meet a serial murderer, the books have made a lot of people lock their doors at night, or think about getting a lock on their windows. The books have also stopped a lot of minor crimes.

Most likely, the worst things I've talked about in this book won't happen to you—but knowledge is power. I wanted to make you aware that safety is often an illusion. You may be tucked away safe behind locked doors at home, but do you know where your identity, your kids, or your money are in the digital domain?

Before you panic, take a deep breath; you already know a lot about protecting yourself in the modern age, and by reading this book you've learned to transfer that knowledge to protecting yourself online.

What's There to Be Afraid Of?

None of the victims we talked to when writing this book were taken advantage of because they were stupid. They just didn't know that they had to look out for these new kinds of crimes. The Internet simply opened a new playing field for bad people. Con jobs such as the pigeon drop and pyramid/multilevel marketing ploys evolved into crimes like the Nigerian 419 email scam. My first goal with this book was just to bring you up to speed on the old tricks in new clothes and give you a general understanding of the dangers and annoyances that computers have created in the modern world.

I tried to provide you with enough information to give you the big picture and help you identify the social-engineering ploys the new bad guys are using to turn you into a victim. The specifics of their tricks and ruses will change, the technologies used will evolve, but the goal remains the same. The bad guys are looking for a sucker. If this book makes you a little more cagey about identity, privacy, and data control issues, you and I have both succeeded.

The original collaborators of the Internet never could have seen the way this incredible technology would be used to compromise people. Even more certain, they never could have imagined how people could hurt themselves online.

Hacking

I began the book with hacking, because it's the computer crime most commonly glorified and vilified by the media. Hacking not only makes great headlines, it has also attracted the attention of Hollywood. As with many "fictionalized portrayals of reality," however, Hollywood got the details wrong. (If you don't think that's true, wait till they make *Security Alert: The Musical*, and see how different it is from this book.) The goal of the information provided on hacking was to show you that hacking is the least of your worries.

Still, hacking is important to know about. It's a cool social statement that created incredible breakthroughs in technology. It's a way many people try to level the playing field in our capitalist society—it's a game for some, a way to make money for others, and it's big business for those selling security solutions to prime targets. Remember, hacking is about being inquisitive, so I hope you treasure the fact that email began as a hack, and that the concept of hacking is usually just about exploring. That said, cracking or criminal hacking does happen, and it's evolving with the lure of identity theft and the simplicity of using viruses to gain access to systems. For home users, installing a firewall, turning off network shares, and using an antivirus program are your best defenses.

Identity Theft

The statistics alone about identity theft are enough to scare you into buying an industrial-sized shredder and paying all your bills in cash. Just during the writing of this book, a company that handles the processing of credit cards got raided and a few million Visa account numbers were stolen, and customers had to trade in their compromised cards. I hope you read Chapter 2, "Identity Theft: Who Owns Me Now?" and emerged with a goal to truly change the way you release information about yourself. You should take a few specific steps to lock down your identity, but very few people are aware of these steps. You may want to share this book with those who are not actively protecting their identity.

Online Fraud

E-commerce is here to stay, and you need to know the safe way around it. You need the same skepticism that keeps you from buying stuffed frogs at a garage sale or a TV from the back of some guy's van. You need to ask questions, seek out third-party reviews, and be a discriminating online shopper. Start by shopping from well-known sites and brick-and-mortar stores that have an online presence, use PayPal when buying through online auctions, and use a legitimate escrow service for big-ticket items. Assume the worst about all other forms of payment for goods purchased at online auctions. Many legitimate payment methods, such as cashier's checks and wire transfers, can be used against you. It's not just about taking your street smarts into the cyberworld, it's about protecting yourself in a new world where old currencies can be used and abused in unimaginable ways.

Viruses

I don't want you to learn about viruses the hard way, by getting a piece of malicious code embedded on your machine and fighting to get rid of it. The day you lose your precious data to a virus is the day you will wish you had used programs such as McAfee VirusScan or Norton AntiVirus. However, antivirus programs are not an end to the problem. You also have to understand a little about how viruses work, know what steps you need to take to stave them off, and then be disciplined to act on those steps. In the beginning, no one taught me the comprehensive way to keep my machines bug free, it was a trial-and-error lesson that I picked up in pieces. Hopefully, this book provides a more complete and simple way for you to learn the lessons of virus protection.

Hoaxes and Scams

Well-meaning friends and drama-king/queen alarmists forward messages to you as warnings: "The bad-times virus will eat your hard drive then spoil all the milk in your fridge!" Your new job is to fact check these types of emails and, if you are so inclined, send a "sorry, this is a virus hoax" email in reply. Other stories and rumors sent via email are just that: fiction, until proven otherwise by a reputable source. No, Bill Gates will not send you a check for $500 if you forward this. You may just ask yourself, "What's the harm?" Well, the short answer is that you clog networks and inboxes by forwarding these hoaxes, wasting resources and time.

Scams are even more malicious. Bad guys are casting a wide net to find gullible victims. Mr. Mose Soseke, the Nigerian government minister who wants to give you a few million bucks, actually does find "partners." He steals from and cons these partners until they catch on or run out of money. Does Warren Buffet invest based on interesting spam he receives? I don't think so.

Dangers of Online Interaction

One of the scariest things we talked about, cyberstalking, is in this book because it does happen and you need to be aware of the fact that violence and abuse can occur in many forms. Crimes online do occur, so I didn't want to pull any punches. The important thing to realize is that such online crimes are rare. The Internet has no more crazies than any other corner of the world. The specter of cyberstalking was raised to make you take a survival skill from your real life and just add it to your cyberlife. Does that pattern sound familiar?

Your instincts will see you through most of the decisions you need to make online—just as it has in the day-to-day world. If you ever felt that you shouldn't ride in an elevator with a certain stranger, you have the sense of preservation. Your right brain is scanning all the time for dangerous situations. I brought up stalking to tell you one thing: If you feel someone is bad news, he or she probably is.

Be careful! The heart can get you in big trouble online. However, there are also wonderful stories of people meeting their soul mates through the Internet. Dating is scary enough, so do a little digging and fact check what people tell you online. If you're planning to meet in the real world, go someplace very public and exercise caution. Getting attention from someone online can make us feel so good that we don't want to see the danger signs. Talk to friends about what you're doing and *listen* to them if they say you are engaging in risky behavior. If I convinced even one of you not to fly across the country to spend time with someone you met online last week, this book is a success.

Dangers to Children

Even if you don't have children and you don't personally feel vulnerable, you are a citizen of the Internet and have a stake in making it a safe place. If you ever come across any images of child pornography, any indications of abuse, anything that makes you feel creepy, talk to someone about it. The cybercitizen is a new breed, and if it that breed doesn't flourish, other forces such as the government will move in to make the cyberworld work, and with that we'll lose some online freedom. We have great freedom in the Internet world, and that freedom must be protected by a little self-policing.

If you do have children, remember that the Internet is a representation of the world: Everything bad in the real world can be found online. If you don't want your kids stumbling across those things on their own, you need to be there with them. Letting the Internet into your child's bedroom is letting strangers into his or her bedroom. Keep the computer in a central location and be an active participant in your child's online life.

So Where Are You Now?

The Internet is primarily a place that is full of helpful people. Never in human history has there been such an extensive medium for sending so much goodness out in the world. People are willing to give their time and energy in vast amounts on the Internet—just look at the number of websites maintained on any topic for free. People do use the Internet to give, and that giving spirit impacts what we do. Just because there are good people online, however, doesn't mean that you don't need to bring a healthy dose of critical thinking to all your actions and interactions online.

Part of your contribution to this culture is to inform your kids, your parents, or anyone who's new to the Internet about the right way to protect themselves online. Newbies need a lesson in online scams and privacy protection so that this incredible tool, the Internet, doesn't become a scary and dangerous place.

Just Do It

Unfortunately, it's not just an issue of gaining knowledge; it's about doing a few things to make yourself an unappealing target for bad guys. I hope you took action on the instruction sets we offered for your protection, and you read, or will read, the Appendix, "Homework"; just to make sure, however, these are the most important things you should do to protect yourself:

Against Hacking

- **Install a firewall.** If you have broadband Internet access, you need to guard the gate. If you have a router distributing your broadband to multiple computers, you are better protected from intrusions, but a firewall also helps you keep track of any malicious programs installed on your computers that are trying to transmit data back to a bad guys. It's free, it's easy, just do it.

- **Turn off file sharing.** Hackers and viruses use open network shares to do a lot of damage with just a little effort. It's an easy tweak, and you probably have it off if you don't know what it is. Double-check just to make sure. You never know what your nerdy cousin did to your computer when he said he was just "making it more efficient."

Against Viruses

- **Antivirus scanners.** Install an antivirus program and configure it to update the definitions at least once a week.

- **Update your software.** Software isn't perfect (no kidding). New holes are discovered weekly, so update your operating system at least once a month.

- **Back up your data.** If you do get hit with a virus—and you very well may—you need to have your crucial data backed up somewhere, preferably on a CD or DVD. Keep all your software install CDs and all the codes needed to activate that software. You never know when you may need to reformat and start over.

Against Identity Theft

- **Flag your credit report.** Put a 7-year flag on your credit report to alert you if anyone applies for a credit card in your name. You may be prevented from getting same-day credit. However, this may prevent you from buying a really hideous plaid couch that you impulsively thought would look great in the living room, and will also keep bad guys from opening lines of credit in your name.

- **Opt out of pre-approved credit cards.** Banks and lenders hammer you with snail-mail offers for new credit cards. Joe ID-thief could steal one of those applications right out of your mailbox, change the address so that you never see the bills, and start charging to the hilt on your good credit.

- **Make your checks safer.** Take your Social Security number off of your checks. (Remember, this nine-digit string of numbers is the key to your identity; release it only when necessary.)

Against Scams and Auction Fraud

- **Buy from reputable online vendors.** Is it really worth it to save three bucks if you get horrible customer service, or worse, if you get scammed? If you are looking for a bargain, do your homework before you buy.

- **Use secure payment options.** You can have a ton of fun and save a bundle bidding online, but use payment methods that are secure, namely PayPal, and for big-ticket items use a legitimate escrow company, such as Escrow.com.

Waking Up from the Illusion of Safety

Awareness and skepticism will protect you more than any firewall or antivirus scanner. In self-defense classes, they teach you to walk with your head up, your eyes open, and your shoulders back to be confident and alert about what's happening around you. It scares away the bad guys because you don't seem like an easy target. The same holds true in the world of Internet and digital crimes. Your goal is to be an unattractive target for the new bad guys.

The computer age just reframes the problems we face as humans. The problems of mankind remain—there is no progress in building a better human, but humankind's technology will progress and give us better and more interesting ways to screw up. Hopefully, this book is a starting place, an umbrella view of some bad things and bad people online.

The world is changing in profound ways, and what we need are more thinkers, not more followers. We don't need centralized authorities telling us what to do with the Internet, how to think, what to post. We need people who are enlightened, realizing that a great equality is settling over the world because of the Internet. You rank up there with university professors in Peking, poets in Edinburgh, homeless chess players in Prague, and bored teenagers in Tokyo. The possibilities for exchange are limitless, as are the possibilities for being overwhelmed by it all.

A new set of users will embrace the possibilities more consciously. Just to ensure that you are among them, I conclude this book with a few steps to follow that will help you control your own safety.

Step 1: Overcome Computer Inferiority

The first step toward accomplishing this goal is to get over your sense of computer inferiority. How many people have I heard say, "Oh, I don't know anything about computers?"

Look in the mirror and repeat: "I'm good enough, smart enough, and, gosh darn it, people like me." I believe that Stuart Smalley (the parody of self-affirmation gurus on *Saturday Night Live*) is encouraging you about your understanding and proficiency in the computer realm.

How much do you know about the inner workings of your car? Does that prevent you from being a safe driver? If you don't know your RAM from your ROM or your USB from your BSD, who cares? This book is about protecting yourself with common sense and a little bit of software (antivirus scanners, firewalls, and some configuration changes to your existing programs). Calling a credit bureau to keep track of your credit report, that's not dependent on your understanding of the disk defragmentation process. Pick up the phone and dial.

Step 2: Do It Now

No time like the present! I use this cliché so that you will remember to take action now. The practical advice in this book is more valuable the sooner you act on it. When it comes to the lessons of this book and protecting yourself from bad guys, do it *now*!

Lock down your PC and your identity. If you follow these steps now, you'll just be doing minimal maintenance from here on out. Do the things outlined in this book and you'll be a much less attractive victim for bad guys.

Step 3: Share What You Know

You need to help your friends and family sort through the miasma of half truths, lies, and hype that's out there about identity theft, viruses, and scams. Lend them this book, debunk myths when people email them to you, and warn people you think may be vulnerable to scams or abuse that there are bad guys online who are looking to exploit them.

Step 4: Don't Do Anything Online You Wouldn't Do in the Real World

People lose their street smarts when you take them off the street. Just because you feel safe in your office or at your home computer, don't let your guard down. Chatting with a stranger online merits the same caution you would use talking to a guy trying to sell you stereo equipment out of his trunk. What people tell you online could be a total crock. You have to assume that and work backward. If you want to trust people online, you have to become an amateur investigator. Seek out third-party corroboration; employ lots of skepticism; and if there's any request for information, money, or a real-world meeting, don't do it. If you have any doubts, any little twinge of doubt in the pit of your stomach, wait awhile. Do a lot of research, and trust that doubtful instinct—not your optimistic hopes that are pinned to this new opportunity/interaction.

Doom and Gloom

Guess what: I love technology. It's exciting and incredibly empowering. Most of us who use computers have had that epiphany—the moment something "worked" and saved us hours of labor or helped us find a piece of information or a person we never could have found in the past. The electronic world is a lot of fun. We lose that sense of joy most of the time, because we spend each day working at our computers or dealing with bills or tasks at our home PCs. We have built up such a thick hide that we no longer consider the miracle of email, no longer view a super-fast machine as amazing, or marvel at the fact that this tool has become a gaming, music-playing, communications toy.

The rate that information flashes across the globe is hampered only by the speed of light. Although I focused on the negative aspects of this new technology, I want you to consider the positive ones as well. The Internet was invented so that scientists could exchange their data and make their discoveries faster. News of a real human virus that's come out of nowhere sends scientists to the site of the outbreak with computers and fiber lines and the brain power of thousands of people at their disposal—all because the Internet connects them. We reap the benefits of interconnectivity. We may only notice this when we are able to buy a newspaper from the day of our birth on eBay, or track down a replica of that prom dress, but we are part of the world in a whole new way. Without a doubt, the good stuff outweighs the bad stuff, and even though it's my job to tell you about the bad stuff, don't let it get you down or scare you away from all this incredible new technology.

By virtue of the fact that you're aware of the need to protect yourself in the digital world, you're at the forefront. You're reading this book and that means you already know how to question safety, and your lifestyle encourages a new curiosity. I haven't given you all the answers to the security problem, but I hope I've taught you most of the questions to ask about your existing systems and that you do ask before you jump into something new. Ask the right questions! That's the big lesson, and you can easily do that.

See, you're feeling better already. You know that the future holds a unique promise for you, and you can handle it.

Homework

Chapter 1, Hacking 101

Install the ZoneAlarm Firewall

1. Go to Download.com (CNET's clearinghouse for downloadable programs).

2. Search for ZoneAlarm.

3. Choose the free version, or the plus version if you want tech support.

4. Click the Download button.

5. Save the file to a location you will remember (a folder you create called Downloads or on your desktop, for instance).

6. Double-click the downloaded ZoneAlarm setup file.

7. Accept all the defaults in the installation. Your computer will automatically reboot.

8. Follow the ZoneAlarm instructions for training the firewall to allow or prevent certain programs from accessing the outside world. Then start the training or configuration process (see Chapter 1 for configuration and training advice).

Turn Off File Sharing

1. Click Start.
2. Choose Settings.
3. Open the Control Panel.
4. Click Network.
5. Toward the bottom of the window that pops up, click the File and Print Sharing button.
6. Uncheck the two options for files and printer(s) so that the boxes are empty.
7. Click OK twice to close the Network windows.
8. Restart your computer if prompted to do so.
9. Close the Control Panel.

Chapter 2, Identity Theft: Who Owns Me Now?

Secure Your Social Security Card

Put your Social Security card somewhere safe. Take it out of your wallet! Finding a Social Security card or number in a stolen purse or wallet is a jackpot for ID thieves.

Lock Down Personal Data at Home

Secure your personal data in your own home. Use a locked firebox and keep it someplace a little more obscure, or just choose a more out-of-the way spot for your really key personal data.

Opt Out of Pre-Approved Credit Card Offers

Call 1-888-5-OPTOUT (1-888-567-8688) to no longer receive pre-approved credit card offers:

1. When you call, press 2 for the Opt-Out option.
2. Choose the Permanent Removal option.
3. Enter your home phone number when prompted.

4. Say and spell your name when prompted.

5. Enter your ZIP code when prompted.

6. Say and spell your address when prompted.

7. Finally, enter your Social Security number when prompted. (In this case, you must submit it.)

It takes 5 days to process your request, and you will only stop receiving mail from companies that use the credit services to acquire names and addresses.

Secure Your Mailbox

I suggest purchasing a locked mailbox. The postman just slides the mail in through the slot, and you use a key to unlock it.

Shred Your Mail

Either buy a shredder or rip up paperwork that contains sensitive data, such as the following:

- Pre-approved credit card applications
- Old bills
- Check stubs
- Family historical data
- Old ID cards
- Old driver's licenses
- Applications
- Pay stubs
- ATM receipts
- Credit reports
- Investment statements
- Documents relating to your passwords
- Medical histories
- Items containing your signature

- Resumés
- Tax forms
- Used airline tickets
- Itineraries

Order Your Credit Report

The three major credit bureaus in the United States are Equifax, Experian, and TransUnion. These companies do not share information with one another, so you should order a report from all three or use a service, such as TrueCredit.com (`www.truecredit.com`), to get a unified report.

- **Equifax Credit Information Services, Inc.**
  Call 800-525-6285 / TDD 800-255-0056 and ask the operator to call the Auto Disclosure line at 800-685-1111 to obtain a copy of your report.
  P.O. Box 740241
  Atlanta, GA 30374-0241

  `www.equifax.com`

- **Experian Information Solutions, Inc.**
  888-397-3742 / TDD 800-972-0322
  P.O. Box 9532
  Allen, TX 75013

  `www.experian.com`

- **TransUnion**
  800-680-7289 / TDD 877-553-7803 Fraud Victim Assistance Division
  P.O. Box 6790
  Fullerton, CA 92834-6790

  `www.transunion.com`

It costs less than $10 each to order the reports separately from each company. TrueCredit.com lets you order credit reports from all three credit bureaus right from your desktop. It costs just $35 for a one-time report or $35 one time plus $44 annually for credit reports emailed to you weekly.

Change Your Passwords

If you have weak passwords on your financial accounts, change them.
And while you're at it, get your "secret question" changed to something an
ID thief can't find out about you through diligent research. Avoid family
names that can be found on genealogy websites. Make up something
untraceable or unique to you.

Chapter 3, Buying Online: What's Safe, What's Not?

Shop with suspicion online and use escrow and PayPal services.

Chapter 4, The Virus Threat

Install an Antivirus Scanner

The more popular antivirus programs are Norton and McAfee. If you
don't want to pay for one, download AVG by Grisoft:

1. Go to www.grisoft.com.
2. Click Free Anti-Virus Protection.
3. Download the file and accept all the default installation instructions.

Have Your Antivirus Program Run Automatic Updates

If you are already running an antivirus program, automate the update
process.

If you are using Norton AV, follow these steps:

1. Click the Live Update settings.
2. Choose the General tab.
3. Select Express mode.
4. Select I Want Live Update to Start Automatically.

If you are using McAfee, follow these steps:

1. Find the McAfee VirusScan icon in the system tray of your Windows taskbar.
2. Double-click the McAfee VirusScan icon in your taskbar.
3. Click the Pick a Task button.
4. Select Change My VirusScan Settings.
5. Select Configure Instant Updater.
6. Choose Auto Update.

Chapter 5, Hoaxes, Virus Myths, and Scams

There are ways to identify hoaxes and scams. If an email message seems too good—or too bad—to be true, it might be a scam. Before you respond to an email that could be a hoax or scam, check the following websites:

- Symantec antivirus resource center `http://securityresponse.symantec.com/`
- McAfee virus hoax center `http://vil.nai.com/VIL/hoaxes.asp`
- Vmyths.com `www.vmyths.com/index.cfm`
- Hoaxes A-Z `www.vmyths.com/hoax.cfm`
- Snopes.com `www.snopes.com/`

Chapter 6, Safe and Sane Online Interactions

Play nice! Be selective as to whom you interact with online, and use extreme caution when developing relationships.

Chapter 7, Protecting the Family

Educate Your Children

Talk to your kids about the dangers online and be an active part of their web experiences.

Stop Images from Automatically Loading in Email

Turn off HTML in your email program or tell web-based email programs not to display images until prompted to reduce exposure to pornographic images sent by email.

If you are using Outlook Express

1. Choose Tools, Options, and then the Read tab.
2. Select Read All Messages in Plain Text.

In web-based email programs you will have to find the Preferences tab that allows you to turn off images or HTML formatting.

If you are using Hotmail

1. Choose the Options button (along the top tab next to Home, Inbox, Compose, and Contacts).
2. From the Options page, choose Mail Display Settings from the Additional Options column.
3. Where it says Display Internet Images, choose Remove Images Until Messages Are Reviewed.

If you are using Yahoomail

1. Choose Mail Options, General Preferences.
2. From the General Preferences page, scroll down until you find the Security section.
3. Select the option entitled Block HTML graphics in email messages from being downloaded.

Chapter 8, Privacy

Find Online Information About Yourself

Use multiple search engines and do an ego search to see what information is posted online about you, or what has been written about you.

Use a Spyware Detector

Run a spyware detector on your computer to see what monitoring software is installed:

1. Go to www.download.com.
2. Search for Spybot.
3. Install and run Spybot to determine what programs are currently keeping tabs on you.
4. Delete programs that Spybot identifies.

Keep in mind that some freeware, peer-to-peer services, and web tools (such as Gator and Bonzi Buddy) may stop working if you remove their spyware components.

Index

B

G

Q-R

S

T